D1488547

To Jim
Best of Luck
Dave Schultz
Feb/82.

THE HAMMER

Confessions of a Hockey Enforcer

DAVE SCHULTZ

With Stan Fischler

SUMMIT BOOKS
New York

Published by SUMMIT BOOKS
A Simon & Schuster Division of Gulf & Western Corporation
Simon & Schuster Building
1230 Avenue of the Americas
New York, New York 10020
SUMMIT BOOKS and colophon are trademarks of Simon & Schuster
Designed by Daniel Chiel
Manufactured in the United States of America

10 9 8 7 6 5 4 3

Library of Congress Cataloging in Publication Data
Schultz, Dave. Date.
    The Hammer: confessions of a hockey enforcer.
    1. Schultz, Dave, date.   2. Hockey players—Canada—Biography.
3. National Hockey League.
I. Fischler, Stan.   II. Title.
GV848.5.S38A33   796.96'2'0924   [B]   81-14577
                                                 AACR2
ISBN 0-671-43181-1

Acknowledgments

To say that this work could not have been accomplished without the diligence and dedication of Rich Friedman and Allan Turowetz would be an incredible understatement. Rich's patient transcribing of tapes as well as his industrious assistance in editing provided the cement needed to bind the project together. Al's data collection, interviewing, and expertise in helping to shape the manuscript were most significant. We owe them both a huge debt of gratitude.

Others contributed mightily and merit more than a mere ovation. These include Lori Weisman, Paul Fichtenbaum, Gabe Miller, Joe Carbone, George Hall, Tanya Simmons, Herman Zuker, Mike Fleming, Shirley Fischler, Esther Newton, Paul Ringe, Bob Stampleman, Jim Namrow, Errol Somay, Bonnie Dillon, Lloyd MacKay, Darey Feingold, Alice Perlmutter, Cathy Schultz, Woodman Franklin, and Kelly Lynn.

This book could also not have been written without the orchestration of our editor, Jonathan Segal, who took an avid interest in the project from the start and provided vital guidance throughout.

To my wonderful wife, Cathy, and to my beloved children, Chad and Brett; the best is yet to come.

D.S.

Contents

Foreword

The literary union of Dave Schultz and Stan Fischler was not made in heaven. Those who knew us both could not conceive of the possibility of Dave's sitting in my living room with tape recorder spinning, telling the story of his life. One might have imagined Dave Schultz winning the Lady Byng Trophy for good conduct on the ice before that would happen.

After all, as a columnist for *The Sporting News* and *The Hockey News*, I had taken dead aim at Schultz and his behavior more times than I can remember. "You didn't seem to approve of the way the Flyers played," Dave said in typical understatement when we began this project.

So how did we manage to unite behind a typewriter?

Our mutual friend, Allan Turowetz, proved to be the magnet who brought us together. Allan and Dave had met in Buffalo when Turowetz was the resident sociologist for the Sabres. When Dave said he wanted to do a book, Allan pointed him in my direction.

Much as I railed over some of Dave's antics on the ice, I nevertheless was fascinated with him as a character. The more Turowetz told me about the real Schultz, the more eager I became to write his book.

Allan arranged a meeting; Dave and I shook hands, agreed that we could work together, and then went about the business of writing a book. It was not easy, especially when Dave expanded on the fights that led to bloodshed, the victories, the humiliations, the ups and downs of his tumultuous existence.

11

12 THE HAMMER

If there was one quality about Dave that emerged from the very beginning—and that set him apart from so many other athletes—it was his utmost willingness to cooperate at all times. Never have I encountered a collaborator with such tenacity. It became obvious once the project got under way that all problems of the past were buried and that the book would be an unvarnished look at hockey, violence on ice, and Dave Schultz with no holds barred. He was asked to swing away just as he did when he earned the nickname Hammer and he complied.

The results are here for all to see and I, for one, am delighted that we beat the odds and became teammates.

STAN FISCHLER

New York City
June 1981

1

The Enforcer at Work

"THIS CAN'T BE ME."

I would look in the mirror and repeat those words.

Here I was in the fourth year of my big-league career and I had become a distortion of the person I had been for most of my life. It was 1975 and "Dave Schultz" had emerged as a household word for goonery in the National Hockey League.

As difficult as it may be to believe, I had lost control of my destiny. I had promised myself from the very beginning that I would stay the same person I had always been. But it had become evident both to me and to those around me that I had experienced changes in both my personality and my style.

I would open *The Hockey News*, the bible of our sport, and look up the penalty minutes. I was always on top.

I had broken Keith Magnuson's jaw. He was the policeman—the so-called enforcer—of the Chicago Black Hawks, and I had beaten him twice. Wayne Cashman was the meanest and toughest player on Boston's Big Bad Bruins. I destroyed him in the 1974 Stanley Cup playoffs with right crosses and uppercuts. John Van Boxmeer was a big rookie defenseman with the Montreal Canadiens. I had scored a one-punch TKO against him one night in the Montreal Forum. Bob and Barclay Plager—who were supposed to be the James Brothers of hockey—and all their teammates on the St. Louis Blues used to kick hell out of the Flyers; after I joined Philly, the Plagers were nicer than St. Francis of Assisi.

I even gained the attention and earned the ire of the Attorney

General of the Province of Ontario, who demanded that hockey clean up its act.

The word around was that I signed my name with my knuckles. There was something to it.

In 1971, at the age of twenty-one, when I was playing for Quebec in the American League, I was sentenced to 382 minutes in penalties, a record. A year later, when I was with Richmond, I broke my record—392 minutes. Next year I made it to the bigs with Philadelphia. In my second season I set a penalty record for the National Hockey League—348 minutes. A year later I upped it to an astronomical 472.

And I'd look in the mirror and say, "This can't be me."

How could it be? The Dave Schultz I *had* been was a pussycat off the ice: shy, soft-spoken, and reasonably articulate for a kid who never got past high school. This couldn't be the same person who used to cry if his father even yelled at him. I had never been in a street fight in my life (somebody always came to my rescue when I was threatened).

Yet there it is in black and white: eight years in the NHL, 608 games, and 2,706 minutes in penalties. Had that record been translated into a real-life prison sentence, I would have been a "lifer." As it was, I became a fairly well-to-do folk hero who in the 1970s, according to what has been written and in the opinion of some observers, had as much impact on the game of hockey as anyone since Bobby Orr.

As calm as I was off the ice (I always have been), once I stepped into the rink I became a completely different person—some called me a wild animal—who succeeded in his profession because of his fists. What had once been a fast-paced, beautiful, rough but straightforward game had turned into a question of intimidation. Scaring the living wits out of the enemy was almost as important as skating, shooting, and stickhandling. How it got that way for me is what this book is all about.

To say that I *totally* regret all I did would be to misrepresent the truth. My style of hockey brought me wealth, fame, notoriety, and a quality of life I could never have had otherwise. But off the ice I paid the price, as I think this book will make clear. That doesn't mean I'm looking for sympathy, or feeling sorry for myself. It does mean that I'm trying to show that things aren't always as they seem.

I'm going to be talking about the pluses and minuses of the life I led as honestly as I can. I'm not going to cover up, although I'd like to try to explain sometimes what was going through my mind when I was doing the things I did. I love the game of hockey and I wish reckless violence weren't a part of it. I didn't help things much. But if what I say here makes some young people and their coaches think twice about how the game is taught, then I will have contributed.

I will run the risk of being called a hypocrite for that because I'm sincerely trying to be honest. Sometimes you have to have a few years to reflect on things before you can really understand what was going on. Believe me, once you've become successful playing one style—no matter what that style is—it's murder to give it up (and all that goes with it). But eight years later you try to explain to your kid why his father is standing there on TV in some old film, yelling and screaming at some poor guy he has just beaten into a bloody pulp.

How do I explain to my children that that was the way their father earned his living? How do I rationalize my behavior on the ice over an eight-year period? And even if I could explain it, how would my kids handle the antagonism and abuse directed their way because of their father? It's a problem to which I didn't give too much thought—until now.

Already, by 1974, the Philadelphia Flyers were known as the Broad Street Bullies. We—Bob Kelly, André Dupont, Don Saleski, and especially me—were the worst offenders. Built like a fireplug, Kelly wasn't a pretty skater, but he raced up and down the rink like a wild dog. Dupont was a hulking French-Canadian defenseman. Saleski, the tallest of the bunch with a shock of blond hair, reminded us of Big Bird from Sesame Street.

In the first round of the 1974 Stanley Cup playoffs we took the first two games from the Atlanta Flames without any trouble. Atlanta was good, but easily intimidated, and we knew it. It always seemed that teams didn't care to get too physical in the Spectrum. They knew we wouldn't take any rough stuff, particularly in front of our hometown fans. I think the Flames also knew I was just waiting for someone to give me a reason to drop my gloves. That didn't happen in those first two games.

The Flames' general manager, Cliff Fletcher, tried to put up a brave front when the series moved to the Omni in Atlanta for games three and four. "Philadelphia has been getting away with too much bluff intimidation by guys who can't back it up," he said. "I guarantee we'll come out hitting at home." Fletcher was on the spot because, except for a couple of his players, e.g. Bryan Hextall and Rey Comeau, the Flames were not a rough team, and I think he felt Atlanta would suffer at the gate if they didn't give their own fans a brave show. (Ironically, they couldn't win in the long run doing that—it wasn't their game.) Sooner or later there would be an eruption.

It happened midway in the second period. Curt Bennett of the Flames went after our captain, Bobby Clarke. Then Bill Flett jumped on Bennett for falling on top of Clarke. I went nose-to-nose with Atlanta defenseman Noel Price. "C'mon," I said to Price, "I'm gonna hit you." I gave him my madman's scowl, but he wanted no part of me. He stood there, mute. What a pretty picture I must have been.

I was taken aback. Here I am all psyched up to fight and he won't fight me. So I left him standing at center ice and skated to the Flames' bench. "You bunch of assholes," I shouted at them. I looked at the faces: Eric Vail, Jacques Richard, Pat Quinn, Tom Lysiak. "You bunch of homers." They looked so nice and neat in their white uniforms with the red flame on the front that I felt a little ridiculous trying to provoke them.

But my boiling point was at an all-time low. Not only was I ready for a terribly important game, but their front office had goaded me and challenged my identity as an enforcer earlier that day. In an effort to prepare myself for that evening's match I had spent the entire afternoon working myself up. In retrospect, I am certainly not surprised that I challenged the entire Atlanta bench that evening. I would have challenged the entire city of Atlanta, the way I was thinking.

I skated by the Atlanta bench and yelled: "Any of you guys wanna fight?" Luckily, the bench did not accept my challenge, or so I thought. As I skated back toward center ice, I noticed Butch Deadmarsh, whom I had fought when we played junior hockey as teenagers, vaulting over the wooden sideboards and coming at me. My plan of attack was simple—grab a hunk of his jersey with my left hand, hold tight and then, while I kept him in position, start swinging with my right.

His jersey, which had been such a spotless white just a few seconds ago, now was a mess of red splotches. In the fury of the battle we had moved within reach of the Flyers' bench. Now Deadmarsh got a taste of Philadelphia sportsmanship. Our defenseman, Eddie Van Impe— the "nice guy" on our squad—tripped him. Down went Deadmarsh and when he clambered to his feet a couple of guys from our bench took a piece out of him.

Deadmarsh finally limped away as the Flames' coach, Bernie Geoffrion, started yapping away at me. Geoffrion wanted my hide, but since he couldn't come out onto the ice, he must have given somebody on the bench orders, because the next thing I knew another Atlanta guy went over the boards.

I looked up and saw it was John Stewart. Stewart and I had played junior hockey together in Sorel, Quebec, and he had never wanted to fight. Now he charged me like a raging bull. Lashing out with my right hand, I sent him flying onto our bench. Talk about raging bulls—the more I fought the more I lost control.

If you think the altercation was difficult for me, imagine what it must have been like for Stewart, a player who had never been perceived as a fighter in the NHL. I said to myself, "What the hell is this guy doing out here?" And to tell you the truth, I honestly felt sorry for him because Stewart was nothing more than cannon fodder for the Flames. (As you can see, the degree to which a professional hockey player will extend himself and attempt to put on a brave front before the home fans is amazing.) We went on to win the game and take a three-zip lead in the series.

We fell behind, 3-0, late in the second period of the fourth game. As much as I would have liked to concentrate on hockey, I knew damn well it was time for my act. I had a function to perform and I felt I had no choice but to get to it. I had been told often enough that a few good hits or a fight can get a team psyched up. Nobody needed to remind me. I knew what kept me on the Philadelphia Flyers and I wasn't about to lose my spot.

I started looking for action. Bryan Hextall, one of their few bruisers, made the mistake of moving in front of our net, just when I got there. I came in with my stick high. Hextall brought his stick up. We dropped our gloves and started swinging. Hextall was trying to tie up my right hand, so I switched to my left and got in a few shots. Eventually, he tied up both my arms, so I butted him with my head.

"Fer crissake," Hextall screamed at the linesmen, "when are you guys gonna break this up?"

By the time the linesmen separated us, Hextall had a long, ugly gash over his left eye and was bleeding from the nose. He skated to the Flames' bench where the trainer gave him a white towel. He put the towel to his face and it soon looked like a red flag. I don't think there's any question but that that sight took something away from the Flames, and picked us up.

We scored three straight goals and sent the game into sudden death overtime. Mike Nykoluk, our assistant coach, sent me out with

Bobby Clarke and Bill Flett. The fights and the turnabout in the game had me feeling good. I wanted the puck. Clarke gave it to me. It was a two-on-one breakaway with me facing goalie Phil Myre. He gave me an opening, and I shot the puck along the ice on his stick side to take advantage of it. Myre moved too late. The red light flashed. I had scored the game-winning goal; we had won the series. A fight had turned it all around.

The next day it was there in the paper: "Schultz's pounding of Hextall was the turning point of the game." Could a fight actually help a hockey club that much? I was coming more and more to the conclusion that the answer was almost always yes. In the climate I was in it was constantly reinforced. Here I was almost at the heights of hockey—how or why should I think otherwise? My theory was confirmed in the semi-finals against the New York Rangers.

It was a hell of a series. They had the artists, we had the workers. We hit and they hit back. One of their top defensemen was Brad Park, someone who had the ability to make the offense go. I had never taken to Park because I always thought he had too high an opinion of himself. He was a snob on the ice, if that makes any sense. In the sixth game I caught up with him. I ran him in the corner and got a piece of him. As the play turned up the ice, I checked him again and knocked him down. Then I stood over his body. I was worked up. I wanted more of Park. I worked myself free of a linesman and, while the other linesman held Park down, I belted him four good ones in the stomach before the officials pushed me to a neutral corner. This fight had a bit of personal grudge to it, and lots of blind rage, but I also knew that to take Park off with me to the penalty box would be a good trade for the Flyers. And I had incentive—if we beat the Rangers, we'd get five thousand dollars apiece and move into the finals.

As I was preparing for the seventh game of our series, I was dwelling on Ron Harris, the Ranger's fireplug defenseman and resident enforcer. Often, the morning before games, I would think about guys I might have to fight that night. Sometimes I'd just close my eyes and visualize a particular player. The whole fight would unfold in my mind: analyzing the enemy's style, figuring how I'd move in on him and then punch until he was thoroughly punished. The closer it came to game time, the more I would gnash my teeth. This time I was nervous, but confident: I couldn't wait for the opening face-off.

Nobody on our club, not our manager, Keith Allen, nor coach Freddie Shero, nor Mike Nykoluk ordered me to get a specific Ranger before the final game of our series with them. But there was a subtle hint from Nykoluk. He walked over to my stall in the dressing room. "If you get a chance, Dave," he said, "remember that Dale Rolfe is playing real good defense now. Try to intimidate him a little bit. Give him a hit."

I took note of that bit of advice. Midway in the first period, with no score, Orest Kindrachuk, my center, took a shot that Ranger goalie Ed Giacomin grabbed. As Kindrachuk moved in for the rebound, the Ranger defensemen, Park and Rolfe, rushed Kindrachuk to make sure he wasn't going to bump Giacomin. I skated over to the melee, although I had no intention of fighting at this point, but the Rangers had understandably become edgy about me from the previous games. That must have been what Rolfe felt because when I grabbed him just to push him away, he overreacted.

At 6' 4" and 205 pounds, Rolfe was one of the biggest players around, but he rarely fought and had a reputation as a soft touch. That's why I was surprised when he started punching. But once he did, blind rage—and habit—took over. His face became a punching bag; I hit him nearly a dozen times without retaliation. I held his blue jersey with my left hand and kept hitting him with my right. His knees buckled and he crumpled to the ice as the linesman, Matt Pavelich, moved in to separate us. By the time Rolfe got to his feet, he was bleeding from a cut over his eye. I was untouched. Rolfe's eye wound wasn't serious, but again psychologically I think the Rangers were damaged. We outshot them 46–15 and outscored them 4–3. We had done what was believed virtually impossible at that time: An expansion team had beaten a first-rate established club to make it into the Stanley Cup finals.

Whether I had punched us into the finals is moot, but it helped us and that's the point. "The fight [with Rolfe]," said Shero, "was the turning point. It took something out of them." Hearing that didn't hurt my ego.

The Rangers looked at it differently. We were a bunch of ogres and I was King Goon. "If I had to maim someone to win another game and win the Stanley Cup, then it isn't worth it," said Brad Park. "If I had to knock somebody's eye out or give him a concussion or break his arm or put him in the hospital to win, well, I want no part of it. It's a game, it's a sport, it's entertainment. This isn't World War III."

At the time, I would have discarded as sour grapes comments from anybody in professional hockey about the way in which we had won.

Seeing the world from Park's point of view years later, I could fully appreciate his motivation for making such claims. Winning through intimidation is certainly more palatable for the victor and much less acceptable to the victimized.

The key question of course, is how effective would we have been if we had played otherwise?

The difficult part about a philosophical discussion of violence in hockey is that success or failure plays such a big part in it. Brad Park changed his tune quickly enough. When he played for a timid team like the Rangers, it was OK for him to put the rap on the Flyers. Once he was traded to the tough Boston Bruins, where he found himself skating alongside a hatchetman like Cashman, a player who would just as soon take your eye out with the blade of his stick as score a goal, he suddenly stopped pontificating about rough hockey.

When his Bruins went up against the classy Canadiens in the 1977 Stanley Cup finals, Boston had a goon forward named John Wensink who said for publication that he was going to ruin Guy Lafleur, Montreal's great forward. I didn't hear Park rushing to the defense of good, clean hockey that time. Looking at it from his perspective, though, with heavies like Cashman and Wensink on his side, as well as a few other bruisers like Stan Jonathan, Terry O'Reilly, Don Marcotte, and Bobby Schmautz all playing rough and tough, Park was on a big winner for the first time. After years of frustration it's tough to go against winning ways.

And it's infectious. The Park who faced us in 1974 was not the same Park of 1981: He developed into a stickman. Instead of dropping his stick and fighting with his fists, he had turned into a slasher, something I consider far, far more dangerous. During a game in 1981 against Winnipeg, he chased Doug Lecuyer of the Jets across the rink, shaking his stick at Lecuyer like a fencer until someone finally intervened.

When you look back at such events you shake your head and wonder. I know that sounds ridiculous coming from me, but it's true. Whipping Rolfe helped us win a big game and moved us into the Stanley Cup finals, but Rolfe wasn't a fighter; he was basically a good clean hockey player.

I wondered if there might not have been an easier way of winning the game without humiliating him before his teammates as well as a national television audience. How would you or I have felt if we had been in his place and had absorbed the beating and then had to carry the stigma of his team's subsequent defeat? Once again—as in the case of Stewart of Atlanta—I had been locked into a situation in which I was confronted by an opponent whom nobody thought of as a fighter.

Doing what I did was something like kicking a guy when he's down. That feeling would appear more and more often, and eventually take its toll.

When I got home that night, the euphoria of beating the Rangers quickly subsided; I went to bed still thinking of the humiliating pounding I had given Rolfe.

The Atlanta and Rangers series confirmed for me one inescapable fact about professional hockey: Fighting can lead to momentum. (It can also backfire.) I led the way and the Flyers followed behind me. The more I fought, the more I felt the need to fight some more. The pressure was real. I only got compliments when I fought. I became more obsessed with fighting than I did with scoring goals (which I had done pretty well in the minors and in amateur hockey), and I became known as The Hammer.

While all this was happening I infrequently reflected upon and evaluated the consequences of my behavior. I was on a roller coaster and no one pushed the lever to stop the cars. I became absorbed with my identity as The Hammer and caught up with my own reputation. And I have no excuses to offer: I just couldn't stop the time machine at that point. The cheers were too intoxicating. It was easy to convince myself that I hadn't changed, but of course I had. In my few lucid moments I knew I was not the person I had once been proud to be. I was another person, a sometime dragon, sometime hulk, sometime bully—hardly the person I would want my children to be if they ever played hockey. It certainly was not the person I had started out to be as a kid growing up in the wheat fields of western Canada.

2

From Farm Boy to
Rink Rat

I GREW UP ON the thin edge of poverty, moving from town to town across the Saskatchewan prairie. Before I was old enough to go to school I had learned the meaning of hardship and how cruel the sub-zero winds blowing around our hovel could be to a man and his hopes.

Edgar Schultz, my father, was a husky man with a deep voice who may well have been the best auto mechanic in the province, yet he couldn't get a break out of life. Dad came from a family of three other brothers and two sisters whose parents were practicing Mennonites. My grandfather on my Dad's side ran a Pontiac dealership in the tiny town of Waldheim, which was a Mennonite center.

My Dad became the black sheep of his family and was not really appreciated by his father. He was the oldest of the six kids and did not warm to religion or his father's insistence that he attend church every Sunday. In fact, Dad never went to church. While his brothers went on to college and professional careers, my Dad rebelled, leaving home at the age of sixteen and joining the Canadian Army. He had already become a pretty fair hockey player and while he was in the Army he played on the Army team with the great Syl Apps, a member of hockey's Hall of Fame.

For some reason Dad thought farming would be for him. It turned out to be a disaster. My first recollection of Dad was when I was three years old. I can still see him going out in 40-below zero weather and feeding the pigs and cows. If you are going to make any money on the prairie you do it harvesting wheat, oats, rye, and barley. But the Saskatchewan summers are short; a farmer spends a lot of time with his eye on the thermometer, hoping that the frost won't come too soon. For Dad, it came too soon four years in a row and damn near wiped him out.

One of the farms I remember best was near Medstead, a town of a few hundred about eighty miles north of the city Saskatoon. Anything cruder than our farmhouse in Medstead is hard to imagine. It was built on mud logs and had only three rooms—a kitchen, a living room, and a bedroom. My brother, Ray, my two sisters, Barbara and Janet, and I all slept in the living room.

You would have thought we were growing up in Abe Lincoln's time. There was no electricity on the farm and no running water, which meant that conditions in many ways were sub-primitive. Our bathroom consisted of a single-seat outhouse made of wood that sat some fifty feet from the farmhouse door; going to the bathroom when it was 20 degrees below zero is an experience I wouldn't wish on my worst enemy.

Like Abe Lincoln, I had trouble reading in the house and doing my homework at night. The only source of light at night was one kerosene lamp with a pair of wicks. When we were having dinner the kerosene lamp would hang over the dinner table. After dinner my Mom would unhook it and carry the lamp into the living room until the kids went to sleep.

A primitive wood stove in the kitchen supplied all the heat for the entire house. Dad would fire it up just before we hit the sack and we'd pray that the blaze would last well into the night. He would get up early in the morning and fire it up again. I never wanted to get out of bed in the morning because by the time I did the fire had gone out, my face would be freezing, and I was confronted with washing up, getting dressed and, horror of horrors, going to the outhouse again. If you don't think this toughened me up for the future, you're sadly mistaken. It's still hard for me to believe that we endured such primitive conditions.

We depended on a neighboring farmer who lived a few hundred yards across the road from us for our drinking water, which we carried home in five-gallon pails. For bath water, we would catch the runoff from the rain and melting snow in a "dugout" in the earth past the barnyard, near the road to the pasture. To bring the bathwater to the house we would load a fifty-five gallon drum upright on a skid called a "stone bolt" and pull it with a tractor. We stored the water outside in the barrels and bathed once a week whether we needed it or not, heating the water on the stove, standing up in a tub, and dipping a pail in the barrel. In the winter, when we couldn't store the water outside because it would freeze, we bathed with drinking water by wiping ourselves with face-cloths. Many a morning we would awaken to find the drinking pail frozen solid.

Poor as we were, my folks made sure we never went hungry. My mother, Pauline, was a kind, hard-working woman who fed us lots of home-baked breads, vegetables, and macaroni for dinner. We butchered our own cattle for meat. Breakfast was usually porridge, piping hot.

Ray, who is a year older than me, was the fair-haired boy in the family. He was confident as a kid. I was shy, unsure of myself. When we played baseball, I was afraid of getting hit in the face with the ball. And under no circumstances would I fight. Once, my friend Roger Bergman had a pair of boxing gloves, and Ray and Roger fooled around with the gloves. I wanted no part of them, but they finally asked me to put the gloves on, so I couldn't back off. As soon as the other guy started to throw punches I closed my eyes. I was scared of getting hit and it was obvious that I couldn't box worth a lick. Instead of standing back and punching, I went at him with my head buried in my hands.

I was also intimidated by animals. One day when I was ten I was doing some weeding for a farmer who had a big Holstein bull. I used to sit at the edge of the corral and tease the bull, but this time I was in the barnyard and, all of a sudden, I saw the bull coming straight for me. I was terrified as it kicked up dust at the other end of the corral and moved in for what I figured was the great revenge. For a second I froze, then I got my legs moving and ran across the yard, dove through the fence, ran up the hill and never stopped running until I got back to the safety of the farmer's house.

I was only slightly braver in an encounter with a mouse. Ray and I were sitting on top of a seeding machine. A long box next to us held the seed, covered with a lid. I heard a noise inside; I lifted the lid and there was a little mouse. I tried to chase it but the mouse jumped up Ray's pants leg. Ray went bananas. He jumped off the machine and ran crying toward the house, all the while squeezing the rear end of his pants. My father heard Ray's screams and ran out of the house as Ray ran into his arms. As the pants came off Ray's legs, the mouse fell out, limp. Ray had squeezed it to death.

When Ray wasn't around I loved to take long walks away from the farm. The prairie air was dry and crisp. The land was flat as a table. I would look out to the horizon and see an endless panorama of fields and more fields. I'd walk between the trees, collect leaves, bring them home and press them inside the pages of a book. I loved the smell of grain. To me it was the perfume of the prairie.

Winters were brutal. The snow would pile twelve feet high around the house, and it was nothing to have almost an inch of ice on the inside of the windows. The snow got so deep that nobody could get to the house by car. One day my grandparents came to visit. We had to bring the car to the farmhouse on our horse-drawn sled.

When my Dad's farm failed we moved to my grandparents' town, Waldheim. My father got a job as a mechanic in my grandfather's car dealership. Because it was a churchgoing community, they made sure that by the time I was twelve I went to Bible camp in the summer, and to Sunday school every week.

Compared with the farm, Waldheim was a metropolis. It had a main street and a couple of stores, but no hotel and no bar. When Dad wanted a drink he had to drive eight miles to the nearest bar.

Saturday night was a big night in Waldheim. Ray and I would walk down to the hardware store to watch the hockey games on television. A bunch of the farmers would gather around the hot stove, smoke their pipes, and root for the Toronto Maple Leafs. It was my first chance to become a hockey fan, and ironic as it may seem, my favorite player was Dave Keon of the Leafs, the cleanest player in the NHL. Keon would never fight and I loved him for it. Why not? I would never fight either, and for that I can thank my brother, Ray.

He proved his worth to me as a protector after the family had moved to Rosetown, a town of three thousand about a hundred miles south of Waldheim where Dad took a job as a mechanic. We spent our teens there occasionally getting into an odd row. Ray, who was bigger and heavier than me, would fight anyone, anytime. Once, when I was sixteen, a couple of bullies came by in a car and began cursing me. The bigger one shook his fist at me. I was terrified. I desperately wanted my brother and ran looking for him. In a matter of minutes I found him driving around with a friend. "A couple of guys wanted to fight with me, Ray," I whimpered.

Like one of those comic book heroes, he led the search, driving all over town trying to spot them. It was getting dark when we finally came upon a house that had a little shack behind it. We could see a little light flickering through the window and the two bullies inside.

Ray stormed up to the door and ripped it right off its hinges. They couldn't believe their eyes. Ray yelled "C'mon out, you sonsofbitches!"

The big one pleaded with Ray: "No, it's not you I'm after, it's your brother." Ray jumped him and gave him a few good shots. Then the other guy started in with Ray. It wasn't easy for my brother this time, but he held his own and came out of it with only a fat lip.

My first close friend, other than my brother, was Claude Paquette. I met him when we moved to Rosetown. By the time I got to high school, Claude and I had become so close we were like Damon and Pythias. I liked Claude's sense of humor, his outgoing nature—and his 1964 Chevy Nova.

We were about sixteen years old when his older brother, Maurice, saved me and Claude from getting our heads handed to us. We were riding around in Claude's Nova when we saw five guys in another car. They pulled right up next to us and shook their fists at us. That was a signal that they wanted to have a rumble (kids that age back home just loved to fight), but I didn't want any part of it. One of them said, "We'll be waiting for you at Three-Mile Corner," a crossroads about three miles north of town, out on the flat prairie, as good a place as any for a bunch of teenagers to park their cars and slug it out.

Claude and I drove out in his car and Maurice came out in another. I felt queasy about the whole thing even though there were two other fellows to protect me, if necessary. Actually one, since Claude had no intention of fighting, either. I kept hoping the three-mile drive would be about three hundred miles.

When we pulled up to the crossroads our enemies were there, and I took a deep breath. I had hoped that they would chicken out, but more than anything I wanted Maurice to come as quickly as possible. At last I heard the distant roar of his car, and could see it coming down the road. My heart started pounding like a bass drum. Maurice got out of the car and ripped his shirt off. The other guys wouldn't get out of their car. Maurice opened the door of their car and dragged one of them out by the scruff of his neck. Slapping him across the face, he said, "If you ever lay a hand on my brother or Schultz here I'll really give it to ya." He picked up his shirt, walked back to our car, turned on the ignition, and Claude and I pulled away triumphantly.

It was great as long as Ray or Maurice was around, but sooner or later I knew that I'd find myself in a confrontation where I'd have to handle my problems alone. It happened at the community hall in Rosetown. There was a dance at the hall and, as is the custom in these Saskatchewan towns, a major sidelight was drinking. For some time I had been tormented by a fellow named Doug Lang, a big guy who had been in a lot of trouble and really bugged me. I had a few beers and suddenly I felt very brave. I said to myself, "Once and for all you gotta challenge him." I walked over to Lang and, with the most nerve I had ever summoned in my life, I said, "OK, c'mon, let's go."

Lang just turned away. He wouldn't fight me. But another guy who had been watching us, Lee Bannister, pushed Lang aside and moved face-to-face with me. He said, "If you want to fight somebody, fight me." I took a swing at him, missed and my fist hit the plasterboard wall. Then he drove me right in the head with his right fist. My forehead felt like it had been hit with a wooden mallet. The fight ended with that one punch. I was humiliated.

It was then that I knew that I would never be the heavyweight champion of Saskatchewan.

My life as a teenager was relatively aimless. I didn't do well at school. I was too shy to date girls, and since I couldn't fight worth a damn, I wasn't exactly a big-shot with the guys in town.

I had two sources of pleasure. One was solitude! I liked being alone, working with my hands on the farms. I would get jobs in the fields, pulling weeds. I loved working a tractor for eight hours all by myself, surrounded by nothing but the sky, the land—the prairie scene. The other pleasure was hockey. I would go outdoors and skate and skate on the town rink—just a set of sideboards and a little hut with a wood stove where you put the skates on—right off the main street in Waldheim. The town was so small it was hard even to get a pick-up game, but I'd just go out and skate by myself or with Ray and a few other kids. It didn't matter to us if the thermometer hit 30 below zero.

It didn't take long for me to become obsessed with hockey. I'd take a stick with me to school and run down the ice-covered roads hitting a tennis ball or a frozen "street apple," which is what we called a piece of icy horse manure (they make good pucks). For a short time, we lived in the basement of the closed-down hospital in Waldheim, and we even played hockey there: Ray and I would go running up and down the empty corridor playing one-on-one. Sometimes he'd be the shooter and I'd be the goalie, then we'd reverse the roles.

Hockey made me feel good. I liked the feel of the puck on the stick.

I liked skating up and down the outdoor rink with the cold, dry air piercing my nostrils.

Although we weren't a particularly close-knit family, hockey brought me closer to my father. Dad loved hockey from his Army days and he still loved to put on the skates and play with the older guys, referee the odd game—or skate with me. Hockey provided the one clear bond between my father and me.

I was beginning to feel a sense of accomplishment about my hockey skills, something I couldn't get out of any other aspect of my life. School was only rewarding at times. Although I attended diligently, I couldn't wait for classes to be over so that I could get to the rink. Half the time I found myself falling asleep behind the desk. At one point I had ambitions to become an engineer, but it was more of a dream than anything.

My mom and dad were never able to give me real guidance because they worked so hard, but I learned the value of sweat from them. I felt sorry for Dad because of all the hard luck he had and I knew in my heart that, whatever happened, I wanted more out of my life than he had.

By the time I reached my mid-teens there were only two real choices for me, farm work or hockey. In that sense I was like thousands of Canadian prairie kids before me. They instinctively turned away from the farm and toward the rink. After all, it was better to play with a hockey stick than a shovel.

The junior (amateur) hockey system was tailor-made for kids like me. Each town had its own amateur club. The bigger ones had what's known as Junior B (for kids as young as fourteen) or Junior A (for kids as young as sixteen) teams. The good part was that I could get to play regularly, meet new people, live in a bigger town and see more of the world, and even make a couple of bucks. (Although we were considered amateurs, the regulations of the Canadian Amateur Hockey Association were more loosely interpreted than those of the Amateur Athletic Union or the International Olympic Committee. In Canada, you're an amateur "as long as you don't sign a professional contract." Therefore, as an amateur hockey player I was given, like the others, a weekly allowance to cover room and board and minor expenses.) The bad part was that schooling was interrupted; there was too much unplanned time on our hands and we had great opportunities for getting ourselves into trouble.

I fell into this world almost by accident. I had become a good hockey player. I was fast—for my bunch—and I could score goals, so it was perfectly natural for me to think of playing more hockey on a somewhat higher level. If nothing else, it kept me off the streets.

Off I went to Swift Current, a metropolis by my standards, which had all of fifteen thousand people when I got there in 1967. It was a great education in itself. Except for the time when I went to Bible camp at age twelve, this was the first time I had been away from home alone.

My coach in Swift Current, a man named Harvey Roy, taught me my first good lesson: Never shake hands with a limp palm. Squeeze. My second lesson was that solitude could no longer be one of the foremost aspects of my personality. I was now part of a team. I discovered a camaraderie I had never known existed. There were more than a dozen of us traveling the roads in western Canada, visiting such outposts as Flin Flon, Moose Jaw, and Estevan. We won together, lost together, and got intimidated together—especially in Flin Flon.

If nothing else, juniors taught me the hard facts of life about hockey: that toughness is a part of the game. Flin Flon, a mining town in northern Manitoba, had a frontier air about it. The entire area around the town was rock. The houses were all built on rock—without basements—and some of the streets had board sidewalks. All of the sewer pipes ran above ground, giving Flin Flon a weird look. The people who lived there were tough. When we drove the five-hundred-odd miles north to play their team, the Bombers, we didn't expect to win. We did, however, expect to get the hell beat out of us—and we were usually right. What I took away from that experience was that the timidity that had been a key element in my character was a major hindrance in my development as a hockey player. Flin Flon played so tough a style I think it's understandable that a kid in my position might have overreacted based on a pretty dramatic first impression.

Up until then, hockey to me had been a pretty game of skating, shooting, stickhandling, and playmaking. When a stick was rammed into my stomach, a butt end massaged my ribs, and a thick leather gauntlet was pushed in my face, I got a different impression of what organized hockey was all about. Flin Flon had bruisers like Gerry Hart and goal-scorers like Bobby Clarke, but they would as soon extract a pound of flesh from a visitor as score a pack of goals.

I wanted no part of that rough stuff. I still recoiled from baseballs and let other guys fight my battles. I was a coward and I proved it when a brawl broke out on the ice in Flin Flon. I hid in the bench area. If I could have crawled under the bench I would have.

Another time, I couldn't get to my hideout on the bench. Before I could get away from the fight one of the Bombers skated up to me and drilled me one right in the head. When I regained consciousness the referee was standing over me.

"Schultz," he said, pointing to the penalty box. "Five minutes."

I said, "Five minutes, for what?"

"Five minutes for fighting."

I hadn't even gotten my gloves off and I was flat on my face and he gave me five for fighting. If that was the jungle law of hockey, I knew I wasn't going to survive long as a pacifist. The trouble was that I had no idea how to transform myself from a soft-touch guy to a hard guy. At that point in my hockey life I still never thought about fighting.

Although it may sound hard to believe, my conception of hockey was a purist one. No one was more concerned about checking, goal-scoring, and finesse than I was in my youth. My boyish fantasies were filled with aspirations to play the game cleanly like a Dave Keon.

My junior hockey life seemed to be a state of reasonably happy suspension. The game was still mostly fun; I had no idea of making a career of it and I had less of an idea of where I was going. The last thing I thought would ever happen to me was that I would turn from a timid stickhandler into a Broad Street Bully.

3

The Lamb Turns Lion

How do you convert a hockey-playing lamb into a lion?
With great difficulty. I was not cut out to be a fighter. I was aware
of the hockey jungle, having heard of the bad men of the NHL, like
Ted Green and John Ferguson. I recognized what they were doing,
but I remained loyal to law and order as I moved up in junior hockey.

I knew that I couldn't avoid body contact altogether, so I devised a
half-assed form of aggression. Hit and run like hell. It was very effective. I'd skate into the corner after the puck and if an opponent was
there I'd offhandedly give him the back of my glove or toss a half-
hearted punch with my glove on and get out of there so fast the other
guy would hardly know who did it. At least this gave me the *feel* of
physical contact.

Deep down I knew that was not enough; sooner or later I would be
challenged to a face-to-face fight. It happened during a game with the
Brandon Wheat Kings, another junior team from western Canada. At
one point in the game I found myself on a collision course with Butch
Deadmarsh, the very same Deadmarsh I would later meet on the ice
at Atlanta.

Neither of us gave an inch. Normally I would have turned away
from Deadmarsh and followed the puck, but I had become a bit confident as a result of my small collection of skirmishes and, instead of
running from Deadmarsh, I once and for all put up my dukes. The
mere act of getting into fighting position gave me goose pimples. I
felt like a wetnose soldier about to face his first hail of bullets. I was

scared, to be sure, but I also was experiencing a hostile form of ecstasy that I wanted to savor as long as possible.

Before Deadmarsh lifted a finger I swung my right fist around and rammed it directly into his face. For a split second I didn't know what to do. To be honest, the sensation of my knuckles colliding with his cheek made me want to jump for joy. Then I felt awkward about what I had done, and a little ashamed. By this time the linesmen were between us, and the fight, for what it was worth, was over.

It was not a milestone in hockey history but it was my first fight and, most important, I had not lost. The fight itself did not inspire me to go out and waste every enemy player in sight. Quite the contrary. I was still content to go out and do what I was doing well—skating hard and scoring goals. I was still very much an honorable hockey player with decent aims.

The final turnabout in my hockey personality from benign to boisterous developed during the middle of the next season, 1968–69. The quality of my play had improved so much that I was invited to play with the Sorel Black Hawks of the Quebec Junior League. The team I was playing for, the Swift Current Broncos, were in last place and I thought a change might be good for me. This was a dramatic switch in many ways. First of all, it meant moving from my home on the prairies to a city where everyone speaks French. Secondly, I would be playing in a fast junior league that was frequently scouted by the big league teams. The biggest change was the fact that the Black Hawks were a tough team. If some of our guys hadn't been teenagers you could have mistaken them for tavern bouncers. They were big and they were tough, not necessarily in order of importance. When I looked around and saw the collection of bruisers on our team, I knew I didn't have to worry. The sense of security they gave me allowed my game to expand.

I get a lot of pleasure when I look back on that season, because when I was out on the ice I wasn't there just to drop my gloves and start something with someone. I was there to *play* hockey—to put the puck in the net. Which I frequently did. That season I scored roughly fifty goals in eighty games (including the playoffs). During a number of those games, I scored hat tricks and was voted the best player on the ice.

I was also getting into a couple of fights; not, as I said, because I had suddenly become a tough guy, but because I was one of the biggest skaters around (there were a lot of small French-Canadian players in the league) and people started to expect me to be aggressive, to be one of the "protectors" of the team. Although I still cared only about scoring goals, I had found out what it was like to play on a team both aggressive and tough. I liked it.

I was young and I was strong and I was scoring goals with my new aggressive game. The fights? Well, that was just a part of the initiation rites: Show you won't be pushed around and they'll leave you alone. Though for the first time I began to perceive that goal-scorers weren't the only ones to get recognition. The "policemen," the guys who could handle their dukes, got as much if not more ink and applause. For my occasional fights that kind of attention was now, for the first time, coming to me.

In June 1969 I was selected by the Philadelphia Flyers in the fifth round of the National Hockey League's amateur draft. Training camp that September was in Quebec City. I reported in and skated against guys I had only read about in the papers: Ed Van Impe, Joe Watson, Gary Dornhoefer, Reg Fleming. I kept my nose clean. I knew I wasn't going to make the big team, but I wanted to make an impression. In one scrimmage against some of the older veterans on the club, I ran into Guy Gendron, a hard-nosed little Frenchman who had learned tough hockey skating alongside Lou Fontinato on the Rangers in the late 1950s.

Gendron turned around and drove me right in the face with a punch that seemed to pulverize my skull. By the time I had recovered from the blow the whole side of my face had swelled and I felt like an impotent greenhorn. Even though Gendron wasn't very big, it was his way of telling me he wasn't going to take any rough stuff from a rookie. I turned the other cheek.

The physical damage was nothing more than a bruised cheek and I managed to recover my ego soon enough to have a decent training camp. The Flyers must have thought so because they gave me an eight-game tryout with their American League farm team, the Quebec Aces. That was tantamount to the International League in baseball, one step from the top. I failed to make the Quebec team—no goals, no assists, no points in eight games. They gave me a one-way ticket to Salem, Virginia. I was now a member of the Salem–Roanoke Valley Rebels of the Eastern Hockey League.

By any standard, the Eastern League was tough. It comprised eager kids like myself, trying to make it to the NHL, and well-traveled veterans like John Brophy who wouldn't think twice about performing surgery on me with his stick blade. Brophy employed his hockey stick the way a samurai uses a sword. If he had any scruples, he must have buried them the first time he put on a pair of skates. One night a teammate of mine skated around Brophy and John just lifted his stick and rammed it into the kid's face. The kid needed six stiches to close the wound.

I did not expect the Eastern League to be a rose garden. On the other hand, I had absolutely no preconceptions about how I was going to react to the rough stuff. All I really wanted to do was prove that I was a good hockey player.

My debut was at home against the Jacksonville Rockets. Playing those few games in the American League had done wonders for me. I felt as if I were better than most guys I was skating against. I felt strong. I was stickhandling as well as any of them and I was getting my scoring chances. And I was hitting.

Midway in the game I had a run-in with a small French-Canadian, Denis Romanesky, whom I remembered from the Quebec Junior League. By the time we collided my juices were flowing very fast. As we parted from the original collision I realized that I wanted to pick this guy apart and I started swinging before he knew what had happened. I was on a terrific high, psychologically, and felt just as strong physically. Once I started landing the punches to his head my nervousness dissipated. A sort of craziness came over me as I began pummeling him. That craziness turned to exhilaration as he went down in a heap. For the first time in my life I had really won a fight.

It was as if everything had come together at the same time. In a way, I had come to develop a perspective on such events. I could tell the effect that this had on the momentum of the game. It is very important to be able to explain what it is you have done in a particular situation. For the first time, I had begun to develop a rational frame of reference for such activity. Without sounding too philosophical, at the time I felt like the Incredible Hulk and I instantly sensed that the fans and players appreciated me as much as if I had scored a goal. Although I had first felt that sensation in Sorel, it was now even more exciting.

We played the next night and I got into another fight. The fans cheered louder for me than for the goal-scorers. Almost overnight I had become an attraction because of my fists and there was no one to discourage it. The media ate it up and my coach, Colin Kilburn, thought it was just great. We now could stand up to other teams that tried to intimidate us.

The fear of being beaten that had so terrified me as a kid in Saskatchewan was gone, buried under a hail of fists and mounds of press clippings. Almost overnight, fighting had made me a celebrity. There it was in *The Hockey News:* "If there is one thing that can be said about the Salem Rebels this year, it's simply that they are an entertaining hockey club after being a dull one in past seasons."

The key word was *entertaining.* They liked the fights. I had become a showman, the hero to the crowd at the Salem-Roanoke Valley Civic Center, who called me "Sergeant Schultz." I was the talk of the Eastern League. I didn't hear the name-calling at first. I was a hungry young player who had been demoted from the American League and wanted to get back up as fast as he could. I lived for hockey now. I could taste the big time. Cowardly most of my life, I felt now like I was caught up in a fantasy.

For the first time in my life I had a reputation—a reputation *to uphold.* I had won a bunch of fights and now the fans expected more. I started looking for fights.

I couldn't stop. We were playing the Charlotte Checkers at our rink. There were four thousand fans in the building and they anticipated trouble every time I stepped on the ice. Late in the second period I spotted Gary Mills, a short, stocky Checkers defenseman. I knew him from back home in Rosetown, where I used to deliver papers to the home of his brother, a schoolteacher. Mills was big, but I felt I could handle him. He couldn't resist the challenge after I had taken him into the boards. I dropped him with a hard right.

In the third period I went after John Van Horlick, but the linesman intervened before I could nail him. I skated to the penalty box and slammed the door in disgust. The fans ate it up. The chanting was loud and clear: "We want Schultz! We want Schultz!"

At home they loved me. On the road they loved to hate me. I was well on my way to setting an Eastern League penalty record. The numbers in the column "penalties in minutes" became meaningful to me. As the numbers increased, my popularity grew. For the first time in my life hockey writers and sports columnists came after me for interviews.

When I got used to the adulation, I changed my style. I still had enough wits about me to know that fighting alone wasn't going to get me into the NHL. I knew that scoring would be the bottom line when the scouts evaluated my potential. So I went eight games without a fight and scored eight goals and eight assists. That reinforced my confidence and pleased my coach, but the press immediately figured I was going soft. The Roanoke World News ran a full-page banner headline: REBELS SERGEANT A FIGHTING MAN NO MORE."

This would set the tone for me throughout my career. Fans, coaches, the media—they all now expected me to fight. I felt I had no choice but to oblige them. I briefly considered shaking my enforcer image, but whenever I got those thoughts I quickly realized that I had become a celebrity because of my fists and there was no way I was going to go straight. Not now.

I had the best of both worlds. Even though I was getting penalties galore I also was scoring at a healthy rate. I produced 32 goals and 37 assists—69 points in 67 games—a respectable record considering I had spent 356 minutes in the penalty box.

The violence didn't come easy to me so I worked especially hard at psyching myself up. I would talk to myself on a regular basis: "If someone takes a run at one of our players everyone expects you to fight." I'd sit back and think about whom I might have to fight and would actually get a picture in my mind of the fight and how I would win it. It got to the point where it became an obsession. Then, when I did win a fight, I would feel so powerful that I'd want to show everyone.

I had developed a special sense of publicity. I realized that my zany antics—slamming the penalty-box door, gyrating wildly at the referee, appealing to the fans—had a show-biz effect that I enjoyed. Quite often the referee would have no choice but to give me a misconduct penalty.

I was never at a loss for a rationale. I justified my misconducts by saying that in order to fight (which I felt I had to do), I had to get myself psyched up. After psyching myself up, even after a fight I still had a lot of pent-up feelings that had to be let out somewhere and on someone. The misconducts were inevitable.

Besides psyching myself up to fight for the team, there was another thing that was sure to get me into a scrap. I hated to the point of frenzy when an opponent held onto me by hooking or holding me; I would lash out at him and usually a fight would follow.

My capacity to fight, in conjunction with my abilities as a productive, constantly improving hockey player, did not hurt my chances with respect to a potential big-league hockey career.

It also didn't hurt that we were winning hockey games.

The Flyers thought enough of me to move me up to Quebec of the American League for 1970-71. This was big stuff. A good year or two in the AHL could mean promotion to the NHL. The question was how would I behave in such fast company? Would I be able to get away with the antics that had worked so well in the Eastern League? Basically shy and passive off the ice, was I capable of sustaining the role of a tough guy on the ice for more than one season? It would not be easy. I was carrying a reputation with me into the best of the minor leagues. I felt the pressure before I even stepped on the ice. My act had to work. It would be necessary to persuade the opposition that I was someone who should be kept at a distance.

I was smelling success for the first time and understood that I had to make a basic decision about my future direction as a professional hockey player. Idealistically, I preferred staying away from the rough stuff and working on my hockey skills. But realistically I knew that I could make a better name for myself going the other route. My gut feeling was that I could produce enough offensively to win the attention of the Flyers' management while doing all the fighting necessary to establish myself as a major gate attraction. When I moved into the American League my coaches encouraged the bad guy image I was projecting because they felt it was good for the team—I protected the smaller players—and it was good box office. Any latent thoughts that I might have retained about keeping to the straight and narrow were well concealed by this glittering opportunity to jab and uppercut my way to the NHL.

Not one responsible person discouraged my act and, by the looks of the headlines devoted to my slugging, there was much to be said for the role of enforcer. I played along with my image and found that the act worked as well in the American League as it had down in the Eastern. My penalty minutes climbed to 382 in Quebec, a league record. I scored 14 goals and 23 assists in 71 games but the modest totals never inspired the Flyers to demote me back to the Eastern League. They realized that I was doing precisely what was acceptable at the Spectrum. They could live with my mediocre scoring output at that time as long as I demonstrated that I was an effective enforcer.

My metamorphosis into a professional athlete got little feedback from my family. Since I was still in the minors my notoriety was still limited to the American League, so there was little news of my evil doings in the Saskatchewan papers. For the moment, at least, my parents were relatively unaware that their once mild-mannered son had evolved into some kind of beast on skates. They were just tickled that I was able to make a living playing hockey. None of my coaches did anything to curb my outbursts. Like most hockey coaches, they figured that every team needed its "policeman" and I was patrolling my beat precisely the way they wanted it, keeping the opposition "honest."

The Flyers organization never realized the transformation was unplanned. There *is* a place in the world of professional hockey for my style of player. In fact, professional teams search out such athletes in the junior hockey ranks. As soon as a young player's style crystallizes, and he displays rough qualities, he immediately captures the scouts' attention. So even if I had some doubts or misgivings about my new role, the Flyers inadvertently locked me in. A relatively small team, they had been battered for a couple of seasons by bigger and rougher outfits such as St. Louis and Boston. The Philadelphia team desperately sought the type of young bruiser that I now epitomized.

When the Flyers moved their farm team from Quebec to Richmond for the 1971-72 season I was with them, now considered a treasured member of the team. Where I once had been afraid of some of the bruisers on the opposition, now nobody scared me. The transformation was complete. I had become a mean, relentless fighter. I showed no mercy.

One night at our home rink, the Richmond Coliseum, we were playing the Nova Scotia Voyageurs, a farm club of the Montreal Canadiens. One of the best players on the Voyageurs was Chuck Arnason, a center from Dauphin, Manitoba. He had been up with the Montreal Canadiens for a cup of coffee and now he was back in the American League. We went into the left corner together. His elbow came up in a reflex act of protection. It caught me on the chin, not heavily enough actually to provoke a fight if I wasn't doing my routine. But to me, Arnason's elbow was like the red flag to a bull. I came at him with fists flying, mashing him in the face with my right fist. He came back with a right of his own, but it had already been defused by my first punch. He retreated toward his net where the Voyageurs' goalie, Michel Plasse, watched along with Arnason's four other teammates. I couldn't believe that none of them jumped me to protect their buddy from more harm. I hit him again. The punch was so hard that my right hand hurt from the blow. I finally let up on the poor guy.

I knew that from this point on in the game I had to be careful, that one of the Voyageurs' tough guys would try to get back at me. One of them might blindside me or deliver a sucker punch, catching me off guard. I became especially tense and I hated it; I felt like a hunted animal that had to be prepared for instant attack. And if the retaliation didn't come that game, I would be on guard for it when next we played. One of the reasons so many did come looking for me was that they knew any brawl would be a clean one, all fists and no sticks.

In the second period that night Nova Scotia's defenseman Tony Featherstone, a little bigger and a little tougher guy than Arnason, stormed at me with a ten-yard charge, but I spotted him out of the corner of my eye. He walloped me with the first punch, but I rolled with his left and right, catching him square in the jaw. His eyes rolled up to the top of his head and his knees buckled. He was hurt.

There were many others like that one. The sum total was 392 penalty minutes (breaking the record I had set the previous year), 18 goals, and 28 assists. And, finally, an invitation came to play for the Philadelphia Flyers in 1972–73.

Caspar Milquetoast had turned into Al Capone.

If I tried to analyze how my abrupt personality transformation came about, I would say that I always had the potential for becoming an enforcer. Remember, bigger guys like my brother, Ray, had always been there to protect me as a kid. Now I simply reversed that situation. Given the proper climate for aggression, there was only one way for me to overcome my Mennonite background and that was to go completely wild in the other direction. The ambience of the ice arenas not only enabled me but encouraged me to pursue this outrageously violent behavior. This social reinforcement gave me an ego boost I'd never received before but obviously needed. Especially after having paid my dues in the minors.

The Eastern League was a sweatshop. The conditions were brutal and some of the people I worked with were no bargain either. We had a full-blooded Indian on the Rebels named August George. I roomed with him and two other guys for a while in a one-bedroom apartment. Awful. August George didn't believe in washing his underwear, so when it got dirty he just threw it under the bed. He smelled so bad nobody wanted to share a bed with him; he wound up with the box-spring bed all to himself. I slept on a couch that was about three inches too short for me. It was worse than sleeping on a Greyhound bus.

In the minors you played for peanuts. I couldn't even afford a car. I made $250 a week and cut corners wherever I could. To some people, $250 a week might sound fairly substantial. But our season lasted five to six months and so did our pay period.

We had a lot of free time but, like most hockey players, we tended to spend it doing ridiculous things. For a while I lived in a mobile home in a horseshoe-shaped trailer court. A bunch of the other guys on the team lived there, too. It was sociable but all they wanted to do was drink until they got soused. Then they would do nice, normal things like pulling out real bows and arrows and shooting the arrows into the sides of the trailers, like cowboys and Indians.

Booze was a big part of life. One night we were in Clinton, New York, home of the Comets, near the Canadian border. After the game the Comets Booster Club invited our team out for beer and sandwiches. We were in a private club on the main floor. In the basement they had a regular bar. Jim Letcher, our goalie, got bored and went downstairs for a drink. Letcher, I should say, played best after partying all night, sleeping late, and taking a couple of Bennies before he went into the nets. While he was waiting, a guy next to him turned to Jim and said, "I don't want you standin' next to my girl."

Letcher was irritated but he didn't do anything. He came back upstairs and said to some of us, "I'm goin' back down. If I'm not up in ten minutes you guys come down and help me."

Ten minutes went by and there was no Jim. I was worried, and for good reason. When I went to look, Jim was face-to-face with the guy, who had a black patch over his eye. The guy grabbed a billiard pole and cracked it in half over the side of the bar, holding the jagged edge in his hand.

Letcher got his hands on a beer glass and crunched it in his teeth. Black Patch swung at Letcher. Jim went for Black Patch's jugular. The restaurant looked like a fight scene from a grade-B Western movie. I was scared stiff.

The play-acting toughness that I had developed so well on the hockey rink did not carry over to a barroom brawl. I ran up the stairs, shouting to Colin Kilburn to get reinforcements down fast to rescue Letcher. Down the steps the Salem Rebels ran, right into the brawl. Someone called the cops. I shouted, "Let's get the hell outta here" and split for the team bus, which was waiting right outside the door. Black Patch and his friend were still throwing punches at us as we retreated out the door. The bus driver—a very wise man—already had the motor running. We gunned our way past the police cars and out of town.

One night we were playing in Charlotte. During an intermission our coach was arguing with the referee in the runway leading to our dressing room. This cop butted in and Kilburn told him off in no uncertain terms. All of a sudden five cops jumped Kilburn and began beating on him. Then they arrested him and took him off to jail. That left us without a coach for the last period. We couldn't leave town until we bailed Kilburn out. After all, he controlled our meal money.

Another time in Charlotte, a fight broke out beside our bench and Kilburn grabbed one of their players by the hair. When that happened the whole Charlotte bench emptied and skated over to our bench. Meanwhile, their coach ran all the way around the rink to punch out Kilburn. Next thing you know the cops moved in and sprayed us with Mace. Our eyes watered and we started choking. Great fun.

If there is one thing that separates major league hockey from the bush league brand it's transportation. In the NHL you travel by plane. First class. In the Eastern League, you go by bus. Fourth class. Our "luxury liner" had eight seats in the front and fourteen bunk beds in the back.

Can you imagine going on an eight-hour trip with fourteen guys stuck on one bus, drinking beer, smoking, and putting up with August George's interpretation of the sanitary code? The bus stank. The floor was covered with dirt and variations of grime that hadn't been invented yet. When the guys weren't drinking, they played cards. The coach would sit in. They bet like crazy and when Kilburn ran out of cash, he'd reach for a box and pull out more money. That box had our meal money in it. By the time we got to where we were going, we felt like death warmed over.

If nothing else, it was good for getting to know your teammates; good for telling stories. And as bad as the bus was, it was nothing compared to the trips we had taken in junior hockey. The trip to Flin Flon, which was located near the Arctic Circle, gave me a good idea of what Lewis and Clark must have felt like when they blazed the Northwest Passage. The drive, over roads you wouldn't wish on a Sherman tank, took more than twelve hours. Once we made the expedition in a convoy of several cars during sub-zero temperatures. Another time, I sat in the back end of a van that had a heater that never blew the warm air beyond the front seat. By the time we got home I not only felt like, I was convinced that I was, the Abominable Snowman.

The money, bad as it was in the Eastern League, still had it over juniors, where we'd be lucky if we got twenty dollars a week. We had been so poor that even the couple of bucks I was making was a lot for me; but you really couldn't live well on that, and some of the other guys felt a need to steal.

One day we were playing a game in Weyburn, Saskatchewan, and after practice I walked into a corner drugstore with two teammates. One of the two asked to see an electric razor. He said, "How much?" The counterman said, "Just a minute, I'll go back and check."

My buddy grabbed the razor and started running. What could I do? I started running with him. We ran all the way back to our team bus. Just as it was about to pull out a police car showed up. Our coach, Harvey Roy, looked at the cops as if they were crazy. He said, "Officer, none of our boys would ever do a thing like that." The cops believed him.

Another time we were playing in Edmonton and a couple of guys went into The Bay, a big department store there. One of them bought a pair of cowboy boots. He took them out of the box and used the box to put stolen goods in; they walked around and whenever they saw something they liked—records or whatever—they just tossed it into the box. All the guys finally left but one: the fellow with the box. As he got to the door the manager spotted him, put the grab on him, called the cops, and sent him to jail. He had sausages and eggs in jail for his pre-game meal, then was let out so he could play with us that night against Edmonton.

These kinds of experiences will never be included in a Boy Scout handbook but they are a part of the upbringing of most hockey players who make it to the top. I sit back some evenings gazing in disbelief at my scrapbooks, at the cast of characters who shared my experiences from junior hockey on through the minor leagues. The pranks, shenanigans, abrasive behavior, and the downright crazies were not to be believed. But more than the good stories there came a framework for my development and growth, not only as a professional hockey player but also as a human being.

I suppose such a statement demands explanation. As far as I was concerned, the world of junior hockey as well as the minor leagues, from the point of view of pressure, routine, and anxiety, is much like the world of the NHL. It was the boot camp of the pros. My junior and minor league apprenticeship provided me with a frame of reference and a set of expectations about my forthcoming career in the NHL. As a result, the pro ranks were no more than an extension of what I had experienced from the ripe old age of seventeen.

I received a healthy amount of assistance in my maturation as a human being in another area, which began with a chance encounter with a lovely young woman named Cathy McNab.

4

Enter Cathy

I WAS BRUTAL with girls. I may have been the shyest kid in the Dominion of Canada. I didn't know how to talk to girls so I didn't. I let my friend Claude Paquette do the talking. If I had a crush on a girl I'd never get to meet her because I'd be too scared to talk. Claude was the great talker; he got all the pretty girls and I wound up with their ugly friends.

In the summer of 1966, when I was living in Rosetown, my Dad had a beat-up car he'd let me drive once in a while. It was a 1957 Dodge. A beaut. It had no first gear and no reverse, just second and third. If you wanted to back up to park it, you didn't; you went around the block. The driver's seat was okay, but something had happened to the passenger seat; it was in a permanent state of collapse. It was more like a couch than a seat, so if you wanted to sit up you really had to work at it.

One day I was driving the Dodge down our street when I noticed two very interesting-looking girls. One of them was Bonnie Pelletier, a nice girl I had seen around. The other was this absolute knockout blonde, Cathy McNab. They had just come from the town swimming pool and were walking down the street. I don't know how I forced the words out but I managed to say, "Do you want a ride home?" It was one of the most difficult moves of my young life.

They astonished me by saying sure and hopped in the car. The blonde sat next to me. I liked that. It was only a minute to her house. When she got out I asked her, "Do you mind if I give you a call sometime?"

"Sure, why not?" she said.

45

That was the beginning of our romance.

Her father, Bob McNab, was the mayor of Rosetown, a classy guy who owned the town's menswear shop. He was scrupulously honest and wouldn't take advantage of a soul. Her mother, Jean, was a pleasant lady, a nurse. They were a very close-knit family, more so than ours. In the Schultz family you sat down to dinner, ate, and then left. When the McNabs had supper, they'd talk for an hour. Dinner was a time for socializing.

Cathy not only was good-looking, she was an athlete. She could run like the wind and was one of the best sprinters in the province.

I was sixteen and Cathy was fourteen when we met. That fall I left Rosetown to play junior hockey but we kept in touch, writing and telephoning. She saw other guys and I saw other girls but we never stopped seeing each other.

It wasn't always easy. When I went to her house I had this feeling I had come from the other side of the tracks. By our standards, her family was well-to-do. They had a certain class about them. My parents were different. And I was intimidated by her father. I don't think I said a word to him during the first two years I knew Cathy.

When I finally turned pro, Cathy went off to the University of Saskatchewan in Saskatoon. I thought hockey would give me more than a university. Of course, I was wrong. Financially, hockey was good, but if I had gone to the university, might I have developed my hockey talent in a better way?

I proposed to Cathy in the summer of 1971. We were engaged to be married my last year in the American Hockey League, when I was with the Richmond Robins. She had come to see me play in Richmond but she never really gave a damn about hockey. It was something I did for a living, but she seemed to have this notion that, sooner or later, I'd get over it and get a real job.

Cathy's parents were not head-over-heels-enthused about her getting married. Her father told her, "If this is what you choose, then this is what you choose, but I would have preferred that you waited; that you traveled; that you saw Europe. I would have wanted you to have a job first and get married when you were a little older."

There was a distance between her parents and me. I felt uneasy with them, unsure of myself. But at no point did they come out and say, no, you can't marry him. There was never a feeling of "Well, Cathy, if you do this, we won't be there."

They were there. The wedding took place on July 8, 1972, at the United Church of Rosetown. Bonnie Pelletier was the maid of honor;

my brother, Ray, was the best man. We had a reception in the church basement and a wedding dance in the Elks Hall down the street.

Right from the start, we had problems. I made the Flyers training camp that fall, which meant that Cathy had all of a sudden become a hockey wife. It was a shock to her in every way. Even though she had grown up in Rosetown, the whole hockey scene was new to her. The Dave Schultz she had known, loved, and married was not Dave Schultz the hockey player. In my entire junior hockey career she had seen me play only once or twice.

So, now I was in Philadelphia, where we had taken an apartment, and her life had turned upside down. She had left the university—a great sacrifice for her—as well as her friends and, just like that, she was all alone in a new and somewhat hostile environment. She became secondary to my major interest in life: becoming a successful National Hockey League player, and being one of the boys. As far as I was concerned, Cathy was there and was to be loved but on my terms and on my time. She very quickly discovered that these did not coincide with her terms and her time. She found herself playing second fiddle to hockey, the Flyers, and Rexy's, the last of which became her prime nemesis.

Ever since the Philadelphia Flyers set up shop at the Spectrum, Rexy's, near Cherry Hill, New Jersey, had become the favorite watering hole for the players and, naturally, a favorite meeting place for groupies, young girls in their late teens and early twenties. A lot of the Flyers veterans, guys like defenseman Wayne Hillman, would hang out there, so I followed along.

In those first months in Philly I was often depressed. Shero hadn't been playing me much and I was frustrated. I felt as if I was wasting my career away on the bench. I would go to Rexy's with the boys and drink and drink and drink. If I wasn't a confirmed alcoholic, I certainly was completing basic training.

Cathy was all but forgotten. Oh, sure, I'd phone her from Rexy's and say, "I'll be home for dinner in an hour." Then I'd drink some more, an hour would go by, and I'd phone her again. "I'll be home in an hour."

Meanwhile I was getting drunk and she didn't know what the hell was going on with me. I had our only car. She was stuck in the apartment alone, waiting, like so many hockey wives. Cathy didn't like it a bit. She didn't like building her life around me—around my game schedule, the practice, the time the team flew in from out of town. It began destroying her image of herself; it crumbled her sense of worth. She began feeling secluded, segregated, and insecure.

Of course, while I was drinking it up at Rexy's I had no idea of how she was feeling. I was too wrapped up in hockey, in the players, in making it as a Flyer. Self-centered to the bones, I felt I had enough to worry about with my career, never mind worrying about Cathy. When practice ended at noon, we'd go to Rexy's for lunch and would still be sitting there, nursing a drink, at midnight.

After a while the Rexy's routine got to Cathy. She managed to control her anger for weeks, but one night I got home late and she let me have it, but good. She told me how bored she was, how her life was going to pot. She said she felt a need to fulfill herself.

"I want to go back to school," she said, "or, at least, get a job."

My approach to life was very conservative. I believed the way my father believed—a woman's place was behind the stove.

"No wife of mine is going to work," I told her. "No wife of mine is going to the university to take those Mickey Mouse courses."

She'd rant and rave into the night and, finally, I'd just turn my head on the pillow and say, "Why do you always have to talk about this at two in the morning?" With that, I'd roll over and go to sleep. I had to; after all the booze I couldn't keep my eyes open.

It wasn't just my nights out at Rexy's that bugged her; it was the entire hockey scene. Once Freddie started to play me, after the halfway point in that first season, I began fighting more and more. I became a hero in Philadelphia and that confused and frightened Cathy. Having taken on the image of an ogre, a wild fighter, the Broad Street Bully, I was clearly not the same person she had married. "It's like being married to an actor," she said. "I don't identify with the person up there on the screen."

Whereas in Quebec and Richmond she rarely saw me play, now she was seeing me play twice a week at home—as well as on TV when we were on the road—and my behavior bugged her. She was looking at someone she didn't know, like discovering for the first time the dark distant past of someone you have known for years.

Even her parents were getting wind of my antics and when I returned home, Cathy's mother asked me, "Why are you doing all that fighting, getting all those penalties?" I could understand their reaction since the McNabs had always liked my boyish quality. (When Cathy and I were courting in Rosetown I had been gentle, sensitive, and especially quiet. Cathy would introduce me to her friends and I'd be so shy it was ridiculous. One of them told her "Gee, he's really good-looking, but does it talk?")

Cathy asked me, "Dave, don't you get the impression that you're detracting from the beauty of the game?"

That set me off. I said, "Obviously, I'm not; the fans love it. Besides, Cathy, you don't play the game. *You don't know.*"

I ended the conversation on that note and that even further infuriated her. Why didn't I talk with her? For one thing, I felt a sort of hopelessness about resolving what I regarded as an insoluble problem. I considered us in two different worlds with no bridge between and since, by nature, I recoiled at the thought of deep conversations, I pulled away from these confrontations as if by conditioned reflex. Also, I had the suspicion that Cathy, being of keener mind than me, would get the upper hand—at least cerebrally—and win whatever argument we might be having. Since my hockey career was now on the upswing, I didn't want to risk having to make any concessions to her that would jeopardize my position. I also couldn't imagine why she would want to rock the boat.

When I walked down the street people stopped and stared. When I walked out of the dressing room I was besieged by autograph-seekers. When I popped someone in the mouth it was news all over the continent. All I had to do was open my mouth in the dressing room and journalists took down my every word as if they were listening to Socrates. A hockey player in Philadelphia was as important as the mayor. A hockey player who punched out the enemy was more important than the mayor. It was superb for my ego—but for Cathy it was something else. She had become a nameless extension of a famous man.

I ignored her problems because I was too intoxicated with being a hero. I soaked up every bit of the joy and couldn't imagine Cathy's not enjoying the adulation directed at her husband. When she complained I simply told her "You're being stupid." In my insensitivity I thought she should have accepted her second class citizenship because it wasn't that bad a deal. To me she was analagous to a maid working for a millionaire. She got all the fringe benefits, just like the maid, and should have been appreciative of all the blessings.

Then I got my first real jolt. I came home one night and found Cathy in the bedroom, packing her suitcase. I said, "What in hell are you doing?"

Without even looking up, she said: "I'm leaving!"

I was livid. My voice dripping with sarcasm, I snapped, "Well, let me help you." After I got that clever remark out, we started talking. She told me how unhappy she was with our lifestyle, how the marriage wasn't what she had anticipated. Her message began to seep through.

"Okay," I finally said, "let's try harder to make it work."

I genuinely wanted Cathy to be a happier person and I thought (mistakenly) that adopting the role of the sensitive husband would be as easy as snapping my fingers. I still was very naive, and very self-centered. What's more, there was a continuing problem. Cathy wasn't like a lot of other hockey wives. Some of the women were incredibly happy basking in their husband's glory. The transfer from the Canadian backwoods to the bright lights of Broad Street was, for many of them, the definition of what life was all about. They felt no compunctions about bathing in their husband's glorious waters. Cathy resented their attitude and, as much as anything, she resented Bobby Clarke and some of the other veterans.

Clarkie was like a sergeant with a company of soldiers. Fighting the battle was the be-all and end-all of his existence. He wanted our team to be a *team*. As far as we were concerned, the wives were a fact of life, but they were to be segregated into the under-class section.

We, the players, pretended to have a very special closeness about us that set us apart from the wives. You could see it at the team parties. There was an imaginary line that wives did not cross. Guys would be gathered around the bar. If a wife dared to go over to get a drink, all conversation would stop until she went back to the "girls."

Clarkie felt that interaction between the wives and players was no good. Winning was the most important thing; if the wives detracted from that objective, tough. That is, it would be tough on *them*.

One summer the team was invited to spend a couple of days in Brick Town, New Jersey. The Flyers were asked to play an exhibition game to promote a rink there. Clarkie told the guys about it. There were no words spoken but it was clear that Clarkie and a few other guys didn't want any wives or kids to come.

Cathy and Mary Ann Saleski and a few other wives came down for the game. Nobody actually told us that we shouldn't have brought them but we got the message at breakfast. Clarkie and our goalie, Bobby Taylor, were sitting at a booth in the coffee shop. Don and Mary Ann Saleski walked in and sat down in the booth next to them. The minute the Saleskis sat down, Clarkie and Taylor picked themselves up and moved to a booth at the other side of the room. Not a word was spoken but the point was made. That was Clarkie's way of telling us the wives weren't welcome and he would sharply remind a teammate who failed to adhere to his philosophy.

Cathy properly thought little of this philosophy and of those who embraced it. She thought Clarkie exercised too much control over us. "If he asked all of you to line up on the Walt Whitman Bridge and jump off," she said once, "you'd all ask him 'What time?'"

While Clarkie was the foremost exponent of the second-class-citizenship-for-wives philosophy, he wasn't alone on the team in that regard. There were other players who felt that a woman belonged in the house and should be at the beck and call of her husband. They felt that a wife should go only where her husband permitted. It's a caste system: Hockey wives are not considered to be in our class. Most players, coaches, and managers would like them to be—and considered them—subservient. Our games were the social event of the week for them, and Heaven help the wife who dared not come to a game. The only time a wife was allowed to miss a game was when she was sick or having a baby.

If you ask Cathy who was the most enlightened player on the Flyers, her answer would be, "I don't think there was such an animal." Her feelings were based on any number of episodes.

When I would fly back to Philly with the team from out of town, Cathy and some of the wives would drive out to pick us up. She'd hear whispering that some of the other guys didn't like the wives at the airport and that would enrage her. "To think that they even have the audacity to consider where I should or shouldn't be," she would say. "Who are they to tell you what to do? Why can't you make decisions on your own? Do you ever think about whether you want to do this or you want to do that? It's always 'The guys say this and the guys believe that.'"

It was ridiculous, but that's how mesmerized we were with this team concept. The hypnosis actually began back in junior hockey where the theory was knocked into our heads that the team comes above all and whatever the coach says is gospel. In Philadelphia that was amended to read whatever Clarkie says is law. That tacit agreement would hold as long as we were winning. With the advent of more college-educated players in the league, such unquestioned rule could not take place. Now, when an authority figure tells a smart young player to do something, he doesn't do it, he asks why. And if the answer doesn't suit him, he will go his own way.

Now that I think back, I am astonished that I allowed Clarkie to influence my life in such a manner, and I'm even more amazed that I permitted this childish behavior to overwhelm my marriage to a point where my wife was either furious or depressed about it—or both—and was ready to walk out on me for good. It says something for how screwed up my values—not to mention the values of a lot of hockey players—were during this critical period in my career. I was mesmerized by a peer group of adolescents just like me.

In this respect, I can remember only two players who defied our fraternity lifestyle, Gary Dornhoefer and Don Saleski. For them I have the utmost admiration because neither would toe the line. At the parties Don would stay with his wife, Mary Ann, and, of course, he'd hear about it. Once somebody made a wisecrack: "Look at them, they're glued together." It all seems so provincial, but it does serve to emphasize the ridiculous extent to which the concept of "team" had been pushed. I only wish I had taken some time to sit down with Saleski and Dornhoefer to discuss their attitudes toward the club— though that, according to Clarkie's unwritten rules, would have been verboten.

Most of the wives were aware that some cheating was taking place. The wives didn't accept it and they didn't rationalize it either. They figured that maybe somebody else's husband is doing it but not mine. Most of the women were so totally dependent on their men that they almost had no choice but to play ostrich for fear of breaking up their marriages.

It didn't take too long before rumors started to fly. One had it that Cathy and I had been separated two weeks after we were married. Nonsense. A neighbor came up to her one day and said the word around the community was that she was not my real wife; that my real wife lived in Canada and that Cathy was just living with me in Cherry Hill. Others gossiped that she ran around; that story was apparently started by a player.

The more popular I became in Philly, the tougher it was on Cathy. By now I had become the most penalized player in the league. When people mentioned my name, the automatic reaction was fighting. Yet off the ice with Cathy it was just the opposite. I'm Libra; Libras don't like emotional confrontations. Cathy is a Taurus, stubborn and opinionated. She liked deep discussions; I didn't. I liked to ride with the tide. You might call it avoiding conflicts.

Superficially, we seemed to be adjusting. I was making more money. We bought a nine-room house in Cherry Hill with a swimming pool, three bedrooms, and two-and-a-half baths. But the same problems remained.

While on a West Coast trip in my third year with the Flyers, I found a letter sitting on top of my clothes as I opened my suitcase in a Los Angeles hotel room. I could tell from the handwriting that it was from Cathy.

It was a Dear Dave letter; a long one. She had had it with the marriage. She wrote that she was going home to Rosetown and wasn't coming back. She explained in great detail about how frustrated and angry she was about just being a hockey player's wife. The letter went on and on and maybe for the first time her problems began to have an impact on me.

I read it over and then I picked up the phone. I told her, "I really understand a lot more about how you feel. I'll try harder. I promise."

Every single day of that road trip I phoned and we talked about the problems. We went over her anger and dissatisfaction. This time I didn't say I was too tired to listen. I listened.

She was angry about what she felt was a wife's position on the team. She was upset with the boys' nights out while she was supposed to be sitting at home watching *The Brady Bunch*. Her feelings were best summed up in a simple declaration: "I don't like your being married to the team and not to me." She was tired of my disregarding what she said. She was tired of my telling her, "You have no idea what this is like."

"If I have no idea," she said, "please enlighten me. How else am I going to understand if we don't share these feelings? Talk to me about it."

Now we started talking.

Our marriage went wrong because we had misconceptions about what each other's role would be and what made a marriage work. I was doing what I felt my father would have done. He was my model. I was doing what I saw older, married men on the team doing. Obviously, I was doing something wrong and it's taken me eight years to build it right.

Sometimes I can't believe how blind and narrow-minded I was about Cathy and our marriage. All I wanted to do was talk hockey. She wanted to talk about almost anything else. Her idea of the relationship was to discuss the state of the world with a bottle of wine between us. When she'd bring up the subject I'd say "Who would want to talk about crap like that?" Clever, wasn't I?

Communication between us was very poor because I would not discuss all of my feelings, what was going on in my mind about the game or about fighting or anything else about hockey. I was all wrapped up in it, but I didn't let her in on my secrets. Of course my inner feelings were not especially satisfying in terms of what I was doing. I had crossed the border from clean hockey to goon hockey and I can't say that I was inwardly happy about my destructive style. At times I felt embarrassed about my tantrums on the ice and at other times I felt a sense of shame over what I was doing to the game and its image. With each month—and each set of fights—my list of enemies grew longer and longer. It was not very comforting to know that a horde of hockey players wanted retribution, nor was it any balm for my conscience to realize that a growing number of writers had expressed dissatisfaction with my behavior. Rather than reveal these negative feelings to Cathy, I bottled them up. Besides, I didn't think she wanted to hear all the hockey talk and I simply did not like one-on-one verbal confrontations with her.

What made it so much more difficult for her is that Cathy is essentially a very private person and did not savor any of the public acclaim that was massaging my ego.

Cathy's mere presence in the kitchen or dining room of our home sometimes acted as a catalyst for some of my misgivings and started me thinking about all the negative things that I had done. But, as we all know, nobody likes to deal with issues that contradict his or her style of behavior. Although I felt I owed her a thorough explanation, a sense of compassion, and feelings of empathy, to open up the can of worms would take away from my ability to concentrate on the essential business at hand. As a result, I worked hard to repress all of my feelings.

And of course there were the groupies. It was nothing for a good-looking woman to sidle up to a player at a place like Rexy's. A lot of the groupies actually knew the game and were very familiar with the players. Some of them liked to brag about how many different players they had been to bed with. The groupies generally liked to zero in on bachelors, but that doesn't mean that the married guys—most of them—wouldn't get involved.

Although I had never paid too much attention to it before, I now came to realize that life as a hockey player's wife gave Cathy an appreciation of the women's movement. I now realize that if I was an example of how men subordinate women, then women are in trouble. Cathy could be a case study for the National Organization for Women.

After I joined the Flyers in my rookie year, it took Cathy quite a while to adjust to the life of a hockey wife because she had no idea how many allowances she was going to have to make or how painful and debilitating so many of them would be. Before she arrived in Philadelphia she had an identity of her own and was a university student with friends who had a lot in common with her. Cathy and I had a partnership that was severely ruptured by the big league hockey scene. How could our partnership help but dissolve if I was always out with the boys sharing with them things I once shared with Cathy?

How could she have confidence in herself as an individual if all she was ever doing was waiting for me to come home or waiting for me to return from a road trip or waiting for me to finish signing autographs? She couldn't, any more than any woman could under similar circumstances.

Everything involving her sense of worth was based on her relationship with her husband. When we went out and met people, they would introduce us as "Dave Schultz *and his wife*." This infuriated her. "Do I stamp 'The Wife' on my forehead?" she would say. "Or do I go forever nameless? Or do I get 'My name is Cathy' pasted on my chest?"

Some people might suggest that anyone who is secure enough with herself as a person would be able to ride through such times on the strength of her belief in herself. They are wrong, and only someone who has never been through an experience as Cathy's would make such a statement.

Like myself, the other Flyers expected their wives to be good mothers and respectful hostesses, to speak when spoken to and provide all of the necessary arrangements for their husbands. As a result, Cathy wasted eight years of her life on these archaic, traditional values. Even worse is the fact that I rarely if ever allowed her to express her feelings to me; so many times I simply ignored her, feeling absolutely no shame about it. Apologies are empty and although repairs have been made, those years that Cathy wasted cannot be recovered.

I haven't even begun to talk about the problem of lack of privacy that haunted Cathy and me, but I'll just let one experience sum it all up. One time the two of us, Orest Kindrachuk and his wife, Lynn, and Bobby Taylor and his wife, Marilyn, took a trip to the Boardwalk in Atlantic City. We wanted to get away from it all, go on the rides, have a good time.

After the first ride a couple of people recognized us and began following the six of us around. After each ride a larger group would follow. It became comical. We would stop short for some reason and people would fall all over each other stopping short, like in a slapstick comedy routine. Finally, one person approached me for an autograph and then everyone approached.

Now there was a long line of people asking me and the other guys for autographs. Cathy was standing aside the way she always did when, quite unexpectedly, a little old lady came up to her and said, "Your husband is wonderful. What a sweet thing you are. Could you get an autograph for my grandson?"

Cathy resented the fact that the woman wanted her to go right up to the front of the line, bypassing all the other people, to get my autograph for her. She told the lady she was sorry but she couldn't do it. The woman hauled off and kicked Cathy right in the ass.

So much for the glamor of being a hockey wife.

5

A Brief Flirtation
with the WHA

THE BEST THING that ever happened to professional hockey players in this century was the birth of the World Hockey Association in 1972. For the first time since the 1920s there were not one but two markets for players, the old National Hockey League and the just-hatched WHA. A player who had been making sixty grand from the NHL suddenly discovered (usually with the help of an agent) that he could get eighty, ninety, and maybe even a hundred grand from these big spenders in the new league.

At first most of us figured the WHA for a pipe dream, but in April 1972 we began to take the league seriously. That was when a Winnipeg businessman named Ben Hatskin made it clear that he wanted to take Bobby Hull, the biggest name in hockey, away from the Chicago Black Hawks and sign him for his new WHA team, the Winnipeg Jets.

The word was that all of the WHA teams would chip in a hundred thousand dollars apiece for Hull's contract and Hatskin, himself, would add to it, producing a total of something like a million dollars for the Golden Jet. In May, Hull said, "I've made a deal with Winnipeg and if they make good on it, I'm gone. They'll have themselves a hockey player."

They did, all right, in June—when Hull officially put his John Hancock on a WHA contract, and the NHL was suddenly minus one of its biggest gate attractions and greatest stars. The event made a deep

57

impression on me because I had been hearing about the new league for several months, going back to when I was still playing for Richmond in the American Hockey League.

Until my Richmond playing days, I had done all contract negotiation on my own and had absolutely no truck with player agents. In that era management not only frowned on players' dealing with agents, but would think nothing of blacklisting a guy who dealt with a personal rep. But the coming of the WHA changed all that and, almost overnight, agents were everywhere on the scene.

One of them was a rather unusual gentleman (by the normal standards of sports attorneys) named Howard Casper. Howard would walk around in a raincoat and no socks. He liked open-necked shirts, sports jackets, and big, black cigars. Until he got involved professionally in hockey, Casper had been a very successful labor lawyer in Philadelphia, and a sports nut. Howard became pals with André Lacroix, a slick little center who played for the Flyers and then the Chicago Black Hawks in the late 1960s and early 1970s. Lacroix asked Casper to give him some advice and Howard eventually persuaded Lacroix to jump the Black Hawks for the Philadelphia Blazers. Overnight, Lacroix became one of the highest-paid players in the WHA.

Lacroix had been one of the more respected members of the Flyers when it came to business, and when he talked to other guys about how well Casper did for him we all began to listen. By the time Casper came down to Richmond to talk to us he already represented—or claimed to have represented—several Flyers. He realized that several members of my team soon would be good enough to play in the NHL—or the WHA. Casper's pitch was to the point: If you want to do well now that the hockey war is on in earnest, listen to me. I told him that I wanted his representation, but I didn't want to sign anything. He said that was all right with him.

The next I heard from Casper was when he phoned a few months later and told me that the New York Raiders, the new WHA team in Manhattan, were interested in signing me to a contract. I was more than a little interested because the Raiders would be coached by Camille Henry, the former New York Rangers scoring star, and would be playing in Madison Square Garden. That was a big jump from Richmond. Casper told me to sit tight while he pursued the matter further.

While I waited the action became hot and heavy in the NHL–

WHA war. After Bobby Hull quit the NHL a bunch of other former NHL stars deserted the old league. Teddy Green, former captain and mainstay of the Boston Bruins, had signed with the New England Whalers; Gerry Cheevers, the Bruins' goalie, jumped to the Cleveland Crusaders. Meanwhile, I returned to Rosetown and awaited the call from Casper.

He finally got back to me and told me that a bunch of WHA owners were going to be meeting at the Château Frontenac hotel in Quebec City and some of the Flyers—Bob Kelly, Bill Flett, and Brent Hughes—would be there, too. Indications were that they were seriously considering a jump to the new league.

Knowing that Hull had jumped to Winnipeg and others were following suit—Bernie Parent had been lured from the Toronto Maple Leafs for $750,000—I figured that I might as well go to Quebec and see what was happening. When I got to the Château Frontenac, Casper told me that something definitely was brewing with the Raiders. He was talking to the Raiders' two top operating officers, Marvin Milkes and Herbie Elk.

Milkes, general manager of the New York team, had been a baseball man all his life and was new to hockey. He was a sweet, little man who walked around smoking big, black cigars while taking advice from his assistant, the large, heavyset Elk, a real hockey man, who also had a big, black cigar stuck in his mouth. They looked like Mutt and Jeff and between them they must have violated every air pollution law in the country.

Milkes didn't know me from a hole in the wall, but Elk had quite a line on my background. While scoring totals were important, the WHA bosses put heavy emphasis on penalty numbers as well. They were impressed with my penalty totals in the minors (proving that those numbers under the listing "penalty in minutes" are meaningful at contract time), and Elk knew that I had been the terror of the Eastern and American leagues. Elk also knew that I could score goals as well as hit people and told me, "Dave, you play the way you did in Richmond and Quebec and you'll be the hit of this league."

Casper seemed impressed with the Raiders' offer and suggested that I give it serious consideration; things were happening fast and I would have to make a decision on my future in a matter of hours. The Raiders' deal was a two-year contract at thirty thousand a year; not bad for a guy who had been making only ten grand in the minors.

When Casper informed me that Flett and Hughes also were jumping from the Flyers to the Raiders and that Kelly was thinking of signing with the Chicago Cougars of the WHA, I realized that this new league was for me. Flett had proven himself a good goal-scorer in the NHL and Hughes was not a bad defenseman. Although he was still rather crude, Kelly had already made a mark in the NHL.

I could tell that Casper wanted me to put my name on the contract and I saw no reason to back off at this point. So I signed on the dotted line. I had faith in the guy, for better or worse, and as far as I was concerned I was now a member of the New York Raiders. Flett, Hughes, and I flew down to New York with Casper for a big press conference in Manhattan announcing the deal.

It was held at the Statler-Hilton Hotel, right across the street from Madison Square Garden. Camille Henry was there and more newspaper guys than I had ever seen in one place at one time. The WHA had made a big deal out of the signings—for good reason, since they had taken two good names from the Flyers. They also made a big fuss about my potential as a bad man. Elk ran around telling the writers that I was the sleeper in the package.

I didn't know it at the time, but sitting in the back of the room, taking note of everything that was going on, was Gil Stein, the attorney for the Flyers.

The next day the headlines reported that the Raiders had gotten three big ones. Well, they did—for one day. As soon as we finished with the press conference in New York, Casper hustled us onto a train to Philly. He said the Flyers wanted to talk to us even though we had a contract with the Raiders. "Don't worry," said Casper. "Let's see what the Flyers have to offer."

Ed Snider, owner of the Flyers, and Keith Allen, their general manager, sat down with us at their office in the Spectrum. "I heard you signed with the Raiders," Snider said, "but we'd really like to use you up here. You can make the Flyers this coming season. Freddie Shero wants you."

Allen agreed that I could make the big team for 1972–73. The money? They said they'd come up with twenty-seven grand, and thirty-two thousand for a second year.

I talked to Casper and we agreed that the Flyers' twenty-seven grand was worth a hell of a lot more than thirty grand in the WHA. I wanted the Flyers. I asked Casper, "But what about the Raiders' contract?"

"Don't worry," he said, "there's an escape clause."

The Raiders, the way Casper put it, had to come to all our terms within nine days, and that meant producing a lot of bucks, which they would have had trouble doing. We didn't think, since the league had not even started operations, that they were in a position to cause any big trouble. In effect, I had two contracts, one with the Raiders and another with the Flyers. Yet at this point there was no guarantee that the WHA would ever really come to fruition. At the time I had no compunctions about dropping the WHA club from my life and putting my name on a Philadelphia contract.

When the Flyers announced that they had signed me, the Raiders announced that they were suing me.

Not to worry; Gil Stein, the Flyers' general counsel, would handle it. He must have done a good job, because that was the last I heard about it. Kelly signed with the Chicago Cougars of the WHA, but they never even got to announce it. The Flyers came up with a counteroffer immediately. I can't tell you that all of it ever made total sense to me, and it made me wary of future deals, but the WHA be praised—it got me to the Flyers.

When I started playing good hockey for the Flyers and getting a lot of ink, Philadelphia's owner, Ed Snider, came to me and said he was ripping up my contract and signing me a new and better one.

By this time, I had changed agents and switched to Alan Eagleson, who was not only a sports attorney but also Director of the NHL Players Association. I did this primarily because I figured that Eagleson, as head of our union, was in an excellent position to make the best possible deal for me. Although Eagleson had been criticized for having a conflict of interests—on the one hand representing the entire union, and on the other hand representing individual players—he had done well by many of his clients, and had a good rapport with many NHL owners, including Snider.

Eagleson arranged a six-year deal starting at $75,000 escalating to $82,000, $90,000, $100,000, $110,000 and, finally, $120,000. That wasn't a bad contract for a guy like me who scored only nine goals in his rookie year, especially when you consider what happened to a gifted hockey player like Normie Ferguson, who was named Rookie of the Year in a poll of NHL players in 1969. Fergie jumped from the NHL California Golden Seals in 1972 to the team I was supposed to play with, the New York Raiders. A year later the Raiders were sold and became the New York Golden Blades, then they left Manhattan to play in Haddonfield, New Jersey, as the Jersey Knights. When the club folded in New Jersey, Ferguson went cross-country with them and put on the uniform of the San Diego Mariners.

Like many others, I was surprised that the WHA lasted as long as it did (until 1979). From the first day of its existence, there had been rumors that it would fold, and I watched with interest as the WHA tried to compete with the Flyers in Philadelphia. The Blazers had signed Bernie Parent as well as Derek Sanderson, but even with names such as those we put them out of business and Bernie came back to us in 1973–74.

Sanderson was a classic example of a professional athlete who became a victim of his overnight wealth. He was a sensational junior in Niagara Falls, Ontario, and a smash hit the moment he reached the NHL with the Bruins. In almost no time he became hockey's first sex symbol—they called him "the Joe Namath of Hockey"—and the 1968 Rookie of the Year.

A major contributor to the Bruins' Stanley Cup winning teams in 1970 and again in 1972, he was revered around the league for his artistry and fearless play. But even in his heyday, Derek was a troubled personality. He chain-smoked to a point where he would have a new cigarette lit before the one he was smoking was out. He hated flying, but since the teams were always jetting from one city to another he began drinking to soothe his nerves. That created more problems. He remained a bachelor whose substantial gifts as a player were diminished by his abuse of his body and the diversion of his attention from hockey to his pursuit of big bucks and the life of a big-time operator.

When the World Hockey Association came along he opted for the $2.6 million deal offered by the Philadelphia Blazers. Almost immediately Sanderson became the big-time playboy with a chauffeur-driven Rolls-Royce and assorted other trappings of the rich and famous. I am convinced, and so are others, that Sanderson the hockey player became softened by Sanderson the millionaire. The distractions of big money disturbed his concentration. He became fat—both literally and figuratively—and he was never the same quality hockey player after that.

When we met as teammates in Pittsburgh (he had been with New York, Boston, and St. Louis after leaving the Blazers), he had become thoroughly dissipated. The Derek Sanderson who once could play thirty minutes of a sixty-minute game without requiring a second wind could hardly sustain a two-minute turn on the ice.

Others, like Parent, got lucky in the WHA. When Bernie got back to the Flyers he became a better goalie than he had ever been and proved to be one of the chief factors behind our success.

The professional player representative has been called many different names by people both inside and outside the sports world; some, I might add, are far from complimentary. Many agents function as contract negotiators, financial planners, and income-tax reviewers. Still others serve as surrogate fathers, career counselors, and problem-solvers. The fact is that the agent has managed to secure a good deal of power and influence in the world of sport.

There are some players who will argue that agents are the most overrated characters in sport. General managers will tell you that they are necessary evils. Agents—like bankers, politicians, and generals—can be lilywhite or thoroughly crooked. My own experience was that agents helped me. I was a naive kid from the Canadian boondocks who wouldn't have known a contract from the daily newspaper when Howard Casper arranged my entrance into the National Hockey League.

On the other hand, the behavior of other agents has been particularly disturbing. Anybody who played in the NHL in the late 1970s will tell you that agent Dick Sorkin was hardly a personality to give credibility to his profession. In November 1977, Sorkin was sentenced to up to three years in jail for fraudulent practices. Nassau County (N.Y.) District Attorney Denis Dillon had ordered Sorkin's arrest in June 1977 on charges that he stole more than six hundred thousand dollars from his clients. Those clients included such hockey players as Lanny McDonald, Tom Lysiak, Gary Inness, and Bob Nystrom.

Dillon's investigation revealed that Sorkin received his players' paychecks from the various teams. He was authorized to take this money, pay the players' bills, provide them with cash for spending money, and invest the balance. Dillon charged that Sorkin instead took the money and converted it to his own use.

Sorkin was typical of the characters who almost by magic materialized on the hockey scene with the birth of the WHA. A former sportswriter, Sorkin amassed more than three hundred clients within two years of the formation of his business, which by 1975 was valued in the millions. But then it took a nose dive. Money he invested in the stock market disappeared, and by 1976, Sorkin later admitted, he had lost more than a half-million dollars on Wall Street. At the time, Sorkin's clients were unaware that their money was being gobbled up. Next, the agent began betting on various sporting events in an effort to recoup his losses, but his luck remained bad. He had lost an estimated two hundred thousand dollars to his bookmakers and players soon got wind of the calamity.

The bottom fell out of Richard Sorkin, Ltd., in July 1976, when prize clients such as Tom Lysiak of the Atlanta Flames dropped out of his fold. "One day," said Lysiak, "I discovered that I was four car payments behind."

One by one, players quit Sorkin, reciting sordid tales of unpaid bills. "There were bills I assumed had been paid," said Inness. "Then I had to turn around and pay them myself."

On the other hand, there are agents who have made dozens of players wealthy. The average NHL salary leaped from thirty-five thousand to ninety-five thousand a year within a couple of seasons in the 1970s. (Having two leagues competing for players also had a lot to do with that.) Superstars such as Phil Esposito, Marcel Dionne, Gil Perreault, and Denis Potvin were earning more than two hundred thousand a year. By 1980, Dionne's salary was estimated to be in excess of half a million dollars, and two Swedes, Anders Hedberg and Ulf Nilsson, who had never played a game in the NHL, signed up with the New York Rangers for comparable sums. And can you imagine a teenager named Wayne Gretzky getting himself a twenty-year personal-services contract worth millions? You don't think he could have done that without an agent, do you?

Agents created a balance of power. In the pre-WHA days, all the power rested with the general managers, and before that the NHL had been a six-team monopoly that controlled every kid who played hockey. They dictated terms to the players, most of whom wouldn't even think of having representation. If you want to know why things may have gotten out of hand in terms of player salaries, remember how restrictive owners were; you'll understand why athletes feel they're only getting what was denied them all these years.

Gordie Howe was one of the greatest players who ever lived and when he signed with the Detroit Red Wings in the mid-1940s, *his bonus was a team jacket*. Some of the older players on the Flyers would tell me that in the old days when they signed a contract they never knew what they were getting into and if anyone complained, management would give him a one-way ticket to Springfield.

Larry Zeidel, who played for the Flyers in their first year, told a story about how he once asked for a raise when he was playing for the Detroit Red Wings. "Jack Adams was the general manager and he went crazy when he heard what I was saying. He pointed to the scoreboard where some guys were fixing the lights and said, 'There are electricians out there making two twenty-five an hour and they've got a trade. You don't even have a trade.' "

But the advent of the agent suddenly put the managers on the defensive.

When Emile Francis was coach and general manager of the Rangers, he was arguing Brad Park's contract with Park's representatives, Marty Blackman, Steve Arnold, and Paul Marcus. For several minutes, Francis harangued them about how Park didn't deserve a lot of money because he never led the Rangers to the Stanley Cup. After listening to Francis' argument, Marcus pointed a finger at Francis and said, "Did you ever stop to think *it was the coach's fault?*"

P.S.: Park got a hefty raise.

What should appear obvious by this point is that the player-representative is a central concern for the young, naive, and often-immature junior hockey player who is generally vulnerable, suspicious, and not graced with the long-term vision that more mature professional athletes share. As a result, the counsel, compassion, and concern generated by the agent have a good deal to do with the future success of this junior hockey player. I suppose, when you get right down to it, you can see this partnership as a marriage where both parties are mutually dependent on each other. Sometimes, however, this dependence can be taken one step too far.

A reporter once told a story about how, one night, Howard Casper got a phone call at 3.30 A.M. from one of his hockey player clients who was shacked up in a Vancouver motel room with a hooker. The way the writer told it, the conversation went like this:

PLAYER: Hey, Howard, you got to talk to this broad I got in my room. She's crazy. She wants a hundred bucks. Here, honey, this is Howard, my lawyer.

CASPER (TO SEXY VOICE): What's this hundred-bucks shit? We'll give you fifty and not a penny more. That's our final offer. Take it or leave it. You're not the only game in town, you know!

6

Getting Respect—
and the Stanley Cup

BEFORE I CAME to Philadelphia the Flyers were the Rodney Danger-fields of hockey. They got no respect. The tough teams in the National Hockey League laughed at the Flyers because they invariably signed little players like Jimmy Johnson, André Lacroix, Garry Peters, and Bill Sutherland, and for years they had literally been beaten badly.

It wasn't until 1969, after the St. Louis Blues knocked Philadelphia out of the Stanley Cup playoffs in four straight games, that the Flyers high command began to believe in an oft-quoted hockey jungle law: the bigger you are, the harder they fall. Ed Snider saw how Barclay Plager of the Blues broke Gary Dornhoefer's leg without a whimper of retaliation from the Flyers, and he seethed whenever Bob Plager of the Blues would run a Flyer into the boards and skate away without a bruise.

When Snider had seen enough of that he made a statement that would chart the course of hockey on Broad Street for more than a decade: "I saw what happened. Plain and simply, we got intimidated. I tried not to get too upset about it, but I made up my mind that it would not happen to a team of mine—never again!"

With that, Snider began to build the Broad Street Bullies by replacing crafty but timid small skaters with large, aggressive types who, it was hoped, had some talent to embellish their muscle. The

67

scouts fanned out from the Spectrum and, in time, they produced the desired skaters.

He got Kelly, who had established a reputation as a battler playing junior hockey in Oshawa, Ontario, and would hit anyone in sight. He got Barry Ashbee, an old-school defenseman who had banged around the minors for years and who was practically immune to pain. He got Clarke, a diabetic who would run over his grandmother if it meant getting two points in the standings. He got Saleski, a big sonofagun who couldn't fight very well, but would throw his weight around. And he got me.

When the Flyers told me I had made the big team in September 1972, I was truly shocked—I still suffered from a childhood insecurity that I never was quite good enough to make it to the top. It is ironic because my father—who never achieved his potential—had been convinced for years that I *would* reach the National Hockey League; not only that, but that I would stay there and become a prominent personality in the sport.

I could not spend too much time in a state of euphoric suspension. I had to pull myself together and understand what was expected of me and what this Flyers team was about. If I required any hints, all I had to do was pick up the 1972–73 Flyers media guide and read the descriptive material under the heading "Dave Schultz." There it was for all to read: *"One of the best fighters on skates, Dave might be remembered by Philadelphia fans for taking on several opponents when Quebec played at The Spectrum two years ago."* The blurb then recounted my penalty records and clearly suggested that I was in the NHL because of my dukes and not my finesse.

Since my naivete was rapidly disappearing, I had no problem discerning that the Flyers of 1972–73 would accent sock over style. The club's schedule brochure reemphasized the point, asking "CAN THE MEAN MACHINE CRUNCH THIS BUNCH?" We were "The Mean Machine" and the rest of the NHL teams represented the bunch we were to crunch.

The philosophy was made evident from training camp to the opening of the season. Freddie Shero, in his second season coaching Philadelphia, constantly harped on the necessity of hitting. Over and over again, he would tell us to "finish our checks," which meant checking the opposition even if he didn't have the puck and taking the enemy out at every turn. "Use the body" was a theme that was repeated so often it became permanently etched in my brain. What was less articulated but still understood was that we were never—but *never!*—to turn the other cheek if we were attacked by the enemy. Quite the contrary; the new Flyers believed in the pre-emptive strike: Belt them first and let the opposition worry about whether it has the guts to counterattack. The philosophy stemmed from Shero who had been a boxer himself, as well as a tough defenseman in the NHL and the minors. When Freddie originally became a minor league coach he invariably cultivated a fighting team, and the Flyers certainly would be no different. Now, for a change, Philadelphia had the personnel. Bob Kelly was complemented by Ashbee, Clarke, and Saleski, not to mention Ed Van Impe, one of the most competent stickmen ever to step onto an NHL rink; Wayne Hillman, a hard-bitten old pro; and goalie Doug Favell, who was a slasher.

Shero stressed the all-for-one-and-one-for-all philosophy. Clarke reiterated it, and if there was any doubt after that it was reinforced by Van Impe, Kelly, and Saleski. We not only would stick up for one another but we would carry it to another dimension—intimidation. Employing the collective use of force, we would diminish a team's desire to hold onto the puck. Once the enemy relieved himself of the puck, he could not score. That's how The Mean Machine would crunch "this bunch."

Based on what I read in the Flyers' guide and what I was told by Shero, there was no question as to my role. Shero called me into his office and helped crystallize my position: "David, a hockey player can have three things: agility, skating ability, and strength. You're not very agile and you don't skate very well, so you have to use your strength." That was as good as saying "Fight, dammit, fight!"

If anyone, whether it was Bob Plager or Wayne Cashman, decided to run one of our guys, I now felt it was my job to go after him. Although Ed Snider never actually told me explicitly that he wanted me to step on the ice and wallop everyone in sight, it was implicit, based on Snider's statements to the media and the entire promotional bent that the Flyers were taking in 1972. The words, obviously sanctioned by Snider, were "mean" and "crunch." I was there to do the fighting and, therefore, infuse courage into a team that had been sorely lacking that vital quality in the past.

Despite the assortment of qualms I harbored, that is what I planned to do.

Any fears that I might have suffered as a junior back in Swift Current, Saskatchewan, were now far behind me. The idea was to ensure that every NHL team knew what the consequences would be if they dared to trifle with the Flyers—fists in the nose, cheeks, and forehead by the dozen. Between Shero, Snider, and our manager, Keith Allen, the message was delivered; and with more than a little concern I accepted my role. The fact is that I was so tickled to be in the NHL at that time that I did not have the energy nor the inclination to review the situation critically. At that moment, my life was ruled mostly by emotion.

If either of my sons were placed in a similar situation fifteen years from now and were to ask their Dad for advice, I would counsel them to do the opposite of what I did; get out of the sport or tell the powers-that-be that that is not the way I want to earn my living. I would not want to see any son of mine turn into a professional athletic goon, nor do I want to see either of them blindly accept the dictates of any management without question, the way I often did.

In my case, my father endorsed some of my aggressive behavior. Furthermore, I was so smitten by the big league surroundings that I felt quite willing to plunge my head right through a cement wall for Shero, Allen, or Snider, if they so desired. By the time we had completed training camp and were ready for the opening game of the season against St. Louis, I had a burning feeling inside me unlike anything I had ever before experienced. It was as if Snider's theme— "Never again!"—was branded on my conscience and it was translated into one simple statement: No team will ever intimidate us while Dave Schultz is wearing a Flyers jersey. No player on my team was going to take a licking without my retaliating in some way. This was my job, and any goals that I might get after that would be pure gravy. The coronation of "King Goon" was about to take place.

As luck would have it, my first test was against the Plager Brothers and the Blues. It was obvious right from the opening face-off that the Blues were still feeling their oats and had the idea that they could run the Flyers out of the rink. The crowd "Ooooooed" in dismay as Bob Plager did his number, hitting Dornhoefer and sending him reeling to the ice.

It was as if Plager had flipped a switch in my bloodstream. I was enraged. I stepped on the ice looking for combat at the earliest opportunity, and the Blues knew it. No one, not even the Plager Brothers, who once had frightened the entire Philadelphia hockey club by their mere presence, raised a fist in anger. I was the young gunslinger who had ridden into town and brought peace to the Spectrum. I looked at the Blues and their sudden timidity and felt an inexplicable surge of confidence; so much so that I just wanted them to try something— *anything* . . . but nobody in a visiting uniform obliged.

This was one of the most significant moments in my budding career, but all I could think of at the time was that it was too easy. I knew my job was to beat hell out of people and I waited impatiently for that first fight. I hadn't spent three years in the minors perfecting my technique for nothing, and now that I had the fighting-on-ice routine down pat I wanted to put my methods to good use.

My method of beating up on the enemy was not unique. During my junior and minor league experience, I had watched a number of fighters in action and deduced that there was one method that was best for me.

My technique was predicated on my getting my right arm free to swing at my opponent. The trick was to grab a guy by his collar, thereby keeping him in one place. If I grabbed him high with my left hand, it was hard for him to throw his right. After that I would hold him and hit him, but the most important advantage was maintaining good balance with my skates planted in the ice and not falling; a fall could ruin the whole plan. Another aspect of my method was to allow the other guy to get in a punch or two while I got a grip on him. Once I fastened my hand on his jersey I would take over, and his counter-attack would almost be nullified. I was not as big nor as strong as some of my opponents—I really wasn't as powerful as people believed and I sure as hell wasn't an artistic boxer—so the hook-on-the-jersey method gave me an advantage.

Having intimidated the Blues, I was more anxious to swing my fists than just glare. I felt I had to prove myself. One of my first big tests came against the Chicago Black Hawks, an established club that boasted a wiry defenseman named Keith Magnuson. A rangy red-head, Magnuson had already been in the league for three years and had earned a reputation as a good and very energetic fighter. One summer he even took lessons from a boxing instructor in Chicago, and in Philadelphia they were still talking about the time Magnuson clobbered Earl Heiskala, who was supposed to have been one of the Flyers' early policemen. Heiskala's career as an enforcer lasted as long as it took Magnuson to reach back and waste him with one punch. It took twenty stitches to close Heiskala's face.

My first meeting with Magnuson was typical of the manner in which a hockey fight between two ice cops begins. We bumped into each other behind the Black Hawk net and he got angry. Impetuous player that he was, Magnuson charged at me, but before he reached his target I drove him in the mouth with my right. In a split second his lips were redder than his hair. Blood red.

Apparently Magnuson knew neither what nor *who* had hit him; when they escorted him to the training room for repairs on his face, he asked the doctor, "Who *was* that guy?" Once Magnuson was supplied with the answer he made it clear that our war had just begun.

In the NHL jungle an enforcer learns that winning a battle does not necessarily mean winning the war, if only because the loser of one fight—if he has any gumption at all—is likely to come back the next time with all guns blazing. So it was with Magnuson on another night at Chicago Stadium. I knew he was looking for me and I was ready for him as I carried the puck toward the Black Hawks' zone. As we were about to collide head-on I brought my gloves up like a giant bumper and Magnuson went down, this time with a broken jaw. It was a devastating check that awed my teammates as well as the Black Hawks. Wayne Hillman, who had been in the NHL for sixteen years and a player for five different teams, reinforced my behavior with a compliment I remember to this day: "I've been around for a long time, Dave, and I've never seen anything like you." Upon hearing that I said to myself: "Oh yeah, Wayne, who's next?"

I can't overemphasize the importance of peer group support in these situations. Hockey players, like any one else, need to feel appreciated for their contributions. In a sense my behavior was being exonerated and approved by my teammates.

My double triumph over so significant a foe as Magnuson was a substantial boost for both my ego and the Flyers' and, within a month, our club's image had done an about-face. Kelly and Saleski and I had the NHL on the run. Our team motto was that everyone on the Flyers gets backed 100 percent. Guys who normally would not have played tough suddenly became brave. Others, such as Bill Flett, were quiet tough, but the enemy knew enough not to mess with them. In a game against the Toronto Maple Leafs, Flett warned Toronto's Swedish forward, Inge Hammarstrom, that his arm would be broken if he touched the puck. While this may be hard to believe, the Swede remained two steps behind Flett for the rest of the night. In those days, Swedish players were new to the league and were accustomed to the cleaner style of European hockey; they recoiled at our methods.

In terms of pure toughness Kelly was first and I was second. Saleski really couldn't fight that well because he couldn't stand up. But he blustered so much—and he also knew he had ten Flyers behind him all the time—that he fooled a lot of opponents into thinking he was a holy terror.

The fighting brought us together as a team and soon it was clear that other teams were backing off from us almost as if it were a conditioned reflex. They knew that if anyone laid a stick on our leader, Clarke, he would have to mess with me. I would take on five guys at once if I had to and I wouldn't mind taking five punches in the mouth if it meant helping the club.

During quieter moments I realized that this wasn't the only way to play pro hockey and that advantages gained through this style were worthy of reconsideration. But, as I said, the euphoria of winning and fighting clouded my thinking process, and I was encouraged by the responses of my bosses.

Snider and Keith Allen were so tickled with the results that they went after more enforcers. In December they traded Brent Hughes and Pierre Plante, a couple of average hockey players, to St. Louis for André Dupont, a heavyweight French-Canadian defenseman who was nicknamed Moose for obvious reasons. We reserved judgment on Dupont until he showed us some fight; a good two weeks went by before he made a favorable impression by belting out Dennis Kearns, a Vancouver Canucks defenseman. "After that fight I began to feel accepted on the Flyers," Dupont said later.

Soon they were writing poems about us and we became the toast of the Philadelphia media. Jack Chevalier of *The Bulletin* knocked off this ditty.

Bodies crash against the boards,
Players drop their gloves and swords,
Broad Street Bullies on the loose—
The Hammer, Big Bird, Hound and Moose.

After Magnuson, I hammered Terry Harper, a defenseman with the Los Angeles Kings. I must admit I enjoyed that one because Harper had this annoying habit of smiling, trying to provoke you, while attempting to stay out of fighting range. Harper's idea of a good bout was having the linesmen intervene before any punches were thrown. This time the linesmen didn't oblige and I flattened Harper with one punch.

With all due respect to Kelly, I had become the heavyweight champion of the Flyers. Jack Chevalier took due note of this event by penning this ditty about me!

Dave Schultz' left hand grabs the shirt.

He tells the fellow, "This won't hurt."
And then, although it's impolite,
The Hammer nails him with a right.

By mid-season I had become the Broad Street Bully. The Flyers began consciously to look to me for protection. If anyone on the opposition seemed to be getting belligerent, one of our players would sound the warning: "You want to fool around? You'd better not or Schultzie'll get ya!" I'm well aware that this sounds like excessive bravado, particularly since we had a number of other tough guys. But somehow or other the other guys looked to me as King Goon and therefore used my name in threatening the opposition.

A pattern developed. I would provoke a fight early in the game to clearly establish our policy of intimidation. Once this statement was made and the fighting was over with, our stars—Ricky MacLeish, Bill Barber, and Clarke—seemed to have more room to maneuver and thereby take command. Throughout the league the Flyers became the team everyone hated; the names the fans bestowed on us— Broad Street Bullies, animals, goons, to name a few—said it all but bothered us not a bit. As Shero put it, "If it's pretty skating the people want, let 'em go to the Ice Capades."

As the number of bouts mounted, I became the center of attention just as I had in Salem, Quebec, and Richmond. There was one essential difference in Philadelphia: the intensity of the media. For the first time I was being seen on network television in the United States and Canada and, as it happened, one of my most decisive fights on the ice took place against the Montreal Canadiens in a game covered by the National Broadcasting Company television network.

My opponent was to be John Van Boxmeer, a blond rookie defenseman who had been called up to the Canadiens from their farm team in Halifax. Van Boxmeer was roughly my size, although he was a superior skater and a pretty good stickhandler. Van Boxmeer also seemed a bit arrogant, maybe because, as I later discovered, he had been tipped off that "Schultz ain't that tough." The events proved otherwise.

Our first meeting was in a corner of the Montreal Forum's ice. Our bodies met momentarily and, when I looked up, I noticed someone wearing the white, red, and blue uniform who was totally foreign to me and who, for all I knew, could have been the toughest new fighter in the league. At the moment of contact, I had no intention of fighting. The puck was within my grasp and I watched the rubber slide toward center ice with Van Boxmeer trailing by a stride. Soon he began showing his speed and as he caught up to me his stick kept flicking out like a snake's tongue, swatting me in the leg. I eventually wound up with his stick between my legs. As I said earlier, I hated the jabbing of the stick against my body, and suddenly the pursuit of the puck became irrelevant.

As physically intimidating as I was, I always deplored the use of a hockey stick as a weapon. Somehow the jabbing and hooking transgressions with the stick impressed me as a hockey cultural taboo and my level of tolerance diminished dramatically. *That* is why I went after Van Boxmeer.

In challenges such as these I had one major advantage—I was the aggressor. My enemy, who already knew of my reputation, didn't quite know how to react to me and I sensed that he was on the defensive. Once I realized that he wanted the battle less than I did, I became the predator and he became the hunted. I made the first move: a quick jump step like a leopard striking at its victim. I grabbed Van Boxmeer's jersey just above the big red Canadiens crest. He seemed scared and his face instantly turned red as he shifted to his left, attempting to get out of my reach.

I felt like Rocky Marciano, relentlessly bearing in for the burst of fists. Van Boxmeer was trapped and knew that he had nowhere to run. He had to slug it out, for better or worse.

At the moment that I cocked my right fist back for the first blow I had worked myself up to a frenzy of hatred. I had taken his seemingly insignificant act of shoving his stick between my legs and multiplied it into a cardinal sin in my mind. Rather than being just another hockey player, Van Boxmeer was a mortal enemy.

I unleashed a roundhouse right that struck him flush in the left cheek. Van Boxmeer went down faster than a flash of lightning crosses the sky. For a moment a bolt of fear coursed through my body. I looked down at Van Boxmeer. He was out cold and, for a moment, I thought I had hurt him badly.

A few seconds passed and the Montreal defenseman began to stir. I looked down at the white tape covering my hands and skated toward the penalty box while hundreds of thousands of viewers watched the episode on television. If ever there had been any doubts about my reputation as a fighter they were erased with that one blow, which would cause comment from Montreal to Los Angeles. In most people's eyes, I had become the number one enforcer in the NHL.

There were many challengers, especially among the Boston Bruins. For more than a decade before 1974–75 the Bruins had been notorious for their collection of tough guys. Ted Green, a snarling defenseman, had set the tone in the mid-1960s but it wasn't until the Bruins added such heavyweights as Ken Hodge and Cashman that they could truly be called the Big, Bad Bruins. In the 1970s they added a fast-swinging sidekick named Terry O'Reilly.

To become an undisputed champion, to take maximum advantage of the intimidating image I had tried to develop, I had to take on the toughest Bruins, and it wasn't until the 1974 Stanley Cup finals between the Flyers and Bruins that I finally got my opportunity.

The 1974 finals epitomized aggressive hockey if only because the Bruins were as boisterous as we were, if not more so. I hated them and was scared to death to face them because they had the most vicious collection of athletes I had ever encountered. As successful as I had been in previous battles, I would be remiss by not suggesting that I, too, had the capacity to be intimidated. In conjunction with the Bruins' reputation as a very physically capable team, my aversion to stickwork made me particularly apprehensive about them. In short, although I would never let on about my fear, I was as nervous and concerned about the inevitable forthcoming fights as the Bruins were.

Cashman, a tall blond forward with a perpetual look of innocence who handled his stick like an infantryman with a bayonet going over the top of the trenches, used every device to throw us off our game and, occasionally, would use his henchmen to help out. I would be in the penalty box and Cashman's big-mouth center Phil Esposito would skate over to me and, in threatening tones, say: "Hammer. The boys are gonna get ya. Better watch out, Hammer, the boys are gonna get ya."

Unlike Esposito, Cashman preferred pantomime, pretending to be a surgeon ready to cut my eyes out. Instead of waving a scalpel, Cashman would use his stick, brushing up against me, pushing his stick against my jersey and saying, "You want any? You wanna get me? You'll have to go through my stick first."

Because of Cashman, O'Reilly, Esposito, and their superstar defenseman, Bobby Orr, nobody gave us a chance to beat the Bruins for the 1974 Stanley Cup. That included our hometown writers such as Chuck Newman of *The Inquirer*, who said we would be lucky if we took a game from Boston. I saved his prediction: "The Bruins are rested and healthy. The Flyers are tired and wounded. What's it all add up to? The Bruins in five games, that's what."

We lost the opener at Boston Garden. If we were going to go

anywhere in the series we had to hit them. *I* had to hit them, and before the second game I could feel the pressure building within me to do something to build up our courage. There was only one thing to do and that was lay out one of the Big, Bad Bruins, despite any fears I might have harbored over the challenge.

As I crawled into bed for my pre-game nap my stomach was churning and my teeth were grinding in anger. I was working up to a boil and had a feeling that tonight the Bruins were not going to intimidate the Flyers. I kept promising myself that nobody on my club was going to take a licking without my standing up for the team. I had to single out one Boston player for punishment, preferably a tough one to make it a symbolic gesture. Why not one of their policemen, Terry O'Reilly?

I rested my head on the pillow and began to fix my thoughts on a scene: *It was the second game, play was in motion, the Bruins were swirling in our zone. O'Reilly had the puck. He came at me, all 6'1", two-hundred pounds of him. I crashed him into the boards and our gloves dropped. He was down in a matter of seconds.*

Then I awakened and stared at the ceiling, thinking how nice it would be if I could make it happen. In part, fear was motivating me; hit them before they hit you.

In any hockey confrontation, gaining the advantage with the first blow is absolutely essential. Using the coach's cliché, "'Take the game to them and gain control," I directed all of my energies toward that end. I would rework that O'Reilly scenario a hundred times if necessary in the hope that, at the appropriate time, I could fulfill the obligations of my role.

When I finally touched my skates to the ice for the pre-game warmup I cruised in a circle, from my net to the blue line, peering over at the yellow and white jerseys with the big B on the front. I watched the number 24 cruise in the other direction and wondered what was going through the head of Terry O'Reilly. Had he or the other Bruins prepared for the game the way I did? "Geez, if they're thinking the same way, I'm in big, *big* trouble." Would O'Reilly try to subvert me before I got to him? Not surprisingly, my thoughts had turned away from the skills of the game to those of violence.

The National Anthem was over and now I prayed that Shero would get me on the ice as soon as possible. I needed contact right away. The longer it took me to rub a shoulder into an enemy stomach, the more impotent I would be. The referee dropped the puck and bodies charged up and down the rink. The long-awaited tap on my shoulder finally came. I put my left glove on the edge of the boards and vaulted onto the ice. I looked around and realized that O'Reilly was out there for the Bruins. My senses were dulled as I became intoxicated with the ebb and flow of the game. I no longer was looking for O'Reilly but rather a piece of any yellow jersey.

I ran at one, connected, and quickly recoiled, satisfied by the exquisite feel. Then another hit and I recoiled again, looked up and saw the heavy-bearded face of O'Reilly. There were no amenities since we both knew what we had to do and, instantly, the arms flailed like locomotive pistons. I brought back my right and drove it as hard as I could. O'Reilly fell backward and down. The linesman rushed between us but I could see the blood begin to trickle down his cheek from under the eye.

I had made an impression on the Bruins and would make another one before the night was up. With the score tied, 2–2, in sudden-death overtime, Shero had benched me and the fans realized that. Some of the Boston Garden faithful may have felt that Shero was saving me from retribution, and I didn't want them to think that. One of the Boston fans shouted at him, "Put Schultz on. That'll give us a goal."

I looked at Shero and said, "Yeah, why don't you put Schultz on?"

He looked down the bench. "Okay," he said, "get ready, Clarke, Flett, and Schultz."

The puck moved into the Bruins' end of the rink to their defenseman, Carol Vadnais. I charged at him but he passed it around to O'Reilly. I lunged at him just as O'Reilly tried to move the puck back to Vadnais. I moved myself between Vadnais and the rubber, took it away from them, and blindly passed the puck out to what I hoped would be a Flyer. Cowboy Flett took my pass and backhanded it to Clarke in front of the net. He shot and goalie Gilles Gilbert saved, but the rebound came back to Clarkie and this time he fired it past Gilbert.

The fight and the goal not only gave us a win, but also a psychological lift in the series. No longer were we afraid of the Bruins, as we proved by winning the next two games and taking a three–one lead in the finals.

We were one win away from taking the Stanley Cup, but the fifth game would be at Boston Garden and I knew the Bruins would be playing with the ferocity of a wounded bear. I expected them to be out for blood, preferably mine, and in the first period Cashman proved I was right. He swung his stick at the head of our goalie, Bernie Parent, and a little later took a big cut at Jimmy Watson. He followed that by punching Van Impe in the mouth and I kept wondering why in Heaven's name Shero had me sitting on the bench when letting Cashman do that to my teammates was so contrary to our policy.

When Shero finally gave me the signal I knew I was to go over the boards to restore order; more specifically, to stop Cashman and, if possible, beat his head in.

In no time at all we were facing each other in the classic *High Noon* meeting. My adrenaline was pumping as he moved his index finger under his eye as if to tell me he would cut my eye out. I remembered how he had once stuck me in the throat with his stick and I knew that if I didn't move fast I would be in trouble.

With my gloves off I lunged for Cashman's jersey with my left hand. I got a piece of it just to the left of the crest but Cashman, an old gunfighter, knew what was coming and while I reached he punched. He caught me with two blows but he never stunned me and that was crucial. If he had dulled my senses I would have been finished, but I withstood his first shots and that enabled me to bring up my artillery and fire away. I came back with my right and caught him square in the mug. He turned red before I could smash him with a second and third right. Cashman realized he was in trouble but he couldn't cope with my onslaught.

He ducked, but I nailed him with an uppercut. He tried to wrestle me but I got free and went to the uppercut again. I was tiring but I could tell he was fading faster. I felt giddy as I put all I had behind another uppercut and lifted him right off his skates.

He reminded me of a mortally wounded ship that had just been torpedoed. He fell back off balance and I helped him by dumping him on his side. My body was drained of strength. I didn't resist when the linesman pulled me off the beaten Cashman. I had scored a TKO. We lost the game. But two days later we won the Stanley Cup.

Bathing in my success, I rationalized that I was no different from the so-called hero-villains of the past—Lou Fontinato, Eddie Shore, John Ferguson. I was doing my job, and my job was to play tough and protect my teammates. Although the orders were more implicit than explicit, I nevertheless recognized them as my orders and they worked perfectly for me within the context of the Philadelphia system. I felt I was doing right by myself and my team because the coach told me so. My ego swelled when Shero said, "Dave Schultz gave us courage. You can't measure the value of a man like that."

Coming from Shero those words meant a lot to me. And as time would tell, *that* was part of my problem.

The Van Boxmeer incident had implications not only for me but for Van Boxmeer as well as for the game of hockey itself. My one-punch knockdown became an instant legend around the NHL. I had become the anti-hero of hockey, the barroom brawler who rarely failed to satisfy the fans' insatiable lust for violence. I became the league's unshaven image, a man the fans loved to hate. They screamed, cursed, and wished that I was dead—except in Philadelphia, where they loved me.

One general manager called me and the Flyers "a neurotic group—a crazed, blood-hungry, publicity-made menagerie." (Shero liked to say that the roughhouse image was created by the media. Looking back I really get a kick out of that one.) For sure, the press and TV people were on my case like never before and though I fought and won my battles with a cleaner technique than most enforcers, that didn't impress them very much. I was so caught up in things then that the distinction took on disproportionate importance for me.

Clarence Campbell, president of the NHL, and Sammy Pollock, the general manager of the Canadiens, had watched me beat up Van Boxmeer from their seats at the Forum. They noticed that my right hand was covered with tape. Because I had hurt my fist in a number of earlier bouts, I now wrapped the tape around my knuckles twice before a game, not in order to hurt anybody, but to protect my knuckles. Neither Campbell nor Pollock accepted that. The NHL wrote a new rule—no tape on the hands. (The day the no-tape rule went into effect I broke my thumb in a fight. I wouldn't have broken it if my knuckles had been taped.)

They also put in, thanks to me, new rules on head-butting and on not wasting time before going to the penalty box. They remembered how I had head-butted Bryan Hextall in Atlanta during the 1974 playoffs and figured that I was a chronic head-butter, although that was hardly the case. The straight-to-the-penalty-box rule was stupid because the regulation now left it to the discretion of the referee, and there were referees who were definitely out to get certain players (in my case, Bryan Lewis, Bob Myers, and Dave Newell especially). I couldn't talk to those referees—and I think players should be allowed to talk civilly to a ref—but I respected referees with whom I could at least discuss a penalty. That's why I liked Art Skov best of all. If I carried on inordinately, then I deserved a misconduct. But in every other sport an athlete at least has his say.

After the Van Boxmeer fight people began to suggest that I might be crazy, and maybe I was during certain periods on the ice; but I never meant to hurt anyone badly (even Park or Harper, who I didn't like personally). Sure, when I slugged away, I wasn't pulling my punches, but I was *not* a dirty player like those who carved up opponents with their sticks. When I fought it was a face-to-face affair and often I waited until the other fellow dropped his gloves first.

I was unhappy with the effects of the fight on Van Boxmeer himself, particularly in terms of the negative image he received and what it did for his major league career. The fact cannot be denied—I nearly ruined him. At a time when NHL teams were putting a premium on toughness, coaches looked with disfavor on a player who was floored with one punch. And there was more to it than that. The game, which was broadcast on the NBC-TV network in the United States, was being handled by Ted Lindsay, a rough, tough left wing who had played for the great Detroit Red Wings club of the late 1940s and early 1950s. Lindsay, who had turned "color" commentator for NBC, enjoyed fighting on the ice the way a kid loves ice cream. According to Lindsay, there was no such thing as dirty hockey. "It's competitive," he would say. "It's not a kid's game. If you haven't got the guts, leave it."

Lindsay said something that, I thought, hurt Van Boxmeer, after the Montreal defenseman was helped to his feet. Now, said Lindsay, we would see how much of a man Van Boxmeer really was. The way Lindsay put it, when Van Boxmeer got out of the penalty box he had to get me; otherwise other players around the league would think he was a coward and run him out of the NHL.

While Lindsay was doing the broadcast for NBC he was, in effect, a spokesman for the NHL, since the league certainly plays a part in advising on the selection of a broadcaster and could have urged Lindsay's rejection. What Lindsay said simply implied that the NHL did not frown on fighting and rough play. In fact, the NHL loved fighting, particularly on national telecasts. Fighting was regarded as good publicity and it, supposedly, sold tickets. Look at the Flyers, the fightingest team in the league. They were also the biggest draw in the NHL. There must have been a connection.

Was it right? Of course not. Not when there were artists such as Henri Richard, Yvan Cournoyer, Bernie Parent, and Rick MacLeish to talk about, but Lindsay was obsessed with the violent aspect of the game and conveyed that message to the viewers. Van Boxmeer's failure to come back and hit me did not mean he lacked courage or was in any way less a hockey player or man. Yet that was the message carried over NBC-TV.

The records show that Van Boxmeer was not very successful for years after that fight although he had until then been a player of great promise. He played very little for the Canadiens and finally was traded to the Colorado Rockies during the 1976–77 season, where he began to get his act together.

Our paths crossed again in October 1979 when he was traded to Buffalo. I met him in the dressing room when he first came in to shake hands with his teammates. It was quite an uncomfortable meeting for me. But once we met face-to-face the past hostility evaporated. We shook hands, became teammates and friends. Van Boxmeer had turned into a good hockey player and for that I was glad. I wouldn't have wanted it on my conscience that I had destroyed a man's career.

I didn't feel so sensitive about most of my other foes. Many of them made a virtual science of fighting on ice, as I did. Some of them had a style similar to my own. They would grab for the opponent's right shoulder in an attempt to immobilize him, and then swing away. Magnuson, Kelly, Pierre Bouchard, Willi Plett, Larry Playfair (who is big, strong, quick, and a good fighter who goes right for you; his punches have quite a sting)—these guys were not afraid to take the first punch, or two or three, as they were going for the opposition's shoulder. Then, once they were set, they'd swing away. I could swing even with a sweater over my head; I'd just aim for wherever my left hand was and punch away blindly.

Others would wade in, swing wildly with both hands, and try to overwhelm you with the sheer number of the blows, however ineffective each individual punch might be. Jack McIlhargey and Kelly would get in five punches to my one; they'd look impressive but they wouldn't hurt, although all they needed was to connect with the other guy's nose just once. Kelly and McIlhargey wouldn't duck, and they'd get hit with a few themselves.

The toughest guys to fight were the ones who fought scientifically, in close. I didn't like fighting Tiger Williams at all for this reason. He'd get in close to you and hit you with uppercuts with both hands.

He often wasted bigger opponents; in a pinch he would stoop to biting. Very tough to defend against.

Then there were the wrestlers. Colin Campbell and I later became good friends, when we were together in Pittsburgh, but when we used to fight he would grab me by the seat of my pants and try to flip me over on my back. Hilliard Graves fought the same way. Dan Maloney, as overrated a fighter as the NHL has ever seen, would grab you and pull you down and then hit you with uppercuts.

Lefties were tough to fight because it wouldn't do me a whole lot of good to grab a lefthander's right shoulder with my left hand. Both of us would be free to swing away because he would be grabbing my left with his right. I fought Terry O'Reilly five or six times, and he was more freewheeling than many lefties, but he also had trouble standing up and would flop. One thing, though: he would never back off.

There are really two categories of fighters: first, those who are sure to be in on the action, like O'Reilly, Williams, Garry Howatt, Kelly, Nick Fotiu, Paul Holmgren, McIlhargey and Behn Wilson. Then there were what I like to call the New Enforcers, the big and awesome boys who did not like to fight but would be deadly if forced to: Larry Robinson, Clark Gillies, Barry Beck, and Jim Schoenfeld.

The most frustrating men to fight were the little guys, like Dennis Polonich. If you beat them, it didn't mean anything because you were expected to. And if they beat you, did you ever look bad. Howatt is small, but the first thing he would do was go for the hair. He ultimately was responsible for the hair-pulling rule—the NHL voted a game misconduct penalty for anyone who pulled hair during a fight—and when we first fought at the Spectrum he had beaten the hell out of Carol Vadnais a few days earlier. Howatt grabbed for the back of my head and I didn't have a hope, but on three subsequent occasions I beat him decisively.

Howatt's teammate, Bob Nystrom, was much more the gentleman although he was every bit as tough as Howatt and a damn good fighter to boot. I will always respect Nystrom for one non-bout we had shortly after I had broken my thumb. The doctor had outfitted me with a cast on my right hand over which my glove was tied. In effect, this meant that my right fist, my power fist in any fight, was immobilized.

If I had had any sense I would have cooled it that night against the Islanders but, temperamental as I was, I couldn't play a calm game against such a team. They played so intensely against us. Sure enough, Nystrom and I crashed heavily against the boards and, even though I hit him clean, he resented the vigor of my bodycheck. He instantly dropped his gloves, prepared to fight, and I, in turn, dropped my left glove. I couldn't release my right glove because it had been tied onto the cast. A lesser sportsman than Nystrom would have let me have it, figuring "Schultz is at a disadvantage, fine!" But as soon as he realized that I was partially incapacitated he held back his swing and the fight ended before it ever got started.

For that act of nobility, Nystrom has a permanent spot in the Dave Schultz Book of Gentleman Tough Guys.

The only person I would never fight was Nick Fotiu. He stands 6'2" and 220 pounds and is a former New York City amateur boxing champion. He is genuinely scary.

Another thing that absolutely petrified—and enraged—me was stickswinging. Dennis Hextall, one of the worst offenders, gave me great respect for the injury potential of wood when he nearly put the blade of his stick through my neck. Of the players still around, Dave Hutchison, Cashman, and Bobby Schmautz are the leading lumberjacks.

My skills as a fighter had become renowned, and I was basking in the glory of success. Unfortunately, however, certain issues, much to my dismay, were beginning to win my attention. What was I doing? How could I have allowed myself to lose control? All of my victims were reasonable people. Many of them were fathers, husbands, good citizens. The inner struggle was beginning to work on me but the publicity, the audience response, and the positive exhortations from my father and friends—not to mention my teammates—kept me going. In addition, my style of play came to be viewed as necessary as well as taken-for-granted by management.

Although some of these descriptive accounts may create the impression that I enjoyed what I was doing, it was not the case. As praiseworthy as some of the media reports had been in Philadelphia, journalists in other NHL cities were destroying me with their critiques. There were more serious and immediate problems. How many of you know what it's like to have dangerous objects hurled at you by an angry audience? Or to have people curse you in the most vile terms? And what about my family and their self-image? How was I going to explain these commentaries to Cathy? How was she to deal with some of the people in our community who viewed me as a thug?

The sum total was an amalgam of conflicting forces. The notoriety would help make me wealthy but I was paying an awful toll mentally. Getting hit in the head with a beer can or an airhorn—that's what happened in Atlanta after I scored a goal—became a regular occurrence, and I soon developed a conditioned fear of the fans' response to me.

At game's end, when we were on the road, I would look warily at the crowd, as one would anticipate sniper fire, and then run off toward the ramp that led to our dressing room so as to avoid whatever missiles were being hurled in my direction. The constant bombardment grated at my nerves to a point where I felt like the ultimate scoundrel wherever we played on the road. I often wondered whether any of my teammates suffered similar feelings of anxiety about being a human target, but the only feedback I got was from several Flyers and it was uttered out of self-protection: "Dave, you go off the ice yourself; if any of us skate next to you we're liable to get hit in the head." Such responses made me feel like an outcast, especially coming from the players who regularly called on me for help but who now wanted no part of their favorite enforcer.

These concerns kept me awake at night, wondering about the world of hockey. As depressed as I was about some of my behavior, I was more disappointed that none of my teammates wondered about the consequences of my experiences both on and off the ice, nor did my coach, manager, or even the club owner. In fact, I was all alone with nobody to talk to, and that is the most serious problem of all. I often felt like I didn't belong; I felt used and exploited. I had the sense that my teammates couldn't have cared less whether I played or disappeared. I wished I had more answers than questions. But how do you confront success?

Alone with my feelings, I drew comfort from one statement made by Shero: I gave the Flyers respect. I only wished the feeling were mutual.

7

Freddie the Fog

FOR THOSE PLAYERS, critics, and observers who have spent years as participants in the National Hockey League scene, the role of the coach has become patently clear. The man behind the bench is ultimately responsible for the success or failure of his team. Invariably coaches have been hired and fired to dramatically change a team's perspective, attitude, and level of motivation. But there's more than that. I had the sense that the coach and his players were not only detached from the administration of a team, but detached from all other aspects of everyday life. We built our own little world—a world with explicit rules and regulations, beliefs, attitudes, and motives. It was as if the Philadelphia Flyers lived on an island all their own and ferried in to the Spectrum for evening matches. Such a world provides immense power and influence for the person who leads that group of men. This was the case with Freddie Shero.

We revered the man. We respected everything he stood for. And we played for *him*. That is central to a coach's success, *that his players play for him*. My teammates respected Freddie, but I should point out that when I played for him I adored him. I don't any more; my assessment of him is far more complex than that.

And here I am going to make every effort to analyze objectively—if that's possible—my involvement with him. Whatever he was when I played for him and whatever he became after I left the Flyers organization could never cloud nor minimize the impact and effect he had on me both as a hockey player and a person.

Although I was part of the Philadelphia Flyers organization when I played in Richmond, I really had no sense of Shero, the person, nor did I take the time to read through Philadelphia newspapers to find out. My first days with Shero at the Flyers' training camp can best be described as a "guess what this guy's all about" experience. He was an enigma to me. He never said much, but in his own way he managed to communicate both information and direction to us. From my first days at camp it became clear that I would spend the next years of my life reading cues and trying to make sense out of this man's behavior without being given specific instructions.

In some ways, I wasn't surprised, because to that point I had never really developed a meaningful relationship with any of my coaches on any level of hockey. That may be as much a comment about me as a person as much as it is a statement about the way my coaches interacted with their players.

Shortly after my arrival in the NHL, I began to hear stories about other coaches and the kinds of relationships they had developed with their players. Scotty Bowman was notorious for the distance he established between himself and his players. Others, such as Don Cherry, came to be perceived as "players' men," working together with their charges *against* their teams' administrations.

Freddie was an interesting mix of the two. Although there was some distance between Shero and the team, the players never felt alone. We always had the sense that Freddie, in his inimitable fashion, would both protect us and provide us with feelings of security at the appropriate times.

Philosophically, Shero was the Vince Lombardi of hockey. Lombardi told his players that there were three factors that counted in their lives: "God, football, and your families are the three most important things in your make-up, but not necessarily in that order." For Freddie the world of hockey *was* his family and on numerous occasions he explained to us that we were more important to him than his own kin.

Think about that for a second. If a coach is prepared to make that kind of sacrifice and display that kind of commitment to his players, how could we help but identify with him and march to his drumbeat? In effect, Freddie's dedication to the game neutralized all our doubts and misgivings, so that we rarely if ever questioned either his strategies or his style of behavior.

Moreover, his absolute commitment to winning at all costs prevailed from the first day I met him to the day that I left the organization. I don't want to bore you with clichés, but the winning-is-everything theory was one that was etched into our collective soul from the moment we hit the ice at the Spectrum on that first day of training camp. You see, some coaches are easily perceived as born losers, but Freddie was adjudged a born winner by all of those around him at that time. Logically, then, the style of our play over the years, our commitment to violence, our reliance on intimidation, fit marvelously well into the more global context of winning at all costs. When people become successful, they rarely have the time or the inclination to evaluate the process that brought them there, and as long as we kept winning for Freddie and ourselves, I was prepared to do everything in my power to maintain that record. If ever I had any doubts, Freddie would squelch them by reminding me of the larger goals and aspirations of the hockey club.

Considering the limited amount of talent he had at his disposal, Freddie did more with less than anyone in NHL history. Look at the lineup we had when the Flyers won the Stanley Cup in 1974: Van Impe, Tom Bladon, Dupont, Joe Watson, Jim Watson, Barry Ashbee, to name a few. There were only four players on the whole team who could legitimately be called special talents—our goalie, Parent, and forwards Clarke, Barber, and MacLeish.

Technically, Shero was excellent because he had paid his dues. He labored for years in the minors, studying his craft and seeking new methods for winning. It was Freddie who introduced the technique of short shifts for both his offensive lines and his defensemen. He wanted his defensemen to skate like hell and get off the ice. Even one minute on the ice could be too long in certain situations.

He brought us together as no other coach could have, and had the good sense to let a natural leader such as Clarke guide the club from within the player ranks.

My relationship with Freddie was mostly positive. He would say to me, "Dave, you are just as important to this club sitting on the bench as you are out on the ice. No, probably more important." He made it clear that everyone contributed no matter how little or how much a guy was on the ice. It made everyone, especially me, want to put out just a little bit more for him. When I knew that I had to be ready for that one or two shifts, I really tried to contribute.

His tolerance—or should I say understanding—of stupidity on the part of the players was amazing. One day a rookie went up to Freddie and said he had problems skating. Freddie asked how come he was having trouble. The kid said he didn't have a pair of skates. "I couldn't believe my ears," Fred told me later. "The kid could go out and buy any pair he wanted, made-to-measure, and have a bill sent to the Flyers. Instead, he borrowed a left skate from one player and a right skate from another. I only found out by accident. I swear, you could cry sometimes. You feel like a summer camp counselor."

When Shero got to Philadelphia he spent the entire season exaggerating fundamentals to make his points. For example, line changes are very important and if executed correctly can make the difference between winning and losing. "Can you imagine?" Freddie would say in that plaintive way of his, "in the NHL and not knowing how to change lines." The players were bumping into each other, stepping on each other, falling over each other. Once Freddie had to explain that no more than two players could get through the gate at the bench at any one time because the gate was only so wide. "If anybody else tries it," he said, "one of you guys is gonna get stuck."

If there was one thing we understood about Freddie it was that he believed in democracy on the Flyers. There was no such thing as a star system with him. He had developed this philosophy during his years coaching in the minors. He liked to tell a story about how, when he was coaching Shawinigan Falls in the old Quebec League, he had a solid old pro named Jean-Paul Denis, whom he liked very much as a player. Denis was the star of the Shawinigan club but it didn't matter to Freddie.

"Every third game," said Freddie, "I'd come in the dressing room and give him hell. Even though he was the star, I'd tell him he was no damned good, chicken, not backchecking, not working, thinking only of himself. This would frighten all the players. They'd say, 'My God, if he says this to Jean-Paul Denis, who's the best player on the team, what does he think of us?'"

That philosophy remained the same throughout most of his coaching career. At any given time you might get a gentle touch of Freddie's hand on your shoulder and you knew that physical message was something very special. Freddie believed that touching was important in developing a mental rapport with his players. It was his way of telling us that he was with us all the way and sympathetic to our problems. I can recall coming off the ice after getting a dumb penalty or missing an easy shot on goal and having Freddie gently touch me, by that telling me that I was still all right, despite my blunder. That gesture made me want to play that much harder for him.

Shero was a student of the game as well as an executor of strategies and plans. While his peers were not paying much attention to hockey activities in Europe, Freddie monitored the successful rise to power in hockey circles of the Soviet Union. That shouldn't come as a surprise, because the Soviets' style of play was one of intense discipline and mobility. For Freddie, staying in your position, taking out the man, and maintaining possession of the puck all were key components to our team's success. The Soviets had developed more adequate techniques for managing such skills, and Freddie wanted to know about them. As a result, Freddie traveled to the Soviet Union, spent time with coach Anatoli Tarasov, whom he idolized, and studied some of Tarasov's writings and hockey philosophies. He was overwhelmed by the stamina, courage, and physiological capacities of the Soviets and could not believe their capacity to demonstrate perfect balance, strength, and poise.

He was astute enough to realize, however, that he had to adapt the Soviets' skills and methods to the NHL. Freddie borrowed ideas from the Soviets and put together his own collection of rules for us, which were simple and to the point, such as:

- Never pass diagonally in our zone unless 100 percent certain.
- Never go backward in our end except on a power play. (Passing backward in our end to a teammate to elude opposition is okay.)
- Never throw a puck out blindly from behind their net.
- Wings on wings between blue lines except when able to intercept a stray pass.
- Never allow men in our defensive zone to be outnumbered.
- No forward must ever turn his back to the puck at any time. Know where the puck is at all times. Only defensemen are allowed to turn their backs for a fraction of a second on a swing to the corner in our end.

But although Freddie had an ideal sense of how these rules should be executed and how these techniques should be learned, some of my teammates were not so believing.

One day he had us out on the ice for practice and told the guys he wanted three-man passing drills with three pucks rather than one. Kelly told Freddie that was impossible.

"Bull," said Freddie. "I saw fifteen-year-olds do it when I was in Moscow." We did it.

At first Shero very rarely played me in my rookie season and I even went so far as to ask him to send me back to the minors so that I could get some ice time. He wouldn't do it. (Out of despair, I was drinking quite a bit at that point.) But he kept reassuring me that I was needed and felt that I was better off with the big club than in the American League.

Eventually he did give me more ice and Freddie, more than any-one, added to my act as an enforcer. Up to that time, most of my fighting and aggressive style of play had been limited to my own perceptions of when and how that should be introduced. Coaches rarely, if ever, instructed me to initiate that style of aggression. It was only after I arrived in Philadelphia that Freddie meshed my style with the Flyers' gears. Reflecting on this point, I suppose that Fred-die was the first person to consciously manipulate me to produce in a manner that would keep me a vital part of the organization for a long time. But once again he managed to communicate it to me in a very subtle way. On the one hand, he never asked me to go out on the ice and start a fight, but by his actions it was more than implicit that he wanted me to fight any opponent who tried to intimidate us.

For example: We were playing Chicago and Magnuson of the Black Hawks ran at our MacLeish after the whistle. By any standards, MacLeish is a good boy with his dukes, but he is even better at scor-ing goals, so why waste MacLeish in a fight? As soon as Magnuson ran at MacLeish, Freddie leaned over my shoulder and said, "Okay, Schultz!"

He didn't have to finish the sentence because I knew damn well that he wasn't suggesting "Okay, Schultz, go out there and get us a goal." If Freddie didn't want me to get into a fight he sure as hell would have told me so when I got back from the penalty box after having belted out Magnuson. But no, not a word was spoken. Freddie liked it; my teammates liked it, and, most of all, the home fans loved it.

Freddie was more like a sergeant in a platoon than someone you could call a pal. He was a leader who was not supposed to be a friend.

Shero once wrote: "We know that hockey is where we live, where we can best meet and overcome pain and wrong and death. Life is just a place where we spend time between games." That part of Fred-die's thinking epitomized the conflict that would eventually distort my perception of what life was about. The short-term successes be-gan to blur my long-term vision about where I was going and what I planned to do for the rest of my life. I actually believed Freddie in the beginning when he told us that hockey was the be-all and end-all of our existence. I wish I could go back in time and take some of the hours that I spent in the hockey world and return them to my family and close friends. Hockey isn't everything, even if you play it for a living. Having an appropriate attitude with respect to the game is only one way of the many in which a person grows and develops. As I was maturing as a hockey player, I felt at times that I was regressing to adolescence and missing out on so many other important things. Believe it or not, I can't even remember the number of times that I was able to sit down alone, read an interesting book, listen to a soothing piece of music, or engage in an intimate and sensitive conversation with my wife. As successful as I was becoming, I had been drained by Shero of all my energy. He had channeled all of my thinking and turned me into an automaton who would respond to his every wish. It wasn't worth it. I begrudge him for taking away that part of my identity.

At times I felt totally controlled and experienced severe feelings of depression over the manner in which he treated me. My whole career was not unlike that of a factory worker who, after taking his lunch pail to work and punching his time card, is told: "We don't really need you today. Just sit there until you're called." I recall one incident when they built an extra seat in the back of our regular team bench. It was designed for the utility player but most times the guys who were supposed to sit in it would forget and the main bench would get too crowded. One night the bench was so crowded that our guys were getting in each other's way as Freddie changed lines.

Freddie was exasperated and shouted, "Will somebody move his ass back there!"

Nobody moved because all eyes were following the play on the ice, so Freddie tried again. "Somebody get back there!"

Still, nothing happened, so Freddie said, "If nobody gets back there right now I'm fining everybody one hundred bucks."

I picked myself up and fell into the utility seat, feeling pretty low about the whole thing.

It's only now that I begin to see how many lows there really were in my career. To this day, I don't know why I agreed to go to the back of the bench. It wasn't because I was a "good guy"; it wasn't because I wanted to save me and my teammates a hundred dollars each; it was because I felt that I was dispensable and was virtually insignificant in the larger scheme of things until the next confrontation on the ice. Even if I thought I might be able to help the team with my hockey abilities, checking techniques, and goal-scoring potential, Freddie wouldn't give me the chance to prove it. This man controlled my self-image. He raised and lowered me, gave me a good feeling about myself and then a bad feeling about myself, on a regular basis. I felt like a puppet being manipulated by a set of strings, the difference being that Freddie was not backstage, an unseen hand, but always in the forefront. Could you live that kind of life? And what in God's name would you do to cope with those kinds of frustrations and depressions?

Besides, what right do coaches have to orchestrate a player's life to such a degree? As an adult, playing in a precarious situation, I felt confident to some extent that I could make some decisions on my own. As an individual who had assumed the responsibility of a wife and family, I felt that I was capable of distinguishing right from wrong in certain kinds of situations. But the structure of hockey does not permit that kind of analysis on the part of the player. From amateur hockey on, we are socialized into thinking that the coach is always right and that rules and regulations and a certain kind of regimentation are keys to success. So many times, I wanted to wedge into some of Freddie's dialogue. And as I looked around and noticed the faces of my teammates, I could sense that they, too, were more than concerned about some of the coach's comments. But to attempt to redirect the conversation would be tantamount to taking issue with the entire system, and would undoubtedly lead to a reputation as a clubhouse lawyer. For these reasons I kept quiet, played the game, and followed orders, although inwardly I was feeling more and more anxious about so many things.

Shero said that the key to winning hockey games was "to arrive at the net with the puck and in ill humor." We did our best to oblige, with excellent results. The Stanley Cup victory over Boston was a case in point, not to mention our continued success-via-intimidation in the 1974–75 season.

Among other things, the championship served to focus attention on Freddie and raised questions about him that may never be fully resolved; chiefly, was he a phenomenon or a phony? Normally such a question would be heretical, considering that the man directed a team from somewhere near the depths of the National Hockey League right up to the very pinnacle. But Freddie, himself, provoked such doubt by his actions, which, at the very least, would have to be regarded as bizarre. Even the Flyers' press guide said as much when it noted that "he is considered somewhat eccentric by some of his peers." Or, as a magazine writer once said, "Mad as a blinkin' hatter." But that is, in effect, how this man operated a good deal of the time.

Most of the Flyers would find it hard to disagree with the description. To us, Freddie was alternately known as The Phantom, Mister X, or The Fog; since "Freddie The Fog" was easiest to say, that ultimately became the nickname that stuck and, by his actions, Freddie saw to it that it did.

One time, when he was trying to figure out some strategy between periods, he took a short walk down the arena corridor in Atlanta. Still deep in thought, Freddie took a left turn, came to a door, opened it, and continued walking until he had figured out the play he had in mind. Unfortunately, he had walked right out of the rink and into its parking lot and found himself locked out of the hockey game.

Slogans were a big thing with Freddie. He played the blackboard the way Van Cliburn plays the piano. From one day to the next we never knew for sure whether he would scribble a message from Peanuts or Dostoevski, but the quotes kept coming. He would scrawl such things as "A winner says, 'There ought to be a better way to do it'; a loser says, 'That's the way it has always been done around here.' " Another one: "Success is not the result of spontaneous combustion; you have to set yourself on fire." And "For a nation to be great it must welcome criticism . . . the same goes for a team." (That slogan had great meaning for us because it provided a shield for us against the barrage of criticism we were absorbing.)

Freddie would follow up on the slogans with unusual drills. Once he put us through a drill that was offbeat even by Freddie's standards. He assigned one guy to stand in front of the goal and stay there while two other guys tried to mug him. The idea was that the victim was supposed to prove how tough he was. "I want the fellow in front to show he has the ability to keep his own bones from being broken," Freddie said by way of explanation. Billy Clement, one of our fine young centers, didn't quite make it through the drill and wound up with an injured arm.

Shero once had us skate around on one leg for several minutes until Clarkie finally said, "Freddie, this is ridiculous—why are we doing it?"

The coach smiled contentedly and replied, "Why, no reason at all, Bobby. I've just been waiting for someone to come up and tell me it's ridiculous."

As ridiculous as some of our on-ice situations appeared to be, Freddie's eccentricity was manifest off the ice as well. "The Atlanta Incident" is noteworthy. Freddie said he didn't know what happened to him in Atlanta in 1974 when we were playing the Flames during the opening round for the Stanley Cup. What we do know is that Freddie awoke in the morning bruised from head to toe so severely that he had to fly home to Philadelphia while his assistant, Mike Nykoluk, handled the club behind the bench. "I don't know if I had a fight in a bar," Freddie said, "but if I did, it wouldn't be the first time I remember the word *animal* upset me."

I'm not quite sure what happened in Atlanta, but Memphis was another story. "Memphis, now there's a town," I once heard Freddie say. "The only place I was ever mugged by a policeman. I was sitting on a park bench in the middle of the night, not drinking or anything, and two cops came up and gave me a rough time searching me. Later, I discovered my wallet was missing."

During a playoff series with the Maple Leafs, the team was staying at the Royal York Hotel in Toronto but, for reasons only Freddie can explain, he booked himself into the hotel under an assumed name. And he only told two people connected with the Flyers what that assumed name was, and where he was. Reporters were harassing hotel workers about Freddie's whereabouts.

"Shero?" they kept saying. "We have no one booked under that name. But if you want to leave a message, we'll see that he gets it. The Flyers, you say? I'm sorry. As far as I know they are not staying here, but I can give them the message."

Freddie had asked the Royal York employees to tell the newspapermen we weren't staying there, even though we were. The only problem with his idea was that half of the Flyers were standing right there in the lobby being interviewed by the very same reporters.

Meanwhile, Freddie wound up at the Maple Leaf Gardens' coffee shop where he had breakfast with the Leafs' manager, Jim Gregory. By this time, none of us were particularly surprised at any of Freddie's antics, because most of us had been with him a couple of years and when you have a coach who sends his players to a gypsy tea-leaf reader and faith healer then you know you're dealing with someone special.

He had done that because he had great faith in mystical powers and truly thought he could do things like direct the puck by concentrating hard behind the bench. He said it once worked when Bladon was playing defense for us and he was going through a slump. Freddie did one of those mystical wishing numbers the night before a game and the next night Bladon got four goals and four assists.

The magic didn't always work, as proven by the time he sent Kindrachuk to a soothsayer in the hopes Kindrachuk's ailing back could be cured. The gypsy gave Kindrachuk a vial containing stones and

I became a full-time fighter in the Eastern League. That's me (16) as a Salem Rebel, taking on one of the Charlotte Checkers.

My French was fractured but they loved me in Quebec when I played for the American League Aces, or "Les As de Quebec."

As a full-fledged Broad Street Bully, I took on Ron Harris (3) of the Rangers—and anybody else I could get my hands on.

BERNIE MOSER—DUFOR STUDIO

The Flyers' Terror Squad—from the left, Don Saleski, André Dupont, Bob Kelly, and me—in 1974 when we marauded through the NHL.

Bryan Lewis (left) was one of my least favorite referees, a secret I never kept from him. (Art Skov was my idea of a good ref.)

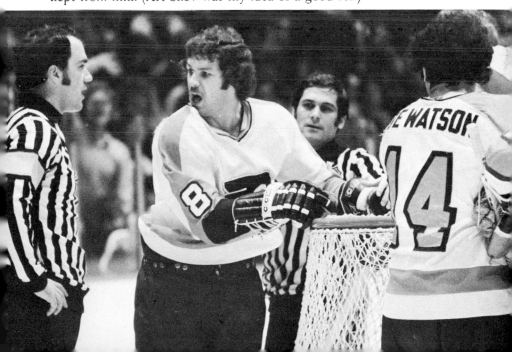

PHILADELPHIA FLYERS

Gentle types such as the Canadiens' Guy La-pointe (5) (above) never bothered me, but others (right) like Dennis Hextall (22) were the kind I'd mentally prepare for—hoping to clobber—on the day of a game.

BERNIE MOSER—DUFOR STUDIO

I always believed I also had scoring ability (although Fred Shero didn't think so). Here, my sudden-death playoff winner against the Flames.

Keith Allen, the man who brought me into the NHL, holds the Stanley Cup on the flight back from Buffalo in 1975. Crowds jammed the streets of Philadelphia to celebrate our triumphal return. Those moments were unforgettable; it was easy then to put out of my mind the anxieties that would cause real problems later, when things weren't going quite so well.

More than anyone, captain Bobby Clarke made the Flyers go, although some of his methods were questionable, to say the least.

BRUCE BENNETT

Fred Shero (standing behind the bench) was my Svengali, but his genius worked to both my advantage and disadvantage. The same could be said for his influence on hockey.

BRUCE BENNETT

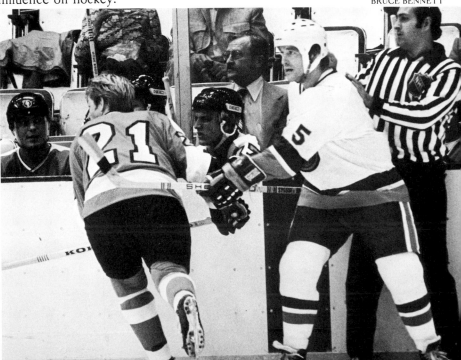

I brought out the worst in out-of-town fans—but I did bring them out. (At home, my tactics got me on the cover of *Philadelphia* magazine in October 1974.) At first I could laugh at the needling, but after a while it had a very damaging affect.

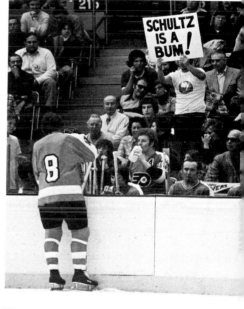

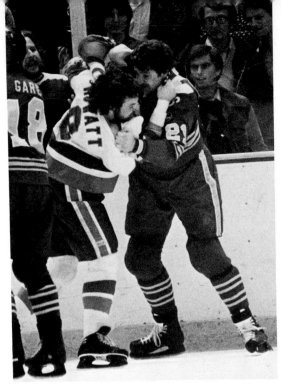

By the time I was playing for Buffalo—my last NHL team—the conquests were rare. Here's my old nemesis Garry Howatt of the Islanders. He is small but tough.

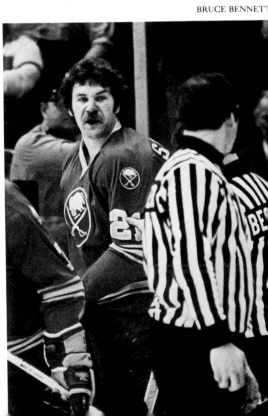

The intimidator had become intimidated. The Hammer was bloodied— and washed up!

copper and suggested if he held it often enough it would give him strength. The only strength it gave Kindrachuk was to take long plane rides to Yorktown, Saskatchewan, where an old friend of his, a chiropractor, would work on his back.

At one time Freddie said he was going to have us scrimmage to music. "I don't know what kind," he said. "We'll have to experiment. I remember liking the military bands back home in Winnipeg and playing better after hearing them before the game. But I just heard on the radio that people who like martial music are idiots."

The only individual who claimed to know what was going on in Freddie's mind was his wife, Mariette, a French-Canadian.

"Don't say you understand me, Mariette," Freddie once said. "I don't understand myself, so how in the world are you supposed to understand me?"

Once Cathy and I were going to dinner and we noticed Freddie walking down the street in our direction. We nodded to him but he kept going. Cathy was amazed. "Doesn't he acknowledge you outside the team?" she asked. But Freddie's shyness and introspection were often misinterpreted. If he was deep in thought or having a serious conversation with someone he would walk a couple of blocks out of his way to avoid talking to anyone else.

Freddie liked to say that his "Fog" image was exaggerated both by the media and himself, and of course our storytelling enhanced that image. A lot of newspapermen who were accustomed to traditional coaches couldn't understand how Freddie could criticize us after we had won a game by a big score. But he knew there were critical moments in the game when, if we hadn't been lucky, we could have been beaten. In the post-game meetings with the writers, he often would take a long time answering their questions; they thought this hesitation indicated he was somewhere out in space.

To say that Freddie was an eccentric is an understatement. His behavior oftentimes left me totally confused, and when I'd return home I couldn't even rationalize for Cathy what had gone on, mainly because I didn't understand it. But the amazing thing was that whatever Freddie predicted inevitably happened. Just as many people don't question a good thing, I decided to live with it, although I must confess that sometimes that "Fog" image was so thick I couldn't even see the person behind it.

It's difficult for me in retrospect to position Freddie in my thinking. There were so many contradictions. On the one hand, this man

was a hockey innovator, a brilliant strategist, a dedicated and concerned individual who existed for his players. On the other hand, he
was a person who sanctioned gang warfare, intimidation, and a style
of play that at times was more a hindrance than a help. I personally
felt intricately involved with that side of Freddie's style because I
was constantly being called upon to execute it. Why didn't he glean
from the Russians, and have us produce, a specific quality of play that
would have avoided such strategy? (But then, if that were the case,
where would I be today? That's one of the biggest contradictions.)

In terms of his critics, and also his supporters, Freddie paid a very
heavy price that, to this time is not very clearly understood. Let me
try to provide a framework for you.

The bottom line on Freddie is that he won two Stanley Cups with
a team that shouldn't have won it either time, if you judge by talent
alone. But, thanks to Freddie, we had something going for us that the
others didn't; we worked harder than any team in the league. We
were the most disciplined and the most aggressive. *We had developed a reputation.* It was this reputation, which Freddie cultivated, that
did irreparable damage to hockey's image. More than anyone else,
Freddie refined the theory of intimidation. I speak from experience
as his number one enforcer. Big league hockey was rough before
Freddie came along, but it was a different kind of rough; fights
occurred as a result of previous fouls. Under Shero, fights were
started for the sake of fighting.

Freddie, who himself was a champion fighter in the Canadian
Navy, sanctioned the gang warfare that became an integral part of
the Flyers' style. A study conducted by the Province of Ontario in
1974 about the causes of violence in amateur hockey revealed that
professional hockey was a prime influence, "particularly the NHL
with its emphasis on winning and use of violence as tactical instru-
ment to achieve that goal."

I partially blame Freddie because the coach, more than anyone
else, is in a position to control the style of his team and if Freddie had
wanted us to play a cleaner brand of hockey he could have told us so.
Obviously, he never did, and we continued to rampage through the
league. Of course, I cannot deny that part of the responsibility is
mine. I'm an adult responsible for my actions. But Freddie did manipulate me. He would send me out on the ice just to stir up trouble
to get the team going, knowing full well that I would do it. If he had
been opposed to that instigating brand of hockey, he never would

have dispatched me with the express purpose of causing excitement.

In my estimate, the most deplorable aspect of the intimidating style was the ganging, when two or three of the Flyers would jump a fellow on the other team. Equally reprehensible was the use of the hockey stick as a weapon of injury. I hated that and I am convinced that Freddie should have warned his players to use their bodies instead of their sticks. Likewise, Freddie should have reprimanded any Flyer who participated in a two-on-one or three-on-one ganging attack.

He didn't. The Oakland Seals had a young defenseman named Barry Cummins who had no known reputation as a tough guy. In a game against the Flyers Clarke skated one-on-one against Cummins, who dumped Clarkie clean. But Clarkie had this habit of swinging his stick over his head as he went down as if he were out of control and needed the stick for balance. In fact, he was trying to get a piece of somebody. This time as Clarke skated away he brought his stick back and got a good piece of Cummins—right in the face. The kid took a dim view of the whack so he retaliated in kind and Clarkie hit the ice. It was a perfect case of tit for tat, except our players didn't see it that way. The law, according to the Flyers, was that anyone who hit Clarkie paid for it—no ifs, ands, or buts.

When Cummins knocked Clarkie down, our whole team—everyone—went after the kid. Can you imagine what it must have been like for Cummins, standing in the middle of the rink with a horde of wild men coming at him, everyone wanting a piece of his flesh?

It so happens I was one of the few Flyers who did not want any part of the mass mugging. Despite all my carrying on I hated that kind of stuff. Cummins was lucky to escape without serious injury and Freddie couldn't have cared less. For all his rhetoric about rough hockey, Freddie never made a distinction between clean checking, clean fighting, and the dirty use of the hockey stick as a weapon. (And why in hell didn't the referee stop Clarke from doing his act with the stick that started the whole thing? Everybody in the league knew Clarke's little tricks.)

In another game against the Seals, in 1975, I got into a fight early in the game with one of their defensemen, Mike Christie. I mention Christie only because he popped up again later.

Later in the game Kindrachuk roughed Christie along the boards and another fight started. Kindrachuk and Christie both got penalties and went to the penalty box. Then Christie and Saleski, who was out on the ice, started jawing at each other. While they were yapping, Kindrachuk sneaked out of the penalty box, entered Christie's area and sucker-punched him. Kelly, among other Flyers, came off the bench and skated to the penalty box where he sucker-punched Christie near the left eye. The Seals fought back and a mass brawl erupted. Poor Christie was mauled. He wound up battered about the eyes and needed fourteen stitches to close the wounds.

It so happens I didn't hit a soul—I just don't like brawls that are so one-sided. I never did. I felt sorry for Christie. This was a side I rarely showed on the ice—until later—and I'm sure few people noticed it.

Freddie kept rattling on with some ridiculous justification, but the fact of the matter was that Freddie would tolerate any kind of cheap shot—especially when the Flyers were way behind.

"Coaching has helped me salve my conscience for the way I played," he once said to a columnist. "I was the kind of player who wouldn't fight unless I was attacked. I'm still ashamed of myself for failing to help Andy Bathgate one night when he was attacked by two opponents. As a coach, I wouldn't have kept myself on as a player, even though I played on winners."

It was inevitable that the more Freddie encouraged our bullying behavior, the more the media harped on it. In time Freddie began to get paranoid about the questioning over our brawling. He would say, "We're gonna fight back. We're allowed to do the same things as the others."

But, of course, we were worse than the others. We were the perpetrators and it is foolish, if not hypocritical, to make it seem any other way. Freddie wanted the brand of aggression that we delivered, and he sanctioned all the craziness that accompanied it.

The pressures that come with success are manifold. Problem drinking for some of us is the outcome of an accumulation of events that are filled with an intense stress and a high degree of anxiety. Drinking is a social response to a variety of pressures heaped upon an individual and is generally symptomatic of deeper and perhaps more serious problems that never surface. The responsibilities heaped upon an NHL coach are awesome. Besides being responsible for the team's success, there are few persons with whom he can share his problems and concerns. Having to deal with twenty individuals on a very regular basis, motivating them, alleviating some of their stresses and anxieties, further pushes the coach into a corner. From the very beginning, Freddie was a loner. I don't know this for a fact, but I would speculate that that style certainly helped to promote what eventually became a condition of problem drinking.

In the early years booze didn't affect Freddie too much as a coach because he worked so hard he could afford an off night here and there. I can prove it by the 1975 Stanley Cup finals between the Flyers and the Buffalo Sabres. One morning we had a practice and Freddie was nowhere to be seen on the ice or in the dressing room. He never showed up because, as it turned out, he was hung over from being with us at a cocktail hour at our hotel. After we finished our meal and drinks Freddie kept on drinking while swapping stories with our rookies.

If it hurt us you couldn't tell by the results of that series; a series, by the way, that the Sabres were favored to win. You see, Freddie had us working on a certain play fifteen minutes a day over and over again long before we had reached the finals against Buffalo. The idea was to score a goal by bulling your way out front from behind the net. Freddie would hand over five bucks to the man who kept beating the goalie and who stayed out the longest. It was a play that would pay rich dividends for us in the final game for the cup. Using Freddie's plan right from the textbook, Kelly got the puck early in the third period with the score tied, 0-0, moved from behind the Sabres' net out in front and jammed the puck into the goal.

In his later years with the Flyers, liquor began to affect Freddie. I don't know, but it could be that he was responding to a power struggle that had been developing in the front office. Originally, the Flyers' hierarchy consisted of only Freddie and our general manager, Keith Allen. But now Clarke had assumed a position of power. There was Ed Snider, our owner, as well as two assistant coaches, Mike Nykoluk and Barry Ashbee, all of whom wanted to have input. So Freddie began backing off and drinking more. By the time he left the Flyers and joined the Rangers in 1978, his drinking problem was hockey's best-kept open secret. It finally became public knowledge two years later, only months before he was fired from his Rangers positions as coach and general manager.

I would be distorting the truth if I said that I knew the "inside story" on Freddie's drinking problem. What bothered me about his problem had more to do with the fact that Freddie never spoke about it. Perhaps I could have dismissed that behavior in other people more easily. But working with Freddie for so many years prevented my doing so. I often wish that I had had the intestinal fortitude to ask him why he was doing what he was doing. I've seen liquor do crazy things to people in professional hockey and I've seen the damaging effects it has had on their careers. Experiencing insobriety night after night is not the way mature men are supposed to behave.

But the bottle has been used as a rationale for maintaining a very strong degree of camaraderie among professional hockey players. It is in the bar, and not in the living room of one's home, where issues are discussed, analyzed, and evaluated. As we all know, drinking behavior is symptomatic of a much deeper set of problems, often having to do with loneliness and self-image, that sometimes virtually destroys people's lives or has a devastating effect on their livelihoods.

That is the price that Freddie and some of my other colleagues in this professional sport have paid. That is what the professional game of hockey can do to reasonably mature men, taking them out of the quiet of their homes and throwing them into a social world filled with delusions of grandeur, promises, and problems never solved.

History will show that Freddie was one of the most significant innovators among hockey coaches for his introduction of videotape as a coaching aid, and his importing of the best of the Soviet style of play to North America. That's what makes it especially sad that he sanctioned so much of the bloody part of the game, and that he experienced a fall from grace in Philadelphia and then in New York after the Flyers' glory years.

Freddie Shero wasn't the greatest guy who ever lived, or the worst. Although his philosophy from a practical point of view was most significant for me, from a human point of view it was more than negative.

Some observers often suggested that Freddie was living vicariously through us, which made it a lot safer for him, but was both physically and psychologically punishing for me. He had great successes but his downfall was also reasonably dramatic. In some ways I have the feeling that the game could get along very well without him, for he is hardly a role model for young coaches and players.

But he also poignantly illustrates the extent to which individuals will go to produce a winning franchise, an end product that is revered and sanctioned by everyone who participates in the NHL. I would never place the blame totally on Fred Shero for the Philadelphia Flyers' intimidation style. And later chapters will reveal that he was a central force but not the only member of the very large cast of characters who should have but didn't curtail such activity. I don't think Freddie's a very happy man, everything taken into account. But for a long time, neither was I. It is my hope that maybe Freddie will have the luxury of sitting back in his living room and reflecting on his experiences and activities in the NHL, as I do now. Perhaps then the inside story from his vantage point will clearly emerge.

8

Hitting the Heights

OF ALL THE MOMENTS I savor when I look back at my career, the one that remains the most satisfying occurred on May 18, 1974, when we defeated the Boston Bruins to win the Stanley Cup. I had come out of the regular season with a respectable total of 20 goals—in baseball it would be the equivalent of being a solid .265 hitter—and the conviction that the best was yet to come. More than that, I had inherited a following: The shy kid from Rosetown had become a civic hero. Mayor Frank Rizzo presented us with the keys to the city and a Stanley Cup victory party was held in our honor.

I had expected the city to go mad when we won the championship, but I never anticipated the extent of the celebration. More than 1.5 million fans paraded up Broad Street, surging west on Walnut and east on Chestnut as well as on the side streets. The players were seated in open cars that attempted to make their way along the parade route; some of them couldn't. The crowd had gotten so berserk around Clarke's car that he and his wife, Sandy, had to turn around and head for safety at the Spectrum.

I was luckier. Our car made it to Independence Square, where the crowd gave us a tremendous ovation. I soaked up every bit of the adulation and slowly the enormity of it all—and the incredible good luck I was now enjoying—began to sink in. A year earlier I had harbored doubts that I even belonged in the NHL, and now I was being hailed as a conquering hero. It was enough to make a guy lose all concept of reality. In a sense, of course, that is just what happened.

At about four in the afternoon the ceremonies ended, and the crowd slowly began to disperse. I sensed at that moment that no matter what happened to this gang of athletes in the future, we now were experiencing the most special moment in our lives.

As difficult as it may be to imagine, the entire season flashed before me in a moment. All of the controversies, conflicts, frustrations, and anxieties paled and a surge of enthusiasm and unbelievable excitement overwhelmed me. I remember other players, after they had won the Stanley Cup, telling television audiences that it is precisely this feeling that every athlete lives for, and now I knew exactly what they meant. The respect, high visibility, and adulation I experienced from Philadelphians was immensely gratifying. "We may stay on top for a few years," I remember saying to Kindrachuk in a lucid moment, "but it'll never be the same again."

That comment was more prophetic than I imagined. It really never would be the same again, and that's part of the problem. The highs that accompany success such as a Stanley Cup win momentarily neutralize existing conflicts, be they on the job or at home with the family. In my case, the Cup win took the sting out of the difficulties I endured during the regular season, as well as any friction with Cathy. At the moment, those conflicts paled in significance. It was difficult to turn my back on the success before me, no matter what traumas I had suffered in the past or what I would be confronted with in the seasons ahead.

Suddenly, Philadelphians were at our feet and there wasn't a restaurant or theater that we visited without being surrounded by fans. At first I reveled in the attention, but in no time I began getting annoyed by the fact that Cathy and I couldn't enjoy a simple meal together. People would walk over to our table and say "I really don't want to bother you," or "If my son knew that I saw you and didn't get your autograph, he'd kill me."

The adulation extended all the way to Saskatchewan. When Cathy and I flew home our plane was met at the Saskatoon airport by a number of relatives, friends, neighbors, and others I had hardly ever seen before who turned out to share in the town's jubilation over me. When we arrived in Rosetown I discovered that I was truly the hometown-boy-made-good.

On Saturday, August 24, 1974, the town gave me a "Dave Schultz Day," starting with a Schultz breakfast at the Legion Hall, a Flyers show and hockey highlights at the Rosetown Theater, Schultz Street Games, and finally a Schultz Burger and Drink to round out the afternoon. In the evening the Rosetown Chamber of Commerce held a Schultzfest and a Schultz Dance at the arena.

It was good to be home with the people I grew up with: Claude and Maurice Paquette, my close friends; others from high school; my mom and dad, as well as my sisters, Barb, Janet, and Glenda. It was exciting to walk Main Street where the high school band in white, blue, and maroon was giving a concert. I went to visit Maurice Paquette, who was getting married, and for whom I would participate in the wedding party.

What made this visit to Rosetown different from any in the past was the new super-hero's role I had attained. Even back home I couldn't shake reporters and had to put up with a writer from Canada's *Weekend Magazine* trailing me around town. The neighbors knew he was going to write about me and became very protective. One lady went over to the writer and said, "Now you write something nice about Dave for a change. He's a fine boy."

From time to time I would shake my head in amazement over what was happening. Unlike in Philadelphia, where I really hadn't been myself for some time, it was easy to keep my feet on the ground at home or at the Chrysler garage where my Dad was putting in a couple of Sunday hours on his car. My father had come east to watch me in the Rangers' and Bruins' playoff series and was terribly proud of his son. When someone would bring up the business of my fighting he would quickly say, "Hey, he can play hockey, too." I wonder what he was really thinking. I suspect he was comparing me to "Wild" Bill Ezinicki, who played on a line with Syl Apps, Sr. (Canada's hockey hero with whom my Dad skated on the Army team). Ezinicki didn't score a lot but he deflected attention from Apps the way I distracted the enemy from Clarke. Ezinicki skated on three straight Stanley Cup-winners in the late 1940s doing that and I'm sure Dad figured me for a latter-day Wild Bill.

When the time came to leave Rosetown and return to Philadelphia I felt a sadness come over me and I realized that, once again, I was leaving the place that I loved most of all, the one that gave me genuine peace of mind. It wasn't easy returning to Philly. Sure, we were now living in a nice home with a swimming pool and two cars, but now that we had hit the heights our home became a haven for the media who never seemed to get enough of me.

When magazine writers came over, Cathy and I would take them out to the pool and relax on the flowered lounge as the questions were fired: "What's Dave Schultz like off the ice?" "How do both of you cope with Dave's hockey image?" "What are the benefits of having played a Schultz brand of hockey?" "In what ways does Dave's identity affect your home life?" "Who was the toughest opponent you ever faced?"

We tried to explain that my character was far different at home than it was on the ice, but I had the sneaking suspicion that few, if any, believed me. It was as if they expected to find me behaving in an antisocial way.

Cathy was terrific with the interviewers. She liked to tell them "He's a pussycat off the ice; a regular Jekyll-Hyde. But if he ever loses his temper around the house the way he does on the ice, then I'll be in trouble." But her attempts at humor were often misinterpreted by the reporters. They wrote down everything she said with no awareness of the nuances, and reproduced even her most sarcastic comments as if they were uttered in seriousness; which, of course, they were not. Once, with tongue well in cheek, Cathy told a reporter that she had yet to be beaten up by me but that I might maul her in the future. Her droll put-on was taken at face value and found its way into the reporter's article.

Meanwhile, the requests came in for appearances (up to twelve hundred dollars just to show up at a shopping center), modeling, and attending hockey schools. I was now self-absorbed; and whenever an opportunity arose for more attention, I grabbed it. When someone approached me and asked if I wanted to make a record I said, "Yeah, sure." He didn't care that I couldn't sing a note. "It doesn't matter," the guy said, "we can fix it."

I had become intoxicated with the sweet juices of success. The mere thought that I could actually produce a commercial record for distribution in the music world—that I would be in the record rack alongside Elton John and Billy Joel—is, in retrospect, ludicrous no matter how rose-colored your glasses may be. That episode alone should have turned me off from the world of hucksters, but it didn't. I suppose when you're winning, anything goes—even at 33 rpm.

They hustled me down to a recording studio and gave me the lyrics to a tune called "Penalty Box." The song started out with a whistle—as in a referee's whistle—and then an announcer calling out my penalties: two minutes for hooking, two for roughing, five for fighting, and a ten-minute misconduct. At this point in the song, I told the woman vocalist to release me from the penalty box. I said, "Love is like an ice hockey game, sometimes it can be rough; you got me checking and holding and hooking and then you blow the whistle on me." Later in the tune, I added, "I'm not defending my style, it's just that every once in a while you've got to leave the rules behind."

As a work of art "Penalty Box" will never replace Beethoven, but my popularity was such in Philadelphia that the record climbed right to the top of the charts. It was number one on a local radio station. The fact that it reached such a high level of success is as much a social commentary on my involvement as it is about the people who purchased the record.

Another promoter figured that if I was so hot on a disk I would be even better in person. He wanted to put me on stage, no less, and once again I accepted. They booked me for a one-nighter at a night club in Cherry Hill, New Jersey, called the Centrum. The idea was for my lousy voice to be backed by a male trio known as the Dovells, with whom I had become friendly.

It all sounded fine until the day I was to go out on stage and perform. Playing hockey before a crowd of 17,000 fans is a lot easier than getting on stage in front of 170 people. When I got to the dressing room I was petrified. I had brought along a Thermos bottle full of booze to get my courage up, and I knocked off a couple of glasses as they prepared me in my dressing room. It was brutal. When somebody yelled, "You're on, Dave," I picked myself up and walked out of the room. Before I could take five steps I was surrounded by teenyboppers. Flashbulbs began popping and I blinked. A kid came up to me and said, "Dave, do ya have a headache?" If she only knew.

Finally I was out there with two male singers on my right and another on my left. I asked myself what in Christ's name was I doing on stage? Before I could think up an answer the band struck up "Penalty Box" and I did my thing, not so much singing as talking into the mike. One tune was enough, then I answered questions from the crowd. I was on stage for half an hour and then, mercifully, they let me off the hook.

The review in *The Inquirer* was not a rave: "Schultz left, looking like he did after Clark Gillies of the Islanders belted him in the face." Ouch. I wished I had never accepted that offer.

Another wild scene was planned by a Montreal boxing promoter who wanted me to go in the ring with Pierre Bouchard, the Canadiens defenseman I had fought a couple of times on the ice. The promoter said he would give each of us twenty five thousand dollars to fight at the Forum and would have the bout televised. I thought it was a hell of a stunt and immediately said I'd do it. Bouchard was an awfully good fighter, but he wanted no part of the stunt. At least one of us showed some class.

As much as I enjoyed my burst of popularity, I knew it didn't wear well with all my teammates. Some of them resented the attention and money I was getting. Several of the more talented players found themselves ignored in favor of a two-fisted left wing who didn't have half their skills. In fact I did very little to encourage the people who were promoting me. A case in point was a novelty shop owner named Phil Stein, a wild Flyers' fan.

One night Stein showed up at the Spectrum with four cronies, all wearing German infantry helmets painted with the inscription SCHULTZ ARMY. There were no indications just how big, or small, this Schultz Army was until the story was written up. Stein then announced he had received more than seventy applications for enlistment into his army. Personally, I felt a little uncomfortable about it, but I let the guy have his fun and more publicity built up. Even though Schultz Army never reached a hundred members it soon became known literally across the continent.

One night I made an appearance on the Mike Douglas television show with Kate Smith. Later, when I appeared on a Philadelphia radio show called "Sports Forum" to take questions from fans phoning in to the station, a record 84,194 people called. They weren't phoning in because I was a 20-goal man; I didn't delude myself. They were calling because I had become Broad Street's biggest Bully. Fighting was the keystone to my success. As I assured one caller, "The team I play on, nobody will have to fight. *I'll* do all the fighting!" Thinking back, I can assure you that it was not a statement that I'm proud of; today I feel quite the opposite.

I had taken center stage over such teammates as Dupont, Kelly, and Saleski because I was a showman. Dupont and Kelly could fight but neither of them fought with a flair. They would peak in their intensity at the start of a fight, whereas I could continue to build my emotional state as the fight progressed so that by the time it was over I was wilder than when it began.

This style should not be viewed as an accident. Few hockey players, I would imagine, prepared themselves for forthcoming confrontations the way I did. My ability to visualize an upcoming altercation and mentally dissect the process in advance of the battle set me apart from other players and had me peaking at the most opportune moment. In a sense, I choreographed my entire fight, developing a crescendo within five seconds of the first blow's being struck and sustaining it beyond all reason. While most players tone down their act by the time the linesmen break up the fights, I would be yapping away at the official and trying my damnedest to get back at the guy with whom I had fought, or I might pursue my rage by jawing with fans; *anything* to continue the scene beyond what should have been its logical conclusion. In short, I purposefully orchestrated my matches and my madness.

That nonsense, along with the fact that I scored some big knockdowns and that I cooperated with the media at every turn—I liked talking to them and they liked writing about me—was what put me up on top.

Once we won the Stanley Cup in 1974 we became the premier attraction in hockey. Among the many rewards for some players was a sudden availability of the opposite sex. The more popular we became, the more women pursued us, particularly the species known throughout professional sport, the Groupie.

The average groupie ranged in age from fourteen to seventeen (many were older, some married) and she was everywhere: training camp, Rexy's, our hangout after practice and after games, in the corridors near the dressing room. Normally groupies would hang out in packs of three or four, but occasionally one could be found stalking the players alone.

The adulation of female fans undoubtedly created additional pressure for Cathy as it did for other hockey wives. The women were neither blind nor naive. They realized that we were constantly being pursued either in person, by mail, or by phone by females who saw something special in us. A wife could only fantasize about what took place on the road and rely upon her husband's word should she attempt to pursue the question.

At home the temptations are not as intense as they are on the road (although many players had things going in Philly—our "boys' nights out" weren't only for the boys). When a club is traveling a player has a great deal of free time and very often doesn't know what to do with it. So what are his choices? He can sit in the hotel lobby and watch the crowd go by, read an interesting book, go to a movie, or sit in his room and watch TV. Or he can go for a beer, which often is the case. One beer leads to two and two to three and before he knows it, he's had five and he has forgotten about everything but the lady who has sidled up to him.

Some guys I played with didn't need any drinks to find some action. There are some hockey players who simply would not consider themselves men if they didn't succumb to the temptation of sex on the road. There are those who screw around occasionally and others who never get involved. A lot of players, at one time or another, have been unfaithful, and when I was with the Flyers it was quite evident. (My guess is that easily half the married players on the Flyers had been unfaithful, whether it was a one-night stand or an affair.) Some of them couldn't wait to get back to the locker room to tell the others of their escapades the previous evening. The theme was that you "got" the woman because of how great you supposedly were in bed. Half of them didn't realize that *they* were the ones who were taken to bed by the women.

There were some guys on the Flyers who would say anything to a woman. Others had a little more class. There were players who got letters from women inviting them to bed—and more. In my four years with the Flyers I got one erotic letter. A woman wrote and said how she wanted to get it on with me in several different sexual positions. I didn't pursue it.

Both Cathy and I had a keen appreciation of as well as a certain contempt for the fans. Many of the fans whom we respected enjoyed the game as much as the contribution the players made. Unfortunately these fans remained in the background and never participated in the ego-stroking; by contrast there were the obnoxious, pushy fans who had no appreciation for the game or the players. They simply had a penchant for being near anyone in the spotlight. Those are the kind of people who wouldn't mind if a player stood before them and insulted them. They would tolerate anything—inattentiveness, rudeness, or indifference—in order to say that they had rubbed shoulders with me.

These are the same people who would push their frightened, whimpering child to the head of the line for an autograph and who would berate the child if he failed to get one.

Most satisfying are memories of the good fans—those who sent cards, or made blankets and outfits when babies were born, as well as fan club members who are genuinely dedicated to the team. I was friendly with one couple who donated five hundred dollars to charity for a pair of my hockey gloves.

There were times when we misinterpreted the fans' good intentions. This was the case when we returned to our home in Cherry Hill after the first Stanley Cup victory party in May 1974 and discovered that fans had not only invaded the privacy of our grounds but had hung signs all over our house. Cathy and I resented what we perceived as the sudden interest of people—neighbors who barely noticed us before—who had come out to see us for the wrong reasons.

Cathy, in particular, always regretted the way she reacted to the fans that night. We should have been graceful and realized that the Cup meant as much to the lives of Philadelphia fans as it meant to us. Instead of getting angry with them, we should have been more understanding.

The good fans provided a positive distraction for Cathy and, considering the state of our marriage as I hit the heights, any upbeat development was to be treasured even if it provided only a momentary satisfaction.

To Cathy, I had become a husband who was completely sworn to the "team, team, team" philosophy of the Flyers. I was also smitten by my own success. I was hardly the husband she had expected when we wed in 1972. As I've described, the very special male camaraderie I enjoyed with the Flyers overpowered my relationship at home.

Professional athletes sustain themselves on the basis of this camaraderie. Whether it be cooling out a frustrating moment at a local bar or sharing memories about past performances in both amateur and pro hockey, or just spinning yarns, athletes feed off each other and use each other to maintain the status quo. If you were to ask any professional athlete about his perception of an ideal team, he would respond in a simple phrase—"a winning team." And that's precisely where we were.

Winning is a cure for any and all problems that pervade a hockey organization or its members, and as a result individual players who unite to produce that victory are naturally attracted to each other.

Under those conditions, Cathy never had a chance, at least the way my values were structured in those days. She became relatively insignificant because the hours spent with my teammates proved to be so rewarding and gratifying. Having to return home to be with Cathy became an added burden. In those days the sad fact was that she did not grab my attention in the same manner that the Flyers did. It is a tragic commentary on where my head and my heart were in those Stanley Cup–winning days.

There were, of course, pressures from some of the other players to stay around as well. Only a handful of the guys were attentive to their women. This may sound ridiculous, I know, but I was fully prepared to allow my home life to further deteriorate in the wake of all the glory that had come my way.

Although I felt confident that I could patch things up at a future date, in retrospect I wish I had cared a whole lot more about Cathy's feelings and needs. The time lost during those years can never be restored. None of the moments when I might have added some sane thoughts to a confusing situation can ever be recaptured. Day-to-day life at home was at times no more than a passing inconvenience. I knew deep down in my gut that I was doing something wrong but the pressures and the long line of successes had blurred my thinking.

This situation would not change—much to Cathy's chagrin—so long as the Broad Street Bullies were winning and laughing. Certainly the situation would remain static as long as Bobby Clarke remained the autocratic captain of the Flyers.

9

Bobby Clarke, Captain (Sometimes) Courageous

IN MY FIRST season with the Philadelphia Flyers, Bobby Clarke was voted the Most Valuable Player in the National Hockey League. If ever there was an athlete who looked like the All-Canadian boy it was Clarke. The image was perfect. He had a gap-toothed grin that always looked good in photographs. He was a kid who, despite the fact that he was a diabetic, made it to the top after doctors had told him to think twice about a professional sports career. He was an incredible worker. Nobody could mean more to a team than Clarke meant to the Flyers in my years there.

Fred Shero once described him as "the only true athlete I have seen in modern sports." He was referring to Clarke's unselfishness. "He's not as interested in his own records as other superstars are," said Shero. "He's not obsessed with scoring."

Clarke was extremely sensitive to his teammates. If one of the lesser forwards was in a slump, Bobby would suggest that the player be put on his line. "Maybe I can give him some help," Clarke would say, "and get him a point or two and boost his confidence.

This episode was more the rule than the exception. Another example: The club once had a rule suggesting that each player make a public appearance free at least four times a season. An older player didn't like that and said so at a team meeting. He said he could make

115

at least a hundred bucks an appearance. Clarkie got up, handed the guy a hundred-dollar bill and snorted: "Okay, let's deal with serious business now."

If you didn't know better you'd liken Clarke to one of those Simon Pure characters in the old Norman Rockwell paintings. Both Clarke and Shero were believers in the old-time inspirational messages. When we won our first Stanley Cup in 1974 Clarke was as much impressed with Shero's blackboard inscription ("Win today and we will walk together forever") as anyone. "It's sort of a corny statement," Clarke said later, "but at the time when you are twenty guys struggling like hell to win the Cup, it was very, very important. It wasn't corny then, it was important."

Shero, of course, was the first to admit how vital Clarke was in his scheme of things. "I'm happy as hell if he talks to me," Shero once said.

Bobby made him happy in many ways, given his brilliant performance day in and day out. And if ever a player led by inspiration, Clarke was the man. But there was a darker side to him, one that many Philadelphians and Flyers personnel chose to ignore or, at the very least, dismiss as irrelevant. I am referring to the manner in which Bobby played the game. Dirty. Very dirty.

Clarke's philosophy was simple—the ends justify the means—and Shero agreed completely. "Bobby is the ultimate competitor," Freddie would say. "Anybody who expects to be great has to be mean. The great ones, Gordie Howe and Rocket Richard, were mean. They took care of the opposition. That's Clarke's game, too. He wants to be hacking and hitting and all of that."

The major difference between Clarke and his predecessors was that ever since Bobby had become the team leader the unwritten rule was that he could dish out the rough stuff but that nobody on the opposition was allowed to retaliate. If anyone did they had to pay the consequences.

A case in point: During a fairly rough game in Detroit, Clarke grappled with Detroit Red Wings defenseman Thommie Bergman. Bergman, a Swede, is one of the last players in the NHL who would harm anyone. You could bet your bankroll that Clarke's worst injury would be a flick of Bergman's eyelashes. But in no time at all Bill Barber and Cowboy Flett rushed over and jumped Bergman. Clarke liked that. "That's the difference between the teams," he said. "Two guys helped me and nobody helped Bergman."

Clarke was often unappealing in his choice of victims. During the

1972 Team Canada–Russia tournament he had roomed with Rod Seiling, one of the mildest players ever to skate in the pros. Seiling was a defenseman who did practically everything possible to avoid fighting. He was basically a textbook defenseman who used his head rather than his body. Seiling and Clarke became friends—until one night when we played the Maple Leafs in Toronto.

We had penetrated the Leafs' zone and were attacking near their net. Clarke moved to a position right in front of the net where Seiling was defending. In a perfectly natural move Seiling tried to move Clarke out of the way. Up came Clarke's stick right in Seiling's face. Down went the Toronto defenseman before fifteen-thousand witnesses. There was nothing subtle about the spearing this time. Even Clarke admitted it later when he said, "I speared him, I poleaxed him and I cut him close to the eye. Things like that happen in the heat of the game, I'm afraid. I called Rod the next morning and apologized." That's a laugh. (Can you imagine what would have happened to me if I had done the same thing to Seiling?) Sometimes, however, Clarke would not even entertain the notion of battle; rather, he would turn to his teammates to bail him out.

That's what you were supposed to do on the Flyers. I was no exception. During the sixth game in the 1976 Stanley Cup semifinal round against the Toronto Maple Leafs (we were leading, three games to two), with only a few minutes left and Toronto holding a commanding lead, I got myself into hot water in my role as Clarke's guardian.

I had already received my share of penalties earlier in the game and wasn't especially looking for more trouble when Tiger Williams, the pugnacious Toronto forward, got into a shoving match with Clarke. Another fuse had been lit. Much as I would have liked to let Clarke fight his own battle for once, I moved right in. "What're ya doin'?" I yelled.

Tiger has big eyes and dark, curly hair and the kind of face that looks like it was chiseled out of stone—with dull tools. I wasn't crazy about fighting him because I knew he was a good scrapper and, by this time in my career, I was getting sick and tired of the ritual. What worried me was that Williams fought scientifically. He liked to box in close, getting in the jabs and an occasional uppercut, which can hurt a guy. As you know, I liked to swing away.

As Clarke backed off, Williams and I grabbed each other. I wasn't able to swing free so I just hung on, hoping to get loose for some punches. Next thing I knew, my head was ringing as if it had been hit with a huge mallet. Tiger had butted me with his thick, plastic helmet on my helmetless head. (That was illegal and he should have been given a match penalty.)

It took me a second to shake off the effect of the blow. I kneed him between the legs. He came back and grabbed me by the hair. Then I felt this unbelievably grotesque pain on my face. Williams had sunk his teeth into my cheek. All this because I had to put up my dukes for Clarke.

There are those who have charged that Bobby Clarke is a coward who would start trouble but never bother to fight his own battles. There is no doubt that Clarke is a ruthless athlete who lives by the bottom line—winning. In the past decade he has been one of the most threatening users of a hockey stick in the NHL, at times employing it in a manner of an infantryman handling a bayonet.

Many have mistaken cowardice for bravery. Canadian chauvinists will tell you that Clarke was a hero in 1972 during the Team Canada–Russia series because he violently sent the Soviet's best forward, Valery Kharlamov, to the hospital with a cracked ankle after whacking the Russian ace with a two-hander. Do you think Clarke could have gotten away with such "bravery" if he had bludgeoned Larry Robinson of the Canadiens in the same way? I think not.

It is an indisputable fact that Clarke rarely backed up his stickwork with his fists. Too often, I was called upon to do the fighting for him and now, I have to admit, I did not appreciate backing Clarkie when he "sticked" one of his enemies and then was challenged by his victim. I felt that if he was going to start something he should have been able to finish it, when he didn't, I lost respect for him.

Fans, referees, and even members of the Hockey Hall of Fame all have taken Clarke to task for his insidious stickwork. One letter written by a Flyers fan appeared in the Philadelphia *Daily News* in 1981 suggesting that Clarke be named to "The All-Afraid Team." The author put it this way: "I've watched many Flyers games and have seen many of his slashes, spearings, high sticking and cross checking, but can't recall Clarke ever willing to stand man-to-man with his victim's attempt at just satisfaction. I'm glad he's on my hockey team, but I wouldn't have wanted him within one mile of me on Normandy Beach."

From my point of view, I didn't like his stickwork and other cheap shots, and I had no respect for somebody who so blatantly let others fight his battles after deliberately inciting them with dangerous play.

In talking with Montreal *Star* columnist Red Fisher once, former referee Red Storey offered an interesting critique of Clarke's behavior. "I was watching Clarke closely," Storey said, "and any time he gets close to somebody, he had a piece of the guy's body with his stick. He doesn't need that. If he didn't have Schultz to come to his rescue, would he be doing it? Let's put it this way: suppose his name was Rocket Richard and he had to fight his own battles the way the Rocket did, would he be doing it every night?"

The answer is no.

The funny thing is that when people talk about Clarke the cute little word "chippy" keeps popping up. *Chippy!* How about "dirty"? The most candid appraisal of Clarke I ever saw appeared in the New York *Post.* "Bobby Clarke is a very dirty hockey player," wrote Mike Shalin. "Perhaps the dirtiest hockey player ever to lace on a pair of skates. . . . The victims of his vicious attacks are too many to name here but all of them have something in common—they have all failed to achieve revenge."

Then Shalin asked a question a lot of people in hockey have wondered about over the years: "Why has nobody taken it upon himself (or themselves) to beat the living stuffings out of this counterfeit angel? Why hasn't someone said, 'Hey, I'm tired of having my face cut up. I'm gonna get that SOB'?"

I knew the answer: Dave Schultz, Bob Kelly, Don Saleski, André Dupont, Mel Bridgman, et al.

In a sense I envy Clarke. Can you imagine what a unique situation he was in for a hockey player—knowing that he could do almost anything to the opposition and not have to worry about answering for himself since there were enforcers like me around to fight his battles?

His comment about rough hockey in print tickled me. For a while, he was writing a column for the Philadelphia *Bulletin* on a regular basis. Once he wrote about me. It was headlined "Schultz Does Lose Control" and I still have it in my scrapbook. One particular statement broke me up. He said, "Using a stick is what I consider violence. Fighting—with the fists—is good for both a team and for hockey." Give us a break, Bobby! To add insult to injury, a few years later, when he became president of the players' union, he did an about-face. In an article in *Sports Illustrated* he said, "Hockey is good enough on its own that it doesn't need fighting."

Bobby argued that if everyone were aware that all parties to a fight would be automatically ejected, it would "prevent guys like Dave

Schultz from trying to get a player like Guy Lafleur out of the game. This way, if Lafleur wants to, he can skate away with grace." Very generous of Bobby. After all the fighting I did for him, fighting he encouraged and counted on, he suddenly turns around and points a finger at me, as if I was ruining the game.

It's interesting how superstars get special privileges. While a stickman and an agitator like Bobby escaped censure, Bobby Schmautz would do the same sort of thing and get blasted. I admire Clarke's great talent and his courage in the face of his illness, but, hey, his stick can take somebody's eye out just like anybody else's.

The two-hander was one of Bobby's standard weapons. It often was employed by him—and by many other Flyers—after the enemy had scored, as an act of retribution. Typical of that style was an episode in a game we played against the Canadiens in February 1974. Murray Wilson of Montreal had just scored a goal and Clarke was right behind him. "After I put the puck in the net," Wilson said later, "Clarke whacked me a good two-hander on the left arm."

In the beginning, Bobby was probably the most dedicated player I had ever encountered. He would do *anything* for the team. He was so obsessed with the team concept and the utter sacrifice of everything—families included—for the team that he discouraged players from having what might have been a more normal home life. I can't really blame him for that because I'm a big boy and I should have made my own decisions. But if we're talking about superstars, heroes, and role models, let's leave Bobby Clarke's name off the list for sainthood.

No individual is without personal flaws and at this point in my life I had become enough of a cynic that I could appreciate some ulterior motives in Bobby's behavior. Clarke has been, is, and always will be an ambitious man, an individual who would much prefer to be the person in power than one being processed by others. I am not taking away from his zealousness, his dedication, or his commitment to the game, for at that level he certainly did act as a role model for members of our team. But he was in other ways as much concerned about himself as he was with the anxieties, stresses, and conflicts of his teammates.

This became evident in later years when Clarke assumed the role of assistant coach. For those of us who had at times been more than suspicious about the close association between Clarke and upper management in the Flyers' organization, this might be interpreted as the proof of the pudding.

How can a team captain-turned-assistant-playing-coach maintain the confidence and trust of his peers? Even while I was there, I always had the feeling that Clarke was watching my behavior and making comments to our owner as well as to others in the high command, all the while encouraging us to believe he was just one of the guys. That's a violation of trust.

When the Flyers finally traded me, I felt—whether it was true or not—that Clarke had had a hand in persuading them to unload me to Los Angeles. And that, for me, is even more significant. I had lost both my respect for and my faith in Bobby Clarke's capacity for honesty and integrity. His dedication had turned to ruthlessness.

What made it at least tolerable at the time were the players around him, my Brother Bullies, the guys who could produce a laugh as easily as they could score a goal or draw a penalty. With them around, hockey was often spelled f-u-n.

10

Brother Bullies

As a youth I had heard tales about the glamorous life a big league hockey player enjoyed but it wasn't until I was actually thrust onto center stage that I fully appreciated all the positive aspects of being a celebrity. My salary, while not the highest in the league, nevertheless provided me with an exceptionally comfortable life. The fans, who revered me as much as any other Flyer, stroked my ego enormously and of course, winning made life even more attractive. There also was an extra added attraction and that was the plain old good times—the laughs that were so much a part of the Flyers' fabric—that made it so difficult to focus on life's more serious issues.

Though it may seem insignificant, it was precisely those fun-filled moments that bonded us together as Brother Bullies. The laughs provided a catalyst for the kind of camaraderie that was essential to our success. We had an unusually colorful cast of characters on our club with Bob Kelly as the lead clown.

Usually the banter was limited to the dressing room, the team bus, or the lobby of a hotel when we were on the road. But from time to time we would plot elaborate schemes that required the cooperation of outsiders. The best example of that was "The Flyers' Great Snipe Hunt" starring Kelly, by far the most gullible Flyer.

According to the scenario, Kelly would be "accidentally" lured into a search for snipes, which, he was told, are little birds that are hunted at night. The plot involved getting Kelly out in the woods, then arrested on a trumped-up charge of illegal hunting and brought before a judge who would demand bail money. At that point the

123

group, assured that Kelly was scared out of his pants, would suddenly appear to get the big laugh.

Van Impe directed the comedy with ample assistance from Bobby Taylor and Clarke. The first scene opened in the dressing room, after a practice. The guys were sitting around, gabbing about nothing in particular, when Van Impe turned to Taylor and Clarke and said, "Are you ready for the snipe hunt?" They went into a whole business about getting flashlights, sneakers, and all the other equipment that goes with catching birds at night. One by one, the players who said they would go on the hunt began practicing their snipe calls. The more they got into it, the more Kelly's curiosity was piqued, until he could resist no longer and begged Van Impe to let him go along. Van Impe said he would consider the request and then added, "For starters, Bob, you have to practice the snipe call." Kelly warbled a few calls and it was clear he was hooked.

Now the plot thickened. Van Impe phoned some friends who were in the Delaware County police department and let them in on the gag. He got the cops and a magistrate to agree to play it straight when they were asked to apprehend Kelly. Even some of the wives became involved. Someone told Kelly that snipes make a delicious meal and that Diane Van Impe specialized in cooking them. Kelly approached Mrs. Van Impe and asked how she handled snipe. "We like it best when the breasts are cooked in wine sauce," she said. "It's really quite delicious." Kelly's mouth was watering.

The night of the snipe hunt, everyone arrived at a hunting area called the Willows ready to go. The garb included old clothes, sneakers, beat-up hats, and all manner of impromptu equipment—including Diane Van Impe's pantyhose, which were hooked onto a hockey stick. Kelly looked the stick over and asked Van Impe, "But will it work?" To which Eddie replied, "It worked before so it should work again."

Kelly was instructed to hide in the bushes with someone while the rest of the guys fanned out in different directions, alternately shouting, "There goes one; there goes another." Armed with a flashlight and a makeshift net, Kelly began uttering his ear-piercing snipe call while beating the bushes. Now all sounds were limited to Kelly and his partner, who was about ten yards away.

Suddenly, a siren was heard and a red emergency light broke through the night. The police had arrived and before Kelly knew what to do a cop moved right in on him. The dialogue went like this:

COP: What the hell are you doing here?
KELLY: Snipe hunting.
COP: Fine, buy where's your license?
KELLY: Hell, I don't have one.
COP: Well, this is a snipe preserve, you *have* to have one.
KELLY (*fumphing*): Er . . . but . . . I had no idea . . .

Meanwhile, one of the other Flyers (a stooge, of course) moved in on the cop's partner and pretended to assault him. A gunshot went through the air, whereupon the first cop shouted, "What happened?" The other cop (who had been "attacked") answered, "The guy ran away but I hit him!"

Kelly was horrified, especially when he realized that one of his teammates was "shot," all because of a snipe hunt. Kelly was now alone with the two cops. They handcuffed him and hauled him off to the stationhouse. Like a common criminal, he was fingerprinted, photographed, and placed behind bars until it was time for him to appear before the judge. Meanwhile, the rest of the guys took in the proceedings from behind closed doors.

With Kelly standing sheepishly in front of him, the judge charged him on five counts of lawbreaking and then, in mock sorrow, added, "I'm just beside myself that I have to miss Monday Night Football all because of you, Mister Kelly."

The judge told Kelly he could get out of jail if he could come up with twenty-five hundred dollars in cash or a certified check. Kelly said he didn't have the cash but he did have a certified check. The judge was amazed and asked, "How'd you get a certified check from a bank at ten-thirty at night?"

Kelly said he had gotten his bonus the other day, gone to the bank, and got ten checks with his name on them. The judge came back fast with a perfect squelch: "Okay, do you have anyone here who can help you, who can act as a character witness?"

Kelly's head dropped because he figured he was screwed again. Finally, he said, "No, Your Honor," and looked like he was about to burst into tears. At that moment all the doors flew open and the rest of the guys burst into the courtroom, laughing their heads off. Kelly was in a state of shock.

He took it beautifully. His resilience, in fact, is what enabled us to trap him again and again. Another time, several players were on a fishing trip in northern Saskatchewan with a friend of the team named Len Warren. The plan this time was for Warren to get to a telephone at the boathouse and call Kelly back at the cabin once the guys got back with the boat. Since we were way out in the woods where they used only old crank telephones, it would be easy for Warren to conceal his voice, and slur over some of the words.

Sure enough, as soon as the boat landed, someone ran out and paged Kelly. He ran to the cabin phone and the dialogue sounded like this.

VOICE (*muffled*): Long-distance for Mr. Bob Kelly.
KELLY: This is Bob Kelly.
VOICE: Just a moment for Mr. Keith Allen [*the Flyers' general manager*].
   There was a pause.
VOICE: Bob . . . sorry . . . *traded* . . . poor connection . . . bye-bye.
KELLY: Where? How?

As the players walked into the cabin, Kelly was in a stupor, talking to himself. "My wife . . . the house . . . leaving Philly. . . ." For a half-hour he walked around in a daze. When it looked like he might slit his throat, we told him it was a gag.

One time Bob drove up to Rexy's, our post-game hangout. The rain was coming down in torrents and as he walked toward the restaurant he noticed the window of Wayne Hillman's car was halfway open. When he got inside he said, "Wayne, I just noticed it's raining in your car on account of your window being half open." Hillman looked at him with a blank expression and replied, "Bob, why the devil didn't you close it?"

"I couldn't," said Kelly. "The door was locked!"

Moose Dupont was also a good target for laughs because of his somewhat broken English and his naturally comic face. Once we were playing the Maple Leafs and Toronto had Borje Salming on defense. Moose was on the bench, needling Salming something awful. Every time Salming skated by, Moose would yell, "Hey, Swiss cheese." None of the Flyers could figure it out so one of them asked Dupont, "Why are ya calling him Swiss cheese? He's from Sweden."

Dupont just shrugged. "Sweden, Switzerland, what the hell is the difference?"

Occasionally, the humor was black, the result of a player's idiosyncracies and nasty habits. Once, when we were playing Vancouver, Van Impe got mad at Richard Lemieux, a fast little center on the Canucks. Eddie decided to spear Lemieux the next time he was out on the ice. Soon this guy came roaring down Eddie's side and Eddie plunged his stick in the guy's stomach. The poor fellow was lying in the corner of the rink moaning and groaning when Joe Watson skated over to Van Impe and said, "Eddie, that's not Lemieux, that's Don Lever, you asshole."

Van Impe's reaction was "Oh!" and he nonchalantly skated away. You had to be there.

Every so often the pranks reached the Marx Brothers' level. Once, prior to a game with the Black Hawks, Clarke and Van Impe got into some slapstick routine while undressing in the locker room. Eddie got good and mad at something Clarke had done and chased him out of the room and down the corridor of Chicago Stadium. They were both naked and they scrambled over and around the seats. Just then Chicago's coach, Billy Reay, walked in precisely when the two of them were flying by in their birthday suits.

Reay scratched his head and said, "How in hell do you sonsof-bitches ever win a hockey game?"

Needless to say, we beat the Black Hawks that night.

While the pranks would have taken place whether Bobby Clarke sanctioned them or not, it helped that he was one of the team's most avid practical jokers. Clarke worked best in a bar with one prop: his dentures.

We would be downing a few when Clarke would go looking for a guy who was drinking either a Bloody Mary or a screwdriver, sometimes even a beer. When the guy would turn away, Clarke would pull out his dentures and stick them in the drink. And when the victim had emptied his glass of liquid refreshment, a set of teeth were staring him in the face. With no front teeth in his mouth, Clarke had a hard time maintaining his innocence.

The low comedy took on other, less harmless forms. Some jibes were directed at physical characteristics. Some of the pseudocomic rituals were geared to bolster one's sense of masculinity or test others. A few of them, such as "The Shave," were downright ridiculous. "The Shave," in which a player was placed on a table and literally shaved—pubic hair and all—top to bottom, was like a fraternity hazing. It never mattered to us that we were humiliating someone or that there was something intrinsically wrong in what we were doing. The laughs justified any prank. I am happy to say the Shave happens less and less in pro hockey these days.

One-upsmanship was very important. By humiliating someone, you were on top. Putting down another guy's clothes was a regular ritual. I once bought myself a nice green suede jacket and green pants and was very pleased with the outfit. The first time I wore it in public, the guys got on me so much (they called me "Christmas Tree") I decided never to wear the outfit again. Believe me, the nagging was incredible.

With such mischief taking place on a continuous basis a player found himself either waiting for his victim to fall prey to the gag or looking over his shoulder, hoping that he wasn't on the receiving end. The artificiality of it all was always just below the surface.

Once, for example, we were on the road, staying at a hotel that had a swimming pool. I was standing at the side of the pool, relaxing in my street clothes. Suddenly I noticed that some of the fellows were up to something and that I was going to be the victim. I assumed they were going to toss me in the pool and I wanted no part of that. I looked around and noticed an empty soda bottle on one of the tables. I grabbed it and smashed the bottle against the tabletop. Holding the bottle with the jagged edge pointed out, I dared anyone to come at me.

I was bluffing—a pretty exaggerated bluff, I'd have to say—but the others weren't sure of my intentions. They stopped in their tracks. We really didn't know each other at all.

Despite all the good times, and with the benefit of hindsight, I must say that we were often a crude, rude, and obscene bunch of professionals. It's hard to believe that a group of grown men—some of them in their thirties—with wives and children would act like a bunch of high school kids. One reason, I imagine, is that some hockey players are permitted to insulate themselves in a world that is far removed from that of the nine-to-five office worker, or a physician or an educator. From September through April the players operate in a virtual vacuum, always together, always shepherded by the coach, the manager, and the press agent. In a cocoon such as that it is rather easy for a young athlete to avoid much contact with the real world around him.

Because the players are idolized they think of themselves as something special—immune from conventional behavior codes. I have seen veterans in their mid-thirties act like teenagers, or worse. For them the coach is nothing more than a camp counselor, trying to maintain a minimum of discipline. A precious few, like Denis Potvin and Ken Dryden, to name a couple, manage to escape this image and sustain themselves in a mature and appropriate way.

Just as in any other occupation, professional hockey has a variety of social types. Some of my teammates were quite content to have a modest meal on their own, read and reflect in the hotel lobby, and then return to their rooms for some TV and a good night's rest. Gary Dornhoefer, a senior member of the team who was very bright and who had been pretty much a loner, was like that. (He later became a very successful commentator on the "Hockey Night in Canada" telecasts.) Such behavior sometimes produced tension, believe it or not, because these players were perceived by the rest of the team as "not one of the boys." They weren't ostracized, but generally these "oddballs" would be accepted in a somewhat distant manner.

Actually, many of the pranks were related to boredom and a player's failure to know how to use his spare time. If I had to do it over again, I would have read more, taken some courses, visited museums, or done other useful things with all the time at my disposal. At the time, I didn't think of that—although my wife did.

Cathy frowned on our tomfoolery and was appalled at the time I was squandering on inanities when I could have been putting the hours to better use. She knew full well that few if any of us ever encouraged life enrichment or personal growth. "I don't think I've ever heard one of your teammates discuss a book he read," she once said. "I don't even think they read books. I've never heard them discuss a theory or an idea or a belief other than those directly related to hockey."

It was not easy at the time to accept the fact that my wife viewed my teammates as self-indulgent adolescents with little integrity, no convictions, and few beliefs. "You and your pals reap all the rewards of society," she would say. "Freedom, mobility, recognition, money. And what do you do with it?"

The fact that these silly pranks often took place at times when I might otherwise have been at home with Cathy did not wear well with her. She did not buy the line that this camaraderie was intrinsic to our success. Actually, while the brotherliness may have looked good from a distance, on closer inspection it really had little substance, particularly when my wife was doing the looking. She was right in saying that we never talked about meaty stuff. We never shared beliefs or ideas or really deep feelings.

Cathy said the hockey wives did more sharing than the players themselves, and she was right. Our camaraderie was superficial; the wives got down to the bare-your-soul kind of stuff.

In all the years I played professional hockey I have made only two really good friends from the game. Considering the nature of our profession, it isn't all that surprising. The players knew deep down that the closeness of even a championship team lasts only until they start losing or until management feels the need to bring in new faces. We all knew that, sooner or later, we could be wearing another uniform. That discouraged us from getting too close.

Some of my teammates believed that a "closeness" automatically developed when a bunch of guys participated in a practical joke. I never shared that view, though I must admit I took part willingly in much of the nonsense.

It should appear obvious at this point that the hockey environment is not conducive to taking issues seriously or making big and critical decisions. Being a part of the team makes you vulnerable to some of the antics and personality traits of its members. I felt it was much easier just to go along with the crowd and, unfortunately, that attitude prevailed not only with respect to humor but also with respect to the way my life had become organized. If only I had seriously questioned some of the patterns and routines, my life might have been far more enriching, rewarding, and acceptable.

11

The NHL vs. Dave Schultz

THE FLYERS' BROTHERHOOD remained intact during the 1974–75 season as we launched our defense of the Stanley Cup, although we had a bit less desire. The change was virtually imperceptible to all but those closely connected with the team and I attribute it to a perfectly natural reaction to success. Once a club has won the Stanley Cup the urge to win it again remains, but a bit of the zeal is lost. Whatever we may have lost in intensity we compensated for with talent. A year later we were a more gifted hockey club and no less tough.

On paper, at least, I looked like a better hockey player. I had scored 20 goals, which was the mark of respectability, and I hoped that would persuade Shero to give me more ice time. "Y'know," Shero told some reporters, "the way Schultz is improving we may ask him to stick to hockey and I'll ask Keith Allen to find me another fighter."

I knew, of course, that Shero was putting them on and that he had no intention of having me change my style. He had made that clear to me when he said I wasn't a sharpshooter or a playmaker, and I never thought to press the issue with him or anyone else in management; that may have been a big mistake on my part. Even if I wanted to go straight, I said to myself, I couldn't: there were too many enforcers around the league looking to take me on and prove they were number one. My enemies were multiplying in direct proportion to my penalty minutes and I soon became the archetypal paranoid-on-ice. I had to be on guard all the time because I obviously couldn't always pick my shots.

When we played the Bruins, for example, I knew that at any given moment I might be set upon by O'Reilly or Cashman. They also had headhunters, like Dave Forbes, Ken Hodge, and Bobby Schmautz, who were a threat to jump me or stick me (with the blade of their hockey stick in the stomach, neck, or groin) when I was distracted or not fully prepared for them. Since I was now acknowledged as King Goon, the fans, the players, and management had high expectations. No matter which arena I visited the fans viewed me with the same anticipation crowds at a bullfight bring to the main event. They came to see me explode, and whether I felt up to it or not I felt an obligation to satisfy their demands.

I had become *capo di capi* of the enforcers. My name had become equated with fighting and other synonyms of violence on ice. I had mixed emotions about my achievement. There was, naturally, something to be said for being top gun. I inspired fear in some opponents and produced a form of respect in others. In any case the reaction I inspired was special, much more so than other Flyer's. Being *numero uno* does have certain advantages for the ego. But the disadvantages also were very real to me: My paranoia was growing and the fear of getting knocked off remained constant. I was also concerned about remaining off NHL President Clarence Campbell's blacklist.

Campbell was a Rhodes Scholar, an attorney, a former referee, and in my opinion a pretty pompous fellow. From time to time Campbell would tell our manager, Keith Allen, to have me phone him at the president's office so that I could present my side of the story after the referee had filed a complaint against me. After one of our conversations Campbell closed by saying, "You are responsible for fifty percent of the bad publicity that the NHL has gotten on the violence issue."

I was perturbed by that remark, especially since I believed it was unfair. I would rationalize that I had never deliberately speared an opponent, while Dennis Hextall of the Minnesota North Stars once rammed the point of his stick into my neck. Nobody carped about Hextall's cheap shots, I would say to myself, nor did they beef about dirty woodchoppers like Schmautz and others who gave the league a bad image, including Forbes. Giving Campbell the benefit of the doubt, I assume he was trying to get me to control myself a little more. And in fairness to him, I have to point out that I wasn't the first player Campbell ever censured. My father used to tell me how in

1955 Campbell suspended the great Rocket Richard of the Canadiens for the final week of the season as *well as the entire playoffs* after the Rocket had abused a linesman during a game in Boston. I understood that the president was trying to protect the NHL's image and deflect some of the media criticism, which, at that time, was growing because of the Flyers and some of the other rough teams.

I did not especially enjoy being the target of Campbell's wrath. Sure, it would have been a lot easier on my psyche if I had been a Lady Byng Trophy winner for good conduct and skill, but within the context of the Flyers' philosophy and knowing how Shero felt about me—and, more than that, what he wanted from me—it would have been impossible for me to be Mister Good Guy and survive in the league.

Consequently, the combination of Shero, the Flyers' pro-toughness propaganda, and the support I received in Philadelphia from the fans as well as the writers (nobody put the rap on me in print in my home city) persuaded me that I had chosen what for me was the most practical if not the purest or most gratifying path. I knew I wasn't honoring the letter of the hockey law but I had convinced myself I wasn't half as bad as some of the other players around. Unfortunately, Campbell's referees didn't see it my way. As I experienced it, the officials exercised little self-control—or objectivity—in the way they treated me.

I know other players felt that they, too, were favorite targets of the referees. If the truth be known, the entire officiating system in hockey is full of flaws. The Flyers, to the surprise of very few, tried their best to exploit these flaws. The essential weakness is that one referee is incapable of detecting more than half of the infractions that take place on a rink that measures two hundred feet long and eighty-five feet wide. With ten skaters constantly in motion the referee—if he is lucky—is only in a position to see the fouls committed in front of him. But since many players often are behind the play, any number of infractions can take place behind his back. The Flyers had made an art form out of the behind-the-ref's-back foul. The officials, then, had to do a lot of faking; that is, whistling off players who they believed had committed a foul. Or, on the other hand, they could—and they usually did—overlook, either deliberately or otherwise, fouls that did take place. That is the human nature of referees.

All this makes for a terribly inconsistent method of handling a game, yet it is one that the NHL has sanctioned for decades and appears reluctant to change. The result is that, week in and week out, during any given season, the referees are sharply criticized for their inconsistency.

Making the best of a difficult situation, the referees often zeroed in on a consistent offender. Since I was constantly in trouble, referees assumed—as far as I could determine—they could penalize me with less fear of contradiction than if they chose to send a Marcel Dionne to the penalty box. I have no way of proving it and I never asked anyone straight out, but I am convinced that the referees gave me the zinger whenever possible. I had a bad reputation and I paid for it. At the time, I would hiss and moan about how everyone was picking on poor Dave. Of course, I should simply have accepted the consequences without beefing. That's the way life is; if you live by your fists, you wind up in the penalty box.

League officials such as Bryan O'Neill, who was Campbell's first lieutenant, admitted they watched the Flyers more closely than others. "We're very conscious of the way Philadelphia plays," said O'Neill. "You'd have to have your head in the sand not to be." But conscious as O'Neill and his officials may have been, the referees still couldn't completely cope with us. According to our unofficial policy, we might commit ten fouls in a period but the referee—because of his intrinsic limitations—would call only half of them, at most. That gave us a terrific advantage, not only strategically but also psychologically.

Aldo Guidolin, who scouted for the Atlanta Flames and then the Colorado Rockies, said that we were able to intimidate the opposition with the uncalled infractions we committed. "The Flyers," said Guidolin, "were especially good at getting away with such behavior right after the whistle had stopped play."

And yet, while we did escape hundreds of penalties during any given season, we were still the most heavily penalized team in the league and, as usual, I led the Flyers in that department. The big difference for me personally in 1974–75 was that I didn't even come close to duplicating my 20-goal-year of the previous season. Fortunately, the club was not suffering because of my drought and Shero kept insisting that I was just as valuable, if not more valuable, by not scoring so many goals. On several occasions I would be sitting on the bench when somebody on the other team would flatten one of the Flyers. At that moment, Shero would walk over to me and say, "Schultz." No more, no less. It meant that the time had come for me to vault the boards and fight the fellow who had flattened my teammate. Shero wanted it and I wanted to do it to help the team. By this time I didn't particularly relish kamikaze behavior as a regular diet, but I was more than willing to sacrifice myself for the Flyers' credo: *Help the team.*

Shero kept a sharp eye on my fighting and, occasionally, when he was aware of Campbell's and the referee's vigilance toward me, he would urge caution. He would invite me inside his office and launch into a talk about a recent fight that I had had. He would tell me how hockey shows you how to react under pressure, particularly when you are the victim of an attack. "Your emotions are tested and your character is tested," he would say.

On other occasions he would caution me if he felt I was getting into too many fights, or if I acted too crazy after being penalized and didn't head directly for the penalty box. "Davey," he would say, "I've been counting on you. It's okay if a man tested you in a fight. You both go off for five minutes. But if I lose you for another ten or fifteen minutes, then I have to spread my whole team. I'm short a man. You just don't think of yourself. I know you are upset, but this is part of the game."

In the midst of one of my slumps, Shero cheered me with a note on the bulletin board: "Individualism is anathema to the Flyers' system." I scored only nine goals that season but the club finished first again and I continued to maraud effectively. My point total dropped by ten and the only area where I showed a gain was in penalty minutes; my total leaped from 348 to 472. "Let's face it," said Clarke, "more people come out to see Dave Schultz than Bobby Orr."

While that was encouraging, the counterpoint was my awareness that I was now typecast for life, that I would never become the well-rounded hockey player I once dreamt of being. I was depressed to realize that I was locked into the system, that my teammates knew that I was locked in, and that, from time to time, they would insult me for what they perceived were my inferior hockey skills. It was not uncommon for them to give me the needle during a scrimmage, for example, if I missed an open net or flubbed a pass. There was nothing I could do. I had created my role and now I had to live with it.

In Philadelphia, where the goon was revered, this was no problem, but elsewhere it had become more and more onerous for me and my Brother Bullies. Public opinion was beginning to jell into a powerful anti-violence campaign and politicians on both sides of the border were getting into the act. In Minnesota, Henry Boucha of the North Stars was clubbed by Dave Forbes of the Bruins and Forbes wound up being tried in criminal court for assaulting an opponent. Boucha was afflicted with double vision, a fractured eye socket, and a twenty-five-stitch gash as a result of his beating by Forbes. Ontario Attorney General McMurtry ordered provincial attorneys and police to rigorously enforce the law against "clear breaches of the criminal code" on the ice.

While the NHL complained that McMurtry had no business sticking his nose into professional hockey affairs, the Attorney General replied that the acts of violence in the NHL are "obviously a very bad example for young kids who ape the professionals."

To a certain extent, McMurtry was right. Just about any youngster who plays hockey has an idol or two from whom he receives inspiration. The advent of televised NHL games meant that kids could see their heroes on the screen and draw their lessons from them in a more vivid manner than in the days of radio. A youngster watching the Flyers at their brutal worst would not be obtaining what I regard as the best example of how a professional athlete should behave. But whether the Attorney General or a District Attorney should try to alter those examples is a question that should be debated by those more familiar with the legal processes than myself.

Interestingly, the furor over violence had no effect on our style. I'm sure that had a lot to do with the principals involved in the Flyers' chain of command. At the top, Eddie Snider had become a major power within the NHL hierarchy. The Flyers had become the most financially successful franchise of the expansion teams and the 1974 Stanley Cup win further added to our eminence. Politically, Snider had become important among hockey barons and, therefore, nobody was going to push him around. Certainly not Clarence Campbell, who was merely a puppet of the owners. Our manager, Keith Allen, favored the rough style of play, and obviously so did Fred Shero. When you come down to it, there was nobody interested in altering the formula that had brought us success. Critics be damned.

Despite all the fuss, we continued to play our brutal game and, once again, it took us all the way to the Stanley Cup finals. Our opponents, the Buffalo Sabres, gave us a good run and even managed to come from behind to tie the series at two games apiece after we had taken a two–nothing lead in games.

Up until the fifth game I was not a factor. I was among six borderline players on the club and Shero, as usual, was giving me limited ice time. The ridicule of my teammates toward me had not abated and was getting under my skin even more. I felt detached from the team and began questioning my ability. Shero was no help in this situation.

He didn't give me any responsibility, and that doubled my concern. I felt the other guys were doing all the work and I had the suspicion that, in private, they were saying "What's the matter with Schultz; why isn't he fighting?" I felt that my hockey play, instead of improving, had deteriorated. I honestly believe it was as much Shero's fault as my own. Coming off a 20-goal year in 1973–74, I needed to play regularly to improve, and I think I could have. But given Shero's decision, I had become too rusty to be consistently effective. As we headed back to Philadelphia for game five I had serious doubts about my future as a Flyer.

A lot of my pessimism was exaggerated and a product of overthink, but I also knew in the back of my mind that goons in pro hockey were now as easily available as pucks. It seemed to me that if I didn't get my act together and show management I was an asset, they'd find another enforcer to replace me. Game five was as good a time as any to prove my worth. I was extremely psyched-up for the game.

Surprise of surprises, Freddie gave me the signal to start. If ever there was going to be a moment when I could restore my stature with the team, this was it. I took the ice with Saleski, who before long shot the puck into the corner so that it would carom out to me. I was at a difficult shooting angle but I let the puck go at the Buffalo goalie, Gerry Desjardins. My shot hit the goalie, bounced up crazily, ricocheted off his mask, climbed over him and down his back. I had my first playoff goal of 1975.

Shero continued to spot me and halfway through the second period I got another chance. Our young defenseman Larry Goodenough had the puck and hit me with a perfect pass just as I had moved into high gear. The rubber crunched off the tape covering my stick blade and I moved into the clear. I was twelve feet away from Desjardins when I released an old-fashioned wrist shot. The puck sailed past Desjardins, the red light flashed, and the crowd exploded. We beat Buffalo, 5–1, and at the end of the game I was voted the number one (out of three) star of the game. My goals had brought us to within one game of the Stanley Cup. They also brought me the kind of headlines I was missing and provided a much needed massage for my ego. Two days later we won another Stanley Cup.

I had produced the biggest goals of a big game of the 1975 finals and felt like I belonged to the Flyers' fraternity once more. It didn't take much to convince me, of course. But in reality trouble was brewing. The two consecutive championships hardly stilled our critics because our tactics remained so distasteful. If anything, the campaigns against me and the Flyers as a group continued with even greater intensity. I remember reading how a Washington *Post* writer named Rober Fachet proposed a solution to stopping the Flyers. He said the answer was to hire twenty thugs and send them out to drive the Flyers' heads into the ice. Fachet was told that the plan couldn't work. A friend told him, "Do you know how many thugs can skate? The Flyers have cornered the market."

In terms of the relationship with my teammates, my position with the Flyers now began deteriorating. Jealousies, which had not been that apparent in the earlier years when camaraderie ruled over all, began to surface. Some players resented the fact that others had selectively bonded together and become business partners. Even Shero began to experience the first tremors of interference from Keith Allen and Ed Snider. Shero now had two assistant coaches, Mike Nykoluk and Barry Ashbee, to contend with, not to mention our unofficial third "coach," Bobby Clarke.

I was a centerpiece in the jealousy because I was getting so much ink (and scored so little) while the genuine superstars were getting so little space in the papers and on television. I would get into a fight and Billy Barber would get three goals in the same game and after the game there would be ten reporters in front of me and only one in front of Barber's stall.

Some people said I could have shunned the publicity, but I simply couldn't. First of all, my policy was never to turn down an interview, whether we won or lost or whether it was to take place in the dressing room or at my home. With almost no exceptions, I made myself available to newspapermen, radio people, and the TV interviewers. I daresay I loved being in front of a microphone or a pencil busily scribbling on a pad. I couldn't help thinking that just six years earlier I had been a bashful nobody who couldn't have gotten his name in print unless I owned the newspaper. I also understood that the more the media talked to me, the more valuable I remained in terms of endorsements and other revenue-producers. I didn't really care whether Barber was bugged by my celebrity status or not.

Early in the 1975–76 season another spate of violent incidents caused problems. The first was a one-sided battle between Detroit Red Wings forward Dan Maloney and Toronto Maple Leafs defenseman Brian Glennie. First Maloney floored Glennie with a flying punch from the side and then bounced his head on the ice twice for good measure. Ontario Attorney General McMurtry moved in again and charged Maloney with "assault causing bodily harm" and ordered him to appear in a Toronto criminal court. Maloney's attack put Glennie in the hospital with a concussion.

The situation was no better in the World Hockey Association, where Bobby Hull sat out a game as a protest against the "brutality" and malicious attacks on his teammates. "If something isn't done soon it will ruin the game for all of us," Hull said at the time. "I've never seen so much vicious stuff going on."

Perceiving the Flyers' successful style, other teams began stocking their rosters with big boys who could hit. "We've got to mold a lineup that can take on a bunch of goons," said Maple Leafs owner Harold Ballard after seeing Glennie cut down by Maloney. "I'm looking for guys you toss raw meat to and they will go wild."

Kurt Walker, a twenty-one-year-old rookie out of New England, became Ballard's resident goon. He was bigger than me by two inches and heavier by ten pounds. Christie Blatchford, a sports columnist for the Toronto *Globe and Mail*, described Walker as a goon, a headhunter, a fighter; not a hockey player. Walker was openly advertised as the Leafs' enforcer so there wasn't a soul in Maple Leaf Gardens when we played Toronto in the first round of the 1976 playoffs who didn't know what he had in mind when he skated out on the ice; he wanted a piece of me. For four full seasons I went looking for fights and was perpetually challenged by bigger and bigger toughies. Frankly, the wear and tear began to have its effect.

I understood that it was merely a matter of time before one of these new Paul Bunyans with skates would tear me apart. Although I have no proof of it, I wouldn't have been at all surprised to learn that an enemy coach had put a bounty on my head. I could envision it while lying in bed prior to a game. "WANTED! DAVE SCHULTZ. PUNCH HIM OUT AND WIN $500."

These new giants were awesome. Walker wasn't alone. Atlanta had a monster named Willi Plett, Chicago had Grant Mulvey. They got bigger and bigger. Some of them, like Larry Robinson of Montreal, were not only enormous but they could play hockey very well, to boot. Besides, they could fight and each of them had the credits to prove it. Some of them—Walker in particular—made no bones about the fact they were after my head. How was I supposed to feel when I picked up the paper and read this comment by Walker: "I know why I'm here. No one has to tell me. Toronto called me up so I could let the guys know the Leafs wouldn't stand for it, so they know we wouldn't be intimidated. I'm there to tell Schultz he can't attack our guys and get away with it."

Walker was not crying wolf. There was a minimum of hockey in that playoff game and a maximum of hand-to-hand combat. As predicted, Walker came at me early in the game and we slugged it out. I was fortunate in that I beat him with one punch. After we had been separated Walker was foolish enough to spit at me (not a part of the enforcer's code of behavior) and for that indiscretion was assessed a "gross misconduct" penalty.

Mel Bridgman, our rugged rookie center, nailed Borje Salming with a check in the second period. Mel knocked Salming in the head, then Salming tried to spear him. When Mel got up the two of them dropped their gloves and started swinging. There was fight after fight. It took three-and-a-half hours to finish the game. (Toronto beat us 5-4). The worst was yet to come. The next day we found out that McMurtry had filed criminal charges against Saleski, Bridgman, and Joe Watson. They were charged with various offenses, including assault and possession of an offensive weapon—a hockey stick—stemming from the second-period fight the night before. (I was a bit surprised that nobody on the Maple Leafs was charged with anything.)

Saleski, Bridgman, and Watson were taken to a Toronto police station where they were photographed, fingerprinted, and formally charged. If I had gotten involved in all the trouble at Maple Leaf Gardens I have a hunch I'd still be in jail.

Not that I always maintained self-control. As the years passed the quality and quantity of hostility directed at me increased. Fans tossed light bulbs at me from the upper balcony at Madison Square Garden. I received a death threat from a group of Bruins fans and in Minnesota I was shot at with water pistols. Even the spectators in the new cities, Kansas City and Washington, began manufacturing KILL SCHULTZ and SCHULTZ WEARS PANTYHOSE signs.

One night at Nassau Coliseum I was skating around in a warmup when some kids threw a roll of pennies at me. I picked them up and hurled them back in the stands. A woman leaped out of her seat and shouted at me, "You ought to be ashamed of yourself."

I sneered back at her, "I'll get you, too, lady."

Sure enough, the next time we visited the Coliseum her husband was sitting directly behind our bench and he was letting me have it in high decibels. I kept my cool until late in the second period when I grabbed a plastic water bottle, squeezed the bottom, and directed a flow of water at my nemesis.

The fan threatened me with a lawsuit, which was good for a laugh.

He said he would drop the suit if I made a public apology to him and if the team would supply him with two season tickets to the Islanders' games. I ignored him and that was the end of it, but it wasn't the end of my difficulties with fans. On another visit to Nassau Coliseum I got into a fight with Garry Howatt along the boards. As I pounded Howatt some fans reached over the glass and grabbed my hair and stick. A couple of my teammates had to harass the fans until the linesman could break up the fight.

Pittsburgh Penguins fans were especially cutting in their comments. There was one regular at Pittsburgh Civic Arena who enjoyed giving it to the visiting teams, but especially to me. He had a seat right behind the visitors' penalty box and whenever one of the opposition got a penalty he would let loose the worst kinds of obscenities.

One night I wound up in the box with a two-minute minor when he let me have it so bad I blew up. I got up from the bench as he leaned over the penalty box barrier and banged my stick on the glass. I never touched the man but he claimed that I caught him in the nose, knocked his glasses off, and caused him to miss a week's work. It wasn't true, but the Flyers had to fight the case and they eventually settled out of court for a few thousand dollars. People like this character seemed to think I was a robot without feelings, that all the abuse just rolled off my back.

Quite the contrary. The abuse I absorbed from the fans had a profound effect on me. It deepened the sense I already had that I was essentially hated everywhere but at home. More than that, I was hated because I was damaging the opposition not with my hockey ability but rather with my fists. It meant that there was not one, not two, but fifteen arenas in which I could expect constant harassment from an assortment of adults and children.

It was the experience of having little kids swearing at me that disturbed me most of all. I could deal with adults, or at least I thought I could, but seeing the angry faces of youngsters bothered me no end. There seemed to be something morally wrong when a performer like me could inspire elementary school kids to vilification with the worst X-rated epithets. What I really wanted, of course, was adulation, given the way I played, that was impossible.

I understood that there was no way the NHL's Public Enemy Number One could expect to be loved by adult or children alike, but knowing that failed to make the sting of a "Screw you, Schultz!" any easier to take. Each insult was treated as a personal affront that I wanted to answer on the spot. Every allusion to my mother or father stung me and demanded—or so I thought—a counterattack. Naturally, this was not only impractical but downright stupid, under the circumstances, but the residue was an endless nagging pain in and around my stomach that could otherwise be defined as depression.

Other players handled the fans in other ways and some were less restrained than I was. Terry O'Reilly and Mike Milbury of the Boston Bruins climbed into the stands in Madison Square Garden and punched out a couple of fans who had attacked them with sticks. Nicky Fotiu of the New York Rangers went after a spectator at Joe Louis Arena in Detroit who had tossed a container of beer at him.

I sympathize with any player who has to absorb excessive abuse from ignorant fans, but no matter how bad the abuse I definitely feel that no hockey player has any right to invade the stands—even when fans get out of hand, as they seem to be doing with greater frequency in recent years. I also realize that it is much easier to say that a player should maintain control than to control yourself in a hostile situation. No other sport generates emotion and anger the way hockey does. The speed, the crashing of bodies, the constant frustrations produced by the game's innate mistakes, the refereeing (generally bad) all combine to produce an emotional cauldron that spills over from spectators to fans. The solution, as I see it, is for the respective arenas to better police the stands. Fans should be made aware that when they purchase a ticket, they are not granted the right to throw missiles on the ice or assault a player. The special police should protect both players and fans from drunks and hotheads. Offenders should be ejected from the arena and banned for at least one full season from returning.

Frankly, I feel I was to blame in part for the increased craziness of the fans. They would see me go through my defiance-of-officials act on the ice and take it to mean that they could be defiant as well. The unruliness of fans over the years is at least partially attributed to the unruliness on ice, in my estimation. This was further accentuated by the media's overemphasis on violent play. Newspapers, radio, and television increased their accent on rough hockey and trained their cameras, microphones, and pencils on those of us who raised havoc rather than the artists on attack or on defense.

More and more, the media also gave a bigger play to the McMurtrys and others who sought to purify hockey from the bloodshed that seemed to be engulfing the professional game. I couldn't ignore the media's new focus even though I rationalized that I was basically innocent of any serious wrongdoing on the ice, like stick-swinging. Self-delusion by this time came easy to me.

Like any athlete, politician, or actor, I learned after being subjected to hundreds of interviews that an occasional distortion might take place and that quotes will be taken out of context from time to time. My problems with the Fourth Estate were minimal until the 1976 Toronto–Philadelphia playoff series. It was then that I had a run-in with a woman reporter that, to this day, fills me with shame. It happened during a particularly bitter game at Maple Leaf Gardens. I was in the penalty box for the start of the third period. In the second period I had been singled out for abuse by the fans and felt oppressed by the insults, the noise, and the general tumult.

As I made my way to the penalty box, I spotted a woman standing to the side of the corridor. I immediately recognized her as Christie Blatchford. In my mind, reporters belonged in the press box, high above Maple Leaf Gardens, not down among the players at the penalty box. I blew up. "Get the hell outta here," I screamed while gesturing with my glove. "We don't need you!"

Had she stayed, I would have completely lost control. Fortunately, a cop moved right in on her and hustled her away from the penalty box area. I can appreciate the fact that she was trying to get a story, but when the game is on? I had no business being abusive and I should have ignored her, but to be the object of a journalist like Blatchford, who would intrude on an off-limits area such as the penalty box, was something I could not deal with in a rational way, any more than I could handle a writer like Larry Merchant, then of the New York *Post*, who stung me more painfully than anyone else ever did. He wrote that "Dave Schultz is like the Long Island dogs that kill deer at night, then go home and lie around in front of the fire and lick people's faces." I have never forgiven him for that.

The sum total of the anti-Schultz, anti-Flyers campaign had reached unbearable proportions by 1976 but I would be unfair if I suggested that I (we) didn't bring it on ourselves.

Having sensed that my act was beginning to become jaded, I made one feeble effort to go straight as a Flyer. I knew Clarence Campbell would come down very hard on me eventually. Cathy had also become thoroughly disenchanted with my role as an enforcer, which was still another motivating force for change. What I had hoped to do was persuade Shero to give me a shot at being a good, checking forward and not simply a goon. Unfortunately, I never committed myself to that. Each time I wanted to say as much to someone in management, I got cold feet. I feared my days with the Flyers would be over instantly.

Shero couldn't have cared less about my desire to change. He wanted me to stay as mean as I had been. So to the casual observer, nothing had changed. But I felt there was more of a hockey player in me than he realized and I worked like hell to improve my skills, spending extra time at practices working on my skating and shooting. I would stay out on the ice doing the torturous stop-and-starts in which a player sprints from one side of the rink to the other, digs his skates into the ice, pivots, and then skates like hell to the other side— where he stops short again. I would repeat this ritual until I was just short of collapsing. Then I would practice my shots. Standing at the blue line, I would place a dozen pucks in front of me and—one by one—I would blast them at the empty net. When everyone had gone off to the shower, I would gather the puck behind the net and stick-handle through imaginary obstacles until I finally reached the net, where I deposited the puck. I worked on every aspect of my game.

I knew I was improving but I wondered whether it was perceptible to Shero or Allen. I looked at gifted forwards like Rick MacLeish and Billy Barber with consummate envy. What I was striving to accomplish through hours and weeks and months of practice, they could do in their sleep.

Playing against a Guy Lafleur, Marcel Dionne, or Bryan Trottier was enough to fill me with jealousy but, interestingly, not with any sense of vindictiveness. I never felt the urge to abuse them just because they were obviously superior talents. In fact, I had such a great appreciation of their talents that I rarely if ever messed up a clean-playing superstar.

Though Shero continued to ignore my attempts at improvement, I persisted because I knew there was just so far a man could go as a fighter and I had gone that far. I was getting beaten more and winning less. I had reached the point of no return; my gunslinger's days were numbered in Philadelphia.

One of the painful experiences that many of us have in our lives is that moment when we are compelled to take stock of where we have been, what we are, and where we are going. My time had come. I finally came to terms with the fact that I was losing control of the situation. My playing career, my home life, my responsibilities were all becoming blurred and confused.

In the past I had been able to rationalize all of the conflicts by simply presuming that, if I wanted success, this is the way things had to be. But it had become apparent to me that my fighting exploits would not sustain me much longer in the NHL. I no longer looked forward to the confrontations as I had a couple of years earlier. Now I was experiencing legitimate sensations of fear, intense nervousness, and a good deal of stress. I felt like a prisoner who is somehow locked into his identity and not only cannot leave the role but really does not know how to make his exit. The attempt I had made to prove my hockey skills had made no impression.

Being the target of my teammates' ridicule was hardest to take. They would constantly mock my efforts to improve the quality of my play. Imagine how you would feel if the very same players you had defended with your blood and sweat on the ice, game after game, made you an object of their scorn. That was more than I could take. I was more determined than ever that the time had come for me to go straight.

Freddie wouldn't hear of it. He kept reiterating that my value on the bench was symbolically as important as were my performances on the ice. Besides, from his point of view my role had served his purposes rather well. But the realization that I was coming to a dead end began to gnaw at me and make me feel hostile toward him. More than that, I began to feel uncomfortable with the awareness that I hadn't been clever enough to change my ways earlier on my own: that I hadn't seen beyond the gloss, the wealth, and the notoriety to the core of it all—that accepting the role I did meant a shortened career.

The fighting became more painful with each outing and I began to take issue with the cumulative effects of those experiences. The hostile fan reaction and the belligerent press reviews were progressively lowering my self-esteem and self-confidence. The abuse was taking its toll. I was told I was ruining the game, that I was giving hockey a bad name, that I was providing a negative role model for children. It was all true, but I felt totally used and drained, and regretted not having anticipated this condition three years earlier.

There were nights when I would receive two or more misconduct penalties even though I still was infrequently used. It was on those occasions that I first contemplated retirement, although I never would have expressed my thoughts openly. While on the outside all was still bravado, on the inside my life was in a serious state of disrepair. My marriage was crumbling and the burdens of public outrage were touching my raw nerves. Coupled with a growing sense of fear that some evening soon I would be pummeled into submission by a new gunslinger was the notion that my staying power in the NHL was fast diminishing. Every time I stepped onto the ice I feared retaliation and, to cope with that, I became even more aggressive—if that were possible—to pre-empt the potential strikes. Hockey stopped being fun.

I wondered where I could go from here, what sort of bridge there might be leading from this increasingly insane world to a more peaceful, less belligerent precinct. It would have been easier if there had been someone on the club who could hear me out, but there was not a soul on whose shoulder I could lean. There was no such thing as a team psychologist (although the Flyers hired one in 1981) and certainly nobody sympathetic in the front office.

One night I turned on the television and saw Edward G. Robinson in *Little Caesar*. Robinson was a hell of an actor, but no matter how good he might have been in another role, he always seemed to be typecast as a gangster. I could identify with that, though my role was King Goon.

12

You Can't Win 'em All

ONE OF THE WAYS I maintained my equilibrium was by building a psychologically protective shell around myself. I tried not to pay close attention to the things being said about me. In many ways it was like living in a fairyland. It was only when a crack in that shell appeared that I began to feel and perceive a potential set of problems down the road. The crack had begun to develop in 1972.

In 1975 I could sense, both from subtle hints and from bold media reports, that I was no longer seen by the Flyers as an invaluable enforcer but rather as a handful of excess baggage. Scanning the minor league statistics in *The Hockey News*, I saw that the Flyers' organization was nurturing players who performed as belligerently as I did but whose hockey skills seemed more refined. I began to anticipate that the too-often-mentioned trade rumors might become a reality.

I had so thoroughly restricted Cathy from my hockey world that I couldn't turn to her for solace. I was surrounded by silver trophies, Stanley Cup rings, and empty feelings. I felt a sense of doom, especially because I was locked to the Flyers' organization, which had molded me into its image. My desire ebbing, I began to lose fights. That would prove to be fatal.

Although few realized it at the time, a couple of scattered bouts were extremely significant in my transition from King Goon to a past champion. Bobby Baun, a hard-nosed defenseman from past Toronto Maple Leaf Stanley Cup–winners, once said, "There isn't a guy alive

147

who is tough enough to go through his NHL career without losing a fight." I was no exception.

Until the 1975 Stanley Cup semifinal round between us and the New York Islanders, I never *felt* I had been decisively beaten in a fight. Perhaps I was, but *in my mind* I was the undisputed heavyweight champion of the NHL. I had to feel that way; thinking positively had as much to do with winning a fight as anything else. Not only did I believe I could handle most anybody but I had the credits to prove it. Any significant losses would drastically weaken my position.

So many stories had been written about me by this time that many opponents were psyched out by the time I stepped on the ice. There were exceptions, to be sure, and one of them was the New York Islanders, an upstart expansion team that was only three years old when we first met them in the playoffs. Even their goalie, Billy Smith, was a feisty character who wouldn't hesitate to whack you in the ankle if you were blocking his way.

Until this game my fights with the Islanders generally involved Garry Howatt. This time my target was Clark Gillies, a Saskatchewan boy like myself, who had two inches and twenty-five pounds on me. Gillies and I had a go early in the second period but it didn't amount to much. We both got two-minute penalties for roughing and that was the end of it—until the last minute of the third period.

I should have known better; I had been on the ice quite a bit and was at the end of a shift, which meant I was even more tired than usual. If I had been smart I would have minded my own business, but I let emotion get the better of me. We had done a bit of jawing at each other after the first altercation. Now, with twenty-two seconds left in the game, I noticed that Gillies was in striking distance so I headed in his direction.

Gillies saw me coming and set himself before I could do my standard grab-the-jersey-and-punch-with-my-right-hand routine. I have to give Gillies credit; he used his equipment to the best advantage. He had that long reach and when he stretched me out I couldn't hit him. We did grab each other momentarily but I couldn't handle his great strength and he broke free. Once he got his right hand open he was throwing them pretty fair and he hit me three good ones that sent me reeling. I don't know what would have happened to me if he had connected again but it's possible that he could have laid me right out.

Fortunately, Dupont realized I was in big trouble and jumped in, grabbing Gillies around the arms so he couldn't hit me anymore. The defeat was a major embarrassment to me. One newspaper report called it a TKO for Gillies. Another said the Islanders' left wing had me out on my feet and sagging toward the ice. No matter how they wrote it, the fact was there for everyone to see: I could be decisively beaten.

The stories had their effect on me. *I* realized I could be taken. I made a mental note: "Gillies is too big to fool around with. He's as strong as a bull." I didn't make much more of it than that, or so I thought.

My second problem fight happened a season later in a game against the Flames at Atlanta. Early in the game I was on the ice checking Ken Houston, a rookie built along Gillies' dimensions, who had just been called up from the minors. Houston got around me and went in to score against us. A split second before Houston put the puck into our net I caught up to him and, as often is the case, I bumped him a bit too late.

As soon as I bumped him, Houston wheeled around and looked at me with a what's-going-on kind of stare. That peeved me even more so I said, "Let's go!" and we went. At first it wasn't much of a fight, just a lot of clutching and grabbing. The linesmen moved in and tried to separate us, but we were still holding on to each other. I had my head buried in one linesman and was waiting for the other to pull Houston away. Just then, the linesman who was holding Houston got his skate caught in the webbing of the net and lost his balance, enabling Houston to get his right arm free. I couldn't even see it because I was behind the linesman. Without my knowing it, Houston brought his right arm around and, with a roundhouse swing, punched me in the left side of my head. He hit me so hard that the blow pushed in my cheekbone. Thanks to that clumsy linesman, I made Ken Houston an overnight hero.

The next day Houston's name was all over the papers. One headline said it all: "Rookie Proving a Real Swinger with His Power-Packing Punch." Houston bragged to the newspapermen how he had broken my jaw. What he failed to say was that he had cold-cocked me with a blindside punch from behind the linesman's back. I wound up in an Atlanta hospital for X rays of a broken cheekbone, a first in my hockey career.

My fears had been realized. The words of Bob Baun were ringing truer than ever and, as I had known for a long time, D-Day had come, except I was the one on the defensive. As I recuperated in the hospital, I realized that no person, no matter how tough, is able to consistently place himself in both a precarious and a vulnerable position—and emerge a winner all the time.

It was not so much the cracked cheekbone that bothered me, nor even my hospitalization; it was the fact that players who had once feared me would now think it appropriate to exploit my potential weakness. I tossed and turned in my hospital bed, pondering my future. Rationalizations and excuses would not suffice. In my mind I was constructing scenarios of the enemy dressing rooms with goons on those teams openly promising to take me to task.

With these thoughts came an increasing sense of personal fear. I *could* be beaten and most certainly would be as my career progressed. I was reminded of a film about Al Capone; after the once-feared gangster had been imprisoned, he was set upon by his fellow inmates in the penitentiary. If the edge of invincibility were to be taken away from me, what would I have left? How would I earn enough money to care for my family and meet my responsibilities? The fragility of my situation became painfully clear to me.

The Gillies and Houston fights had a cumulative effect on the public's mind and, I imagine, on the mind of the Flyers' high command. What they demonstrated was that Schultz (forget about how it was done) could be taken. I tried to explain it away. I dwelled on the fact that Houston hit me with a sucker punch; that helped persuade me I could have beaten him otherwise and helped bolster my confidence. But over and over I was confronted with the irrefutable evidence that, at one time, I had not been a fighter; that I had been a coward; that I took lickings when I did fight, and that sooner or later this would come back to haunt me. In the back of my mind was the fear that a good hit or punch could affect me forever.

My bosses—Shero, Allen, and Snider—were aware of my changing fighting pattern and they were very disturbed when Montreal wiped us out of the 1976 Stanley Cup finals in four straight games. They were mad not simply because of the defeat but because the writers were saying that it was the best thing that had happened to hockey because the artists (the Canadiens) had triumphed over the goons.

Snider told me he wanted me to become more of a "class player." He pointed out that I was getting older and that maybe it was time to change my habits. If I didn't get his message right away, all I had to do was look at the kids the Flyers had added to their roster. They already had Mel Bridgman, a big, mean center, and there was Paul Holmgren, an even bigger tough forward.

I dropped into Snider's office during the summer of 1976. My name had been mentioned in trade rumors once again and I wanted to find out from management where I stood with the team. Perhaps I was being naive. Maybe I shouldn't even have wasted my time—and Snider's—by bringing up the subject, but I figured that nothing could be lost by a good heart-to-heart chat; the Flyers' organization in many ways had gone out of its way to accommodate players and their families. I also thought it would be nice to spend the rest of the summer secure in the knowledge that I would be back at the old stand in the fall.

"What about the trade rumors?" I asked Snider.

He looked me straight in the eyes and said, "Don't believe them, Dave, you're gonna be around here a long time." I drove home feeling pretty good.

When I got to training camp in September the sight of Holmgren, Bridgman, and the other big rookies didn't make me feel terribly secure. I was also bothered by the anti-violence campaign, which the NHL had intensified in the past year. One difference was a new league regulation—Rule 54. It said that the referee had the right to punish fight aggressors with game misconduct penalties. Already, it was being called "The Schultz Rule." Obviously it had been written with me in mind, though it didn't seem to concern the Flyers' management very much. Our assistant coach, Mike Nykoluk, got out from behind his big, black cigar one day and said, "Dave has proven he's a valuable man for us. I think he should play his game and not worry."

I took Nykoluk's advice. I didn't worry when the Flyers bused up the New Jersey Turnpike to New York to play an exhibition game with the Islanders and left me home with Kindrachuk and Saleski. Matter of fact I was glad they did because it was September 29 and my son, Chad, was having his first birthday party.

Barry Ashbee, our other assistant coach, was running the scrimmage at our practice rink at the University of Pennsylvania's Class of '23 Arena. After the workout I had planned to pick up a few items for the party and then head back home to Cherry Hill. I was feeling good; so good that I stayed out on the ice an extra twenty minutes just to get in some additional skating. Finally, I skimmed my last puck into the open net and headed for the dressing room. I was looking forward to Chad's party.

Ashbee intercepted me before I got to the dressing room. I couldn't tell for sure from his expression what was going on but I knew there was trouble when he said "Keith wants to see you in his office at the Spectrum." I knew that Allen had been in Springfield to see our farm team so he must have been on his way back. I got out of uniform as fast as I could, jumped in the car, and drove across town to the Spectrum. A dope, I wasn't. When the manager wants to see you it means one of three things—either you're getting bawled out for something, you're getting praised for something (unlikely), or you've just been traded. As I drove to the Spectrum, I weighed the possibilities. Maybe Allen was going to give me a pep talk about the new season. Maybe he was concerned about Rule 54 and its effect on my play. Maybe he had some other plans for me that I hadn't even dreamed about.

Maybe I *was* being traded.

My legs were wobbly by the time I got to his office. Allen wasn't there. "We're expecting him shortly," the secretary told me.

All of the explanations and excuses that I had developed to account for my being summoned to Allen's office were meaningless at the moment. My being there was most unusual for this time of year. It wasn't Allen's style, especially since he was just arriving from out of town. No matter how I tried to cloud and distort the situation, I realized full well that a trade was inevitable.

I was impatient. Cathy was counting on my shopping for the party and getting home at a reasonable hour to set up for the kids and parents who were coming. I got tired of waiting. I told Allen's secretary, "Look, if it's so important, have Keith call me at home. I'm leaving."

As I started out of the office, the secretary's phone rang and it was Keith. He had just landed at the airport. His secretary told him I was on my way out of the office. "Keep him there!" he told her. "Don't let him go."

I hung around and, finally, Allen arrived. "Hi," he said, "I'll be right with ya."

A minute later the secretary beckoned to me. I was tight. My head felt heavy. "Sit down," he said.

I sat. "Dave, we traded ya today."

The words bounced around my head like a handball in a four-wall court.

For a moment I recovered. "Where to?"

"Los Angeles."

I was dazed. Rumors or no rumors, I never thought it would come to this. I had given everything to that team. I had fought my butt off—protecting MacLeish, Clarke, Kindrachuk, the bunch of them—and what do they do, trade me for a couple of draft choices; two unknowns who hadn't even been selected yet. How humiliating! Of course, I had known the day would come. It does for most of us. But no matter how much you know it, it still causes a severe shock. It's dislocation pure and simple—and rejection. You don't think that someone else wants you; you think that somebody doesn't.

I walked out of the parking lot, got the car, and drove home. I wondered how Cathy would take it. That was as important as anything because, by this time, our marriage wasn't going great. I knew she would hate to leave several of her friends. They had been very important to her over the years, much more supportive in many ways than I had been. But I also knew that the Flyers' organization bore the brunt of her frustration and anger for transforming the man she had married. Perhaps a shift in locale would produce a change in our social relationships as well. Cathy always had a sense that people in Philadelphia were inherently exploitive and not genuine in their feelings for both of us. She felt it was always more important to them to be *in the company of the Schultzes* than to *get to know them*, to share things with them and to understand them as people.

Cathy had expected me a lot sooner and was visibly agitated when I drove into our driveway. "Where were you?" she asked. I was concerned about how she'd take it.

"I've got good news and I've got bad news," I said. "The bad news is that we've been traded. The good news is that we've been traded to Los Angeles."

Cathy took it better than I had expected. In fact, she seemed tickled with the prospects of getting out of Philadelphia.

The Flyers returned from their exhibition game on Long Island and came directly to our house to pay their respects. That was nice, but I wasn't happy about the fact that Shero didn't come by and didn't even bother to call. I felt I had displayed a loyalty and dedication to Fred that had forged a bond between us. I know full well that I would have been the first one on the telephone had he been moved out of the organization and not me. It's unfortunate that the world of professional hockey produces such scenarios on a regular basis. Perhaps Shero, who had coached so many teams and seen so many trades, had become jaded by it all. Perhaps, for all he cared, my name was interchangeable with those of all the other men he had coached.

I picked up the papers the next day and there was a remark by Bobby Clarke that disturbed me: "I just hope we don't regret this." To me, the key word was "we." Whether Clarke was actually responsible (not impossible) for my being moved or not is less significant than the fact that *I* was suspicious about his possible involvement. As a captain, he had assumed a lot of power with management. I didn't want to believe it but I couldn't help thinking that, perhaps, Clarke had helped ease me off the Flyers' roster.

One of the features of a hockey player's relationship with his peers is that of trust, of mutual feelings of confidence. I cannot overemphasize the pain that even the thought of Clarke's involvement caused me. The news of my dismissal, I must confess, was often overshadowed by my confused feelings about Clarke. Of course, I had no tangible evidence that Clarke was directly involved in my transfer and I never was able to learn any more about the matter, so I was forced to live with my suspicions. Yet, intuitively, I felt that I was *not* making too much of Clarke's use of the figurative "we."

Leaving Philadelphia inspired passionate feelings of anger. "How dare they trade me?" But during my more pensive moments, I began to reflect about the difficulty of returning to face my former teammates, the uneasiness of skating against guys I had roomed with for years. How could my teammates assault me and take me out of the play with vigor after the many efforts I had made to protect them? And the fans: How could they jeer me after the many exciting moments I had provided them?

Flying to my new team in Los Angeles, I had the sense this was going to be a new beginning for me. The Kings did not play an aggressive brand of hockey. Indeed, coach Bob Pulford, on my arrival, hinted that I had been obtained by the Kings as much for what I could contribute as a hockey player as I could as an enforcer. There was an ever-so-subtle hint that my former antics, which went over so well at the Spectrum, might not be as appreciated in the Forum, home of the Kings.

Supposing I were to play a different, less belligerent game? How would the enemy react? Press releases weren't going to be dispatched by the Kings' office informing other NHL goons that Dave Schultz was preparing to change his ways. How could I shed my former identity, *the* symbol for hockey violence? But the change of uniform provided me for the first time with at least an opportunity to change. I might not be able to make the transition but I had to try.

Pulford, my new coach, was always a bit vague and introverted (that would prove to be a severe problem in the long run), but I understood him to believe that goonery would be appropriate if the opposition provoked such behavior, and that he had no intentions of my being an enforcer on a full-time basis. Ironically, my first game against the Flyers proved that I was still locked into my old role and emphasized that I would never be able to shake it.

We had a stopover at Pittsburgh before we got to Philly for the game on October 19, 1976, and I felt excited about going back. Part of it was that I felt I had something to prove. Naturally, I was concerned, especially after talking to some of my old Flyers teammates who had been traded—Billy Clement, for one—who told me they hated playing against the Flyers.

Frankly, I didn't anticipate bloodshed. I looked over the Flyers' lineup and didn't see many guys who would fight. Only one guy was doing the bulk of the fighting and that was Jack McIlhargey. If a fight were to start, it would be a Flyer who would start it, not me. As for the fans, I figured they would love me when I first came out, but that after I hit somebody things would change.

As it came closer to game time, I got more nervous. When I finally got to the Spectrum there was Phil Stein, the general of the Schultz Army, wearing his German-style helmet with the blinking lights. He had a new inscription painted on: "L.A. TOOK AWAY MY HAMMER: GONE BUT NOT FORGOTTEN."

My instinct was to walk into the Flyers' dressing room but I was herded with the Kings to the visitors' room down the hall. It was an eerie feeling, especially when I heard the sounds of the Flyers carrying on with each other as we had in better times. I wondered what was going through their heads, whether this game had any special meaning to them the way it did for me.

I skated onto the ice for the pre-game shooting drill feeling very much the outcast and wondering what kind of reception I would receive as a loyal member of the opposition.

When I finished the warmup the building was still half empty, but the diehard fans already were putting up their banners. Signs that said "SCHULTZIE—WE'RE STILL YOUR LOYAL SUBJECTS," and "DAVEY—YOU'LL ALWAYS BE THE HAMMER OF OUR HEARTS." By game time, the place was packed. This time, when I took the ice, the crowd roared as if we had won the Stanley Cup.

Less than a minute later they were booing me. I tried to plaster Paul Holmgren into the boards. Nothing personal. Soon after that Don Kozak, my linemate, got a penalty. Lou Nolan, the Spectrum public address announcer, was so used to calling penalties for me that he started out by saying, "Los Angeles penalty to Da— . . . pardon me, Don Kozak."

At 2:13 of the first period Bob Kelly and Dave Hutchison, our husky defenseman, slugged it out. On my next shift I went up against Ross Lonsberry along the boards. We had a few words but no fists were raised. Soon Hutchison was hit with a good check by Bridgman. Hutchison was flipped in the air and when he landed his stick hit near Bridgman's face. Hutchison meant no harm; if Bridgman had been hit dirty, you can bet that Hutchison would have been looking out for trouble, but he wasn't. In fact, as soon as Dave saw Bridgman go down, he knelt down to help him. Before he could, McIlhargey came up and suckered him in the mouth. Dupont moved right up and jumped Hutch. Soon there were four guys on one.

I spotted Holmgren. He goes 6'3", 215. I was 6'1", 190. He knew I wanted him. "Let's go, you sonofabitch," I yelled.

It wasn't one of my smartest moves. Holmgren was wearing a mask to protect an injured eye, plus a helmet, so there was no way I could get through to him with my punches. He got me with a flurry of rights and then threw me down on the ice. The crowd that I had had in the palm of my hand for four years turned against me. As Holmgren pummeled me around the right eye and nose, the Spectrum went crazy with cheers. In Philadelphia, I was now a bum. Before the first period had ended I had been thrown out of another hockey game.

One line in the Philadelphia *Inquirer* said it all: "Dave Schultz was no longer loved. Just another enemy goon."

I had mixed feelings about the Flyers as the Kings continued on their road trip. Rather than dealing with my sense of loss—the fact that you can't go home again—I covered it up by fuming over the way the Flyers had jumped Hutch. When we got to Buffalo I received a phone call from Don Ramsay, a reporter for the Toronto *Globe and Mail*. I should have realized that he was setting me up for an explosive story. You know: "DAVE SCHULTZ SMEARS THE FLYERS." We talked at length and, I suppose, I talked too much, especially about my old buddies.

The story, which broke in the *Globe and Mail* and was picked up by wire services, quoted me as saying this about my old team: "It can be said that they operated on a sort of mass hysteria. . . . One-on-one, they're nothing. . . . Those guys think they can take the law into their own hands. . . . They try to instill a sense of fear in you. . . . Some of the things the Flyers have done are disgraceful. . . . My role there . . . began to sicken me. . . . Continuing my career in Philly may have eventually ruined any plans I had for a career in hockey. . . . "

Some of what Ramsay wrote was taken out of context, but I had sent out some signals and Ramsay had read between the lines. He was not totally accurate but he had been astute enough to detect the bitterness I felt. It was hypocritical of me to totally condemn my former teammates for their behavior on the ice since I had been a major part of it. All the same, my frustrations, anxieties, and feelings of inadequacy, which had been repressed for years, began to surface. I could not accept having been traded. My bitterness often turned to hostility as I played for a new team but watched the Flyers progress without me. I often found it difficult to concentrate. What I had said to Ramsay was a product of my mental turmoil at the time. By chance, he was there to exploit it; at a calmer time, I would not have said many of the things I told him.

It's ironic, but understandable, of course, that the media—which created me as a folk hero in Philadelphia—should start working against me almost as soon as I had packed my bags and left the Spectrum. I shouldn't have been surprised or particularly upset. After all, few athletes got more ink out of less talent from the writing and TV–radio fraternity than I did. And the same—in a perverse sense—could be said for the Flyers. We were a violent team and the journalists, who realized we were a running story, wrote about us more than any other team, including the classiest of them all, the Montreal Canadiens. Thus, in properly doing their job, the media helped create the image of the Broad Street Bullies the way the media helped popularize Hell's Angels.

People made a fuss over us—of course we gave them the raw material to work with—and we responded. When we played on the road local writers would create a mental set; the home team was put on notice and became edgy, sure there would be trouble.

In general the media was fine, properly covering the violence, and I had no objections. What bothered me were the blatant hypocrites. In New York, for instance, Warner Wolf, a local showman, keeps saying there's too much fighting in hockey, but whenever Wolf shows hockey clips on his TV show he invariably features the fights and not videotapes of the artistic plays. He can object to violence all he wants to, but the fight is played back because he thinks it makes for good TV. That's why it's hard to take his "editorializing" seriously.

As a rule most athletes have only a vague idea of the rudiments of journalism and, therefore, often mistakenly believe they are being exploited by the media. In my own case, it took me a while to realize that the reporters who write the stories about the games are not the same people who put the headlines on those stories, that a deskman back at the newspaper edits the story and then writes the headline. (Which explains why some headlines are distortions of what is in the body of the story.)

In the ideal situations, writers on the beat establish a rapport with the athletes and they develop a mutual understanding of each other's needs and of precisely what is and what is not off the record. During my stay in Philadelphia, I felt most comfortable with Bill Fleischman, who covered the Flyers for the Philadelphia *Daily News*. I liked him because I felt he was fair to the team and, conversely, would not hesitate to put the rap on us if we deserved it. Fleischman, unlike some others, would never go out of his way to write an embarrassing story. He would let us know in advance if he was going to write a tough piece and, as is only fair, would ask our side of it.

On the whole we were treated well by the Philadelphia media. Like journalists in every city there were "homers," who wore Flyers-colored glasses, and there were others who pulled few punches. A mistake that many of us make is to view media criticism as a personal affront. I remember a newsman telling me that he could write two hundred positive stories about a hockey player and never receive so much as a nod of appreciation, but the day he wrote something negative was the day the player would complain about a hatchet job.

That was part of our cocoon mentality; we couldn't see beyond our Flyers' crest. We believed that whatever we did was all right and anyone who criticized us was a jackass. In time I came to be more sophisticated about journalists. I came to expect to be misquoted here and there and I knew that there were papers that sensationalized stories as a matter of policy while others were more temperate in their approach.

I'm aware of the excesses of the media and equally aware of the manner in which I, myself, exploited them. I got more ink than I deserved, if ability is any criterion. I would get into a fight in Philadelphia and the next day everyone across the country knew about it. Nobody has to tell me where I would have been without the media. The Fourth Estate made me into a hero, first in Salem and Richmond and eventually in the NHL.

I was always grateful to be recognized. To me, bad publicity was better than no publicity at all. I understood that my notoriety made me more money and to hell with the consequences on my family or my psyche. I could have been wiser.

13

Living Like a King

IN TERMS OF our marriage, the move to Los Angeles was a step in the right direction. Several factors contributed to our getting closer together again. Being in a pleasant environment didn't hurt. We had a lovely house on a big hill in Palos Verdes, California, south of Los Angeles. Emotionally and esthetically, it made a big impression on Cathy. The sky was always blue and beautiful, trees and flowers bloomed everywhere, and it seemed like summer twelve months of the year.

Equally important to her, we were no longer in the limelight. In Philadelphia she didn't like receiving special privileges just because she was my wife. In Palos Verdes she became more of an individual again; most of the people didn't know from hockey and could have cared less. For the first time in four years we were in the shadows and enjoying every minute of it. The press paid little attention to the NHL and there were no demands on me to make appearances.

Fortunately for Cathy, there was no Bobby Clarke captaining the Kings. Our captain, Mike Murphy, was a low-key guy who had absolutely no interest in all the fraternity-like ideas that were such a big deal to Clarke. For instance, the Kings had no such thing as a "Boys Night Out" the way we did in Philly, which meant that instead of going out drinking or carousing, I went home. After years when I had been far more attentive to hockey than to Cathy, things turned around completely.

But I would be lying to suggest that all had been repaired. The years in Philadelphia had definitely left their mark, both on our marriage and on Cathy as an individual. She had become suspicious and mistrusting of all persons associated with professional hockey; my dramatic transformation had jaded her.

Now, after so many years, I was finally beginning to read her emotions more clearly and to resolve some of the problems that had come between us in Philadelphia. It wasn't easy. I had never given her the kind of attention she needed, especially when we were moving through unpleasant times. But, like anyone who goes through a process of sacrificing and compromising to improve their lives together, we were beginning to address the key concerns in our own home.

I became a better person at home because I was more relaxed at the rink. Vague as he usually was, Pulford seemed to be willing to allow me to play hockey. "You're going to be my left wing on a regular line," he once said. "I don't expect you to go out on the ice and start a fight every time." Wow! I couldn't believe it.

That relieved a tremendous amount of pressure. What a difference: In Philadelphia if an opponent speared a Flyer, Shero would send me out on the ice on the very next shift to retaliate against the culprit. In L.A. Pulford still wanted me to play a hard-checking game, but he wasn't going to use me incessantly as a goon. My contribution was fair to middling. After a poor start, I was put on a line with Vic Venasky and Don Kozak. We had a great second half of the season and helped put the Kings in the playoffs.

I felt relaxed in Los Angeles, but I also had quite an adjustment to make. In Philadelphia, every game was like a war and every one of us felt like a soldier going into battle. Because of the intense interest generated by the fans and the media (and Clarke), the players felt a constant pressure to produce. Unlike the Flyers, the Islanders, and the Rangers, the Kings didn't have intense rivalries, which also reduced the pressure. The Kings had adapted nicely to the Southern California lifestyle. With few exceptions, they had a free-and-easy approach to the game. Sure, we wanted to win, but the attitude was win-a-few-lose-a-few. There was hardly much pressure from the press; it was rare that a hockey story appeared in the paper.

Players lived farther apart, which made for less togetherness. Still, we had the occasional party and there was a fair amount of camaraderie, although a couple of episodes caused dissension. One of them involved the smoking of marijuana. Up until this time I had not been aware of any hockey player who indulged in drugs.

I am not going to name names and risk ruining a player's NHL career. Such a vast number of Americans have harmlessly experimented with marijuana that by now it seems almost silly to worry about it. But teams and the league are still too nervous about their image and hypocritical about these things, so I think I should refrain.

The first player I ever saw smoke pot was a forward in his mid-twenties. He was a very talented player who had failed to live up to his potential with his previous team. Obviously, when the Kings obtained him they still believed he could become a star. He never lived up to his expectations. Was it because of the drugs? Who knows? But his consumption was enormous.

It didn't take me very long to find out he wasn't the only guy on the Kings who used drugs. And then, during the 1977 Stanley Cup playoffs, we were between playoff games in Boston and had nothing to do at the hotel. Some of the guys rolled a few joints and I decided to have one for myself. I felt like a little schoolkid, sneaking his first puff on a cigarette.

After we lost in the quarter-finals to the Bruins, Cathy and I threw a party for the team at our house in Palos Verdes. For most of the night it was great fun. Later in the evening one of our big forwards went over to Cathy and asked her, as the hostess, whether she would mind if he lit up a joint. Cathy wouldn't say no so he went off into a corner and rolled one. Marcel Dionne, the Kings' one and only superstar, got wind of what this guy was doing. Understandably, he didn't want to run the unnecessary risk of damaging publicity. Dionne was so incensed he grabbed his wife and stormed out of the house.

Did drug use have any meaningful effect on the Kings as a whole? I doubt it. Of course it's no secret that too much marijuana will hurt your performance (as will too much booze; I can think of one Philadelphia forward in particular who was sent packing for his alcohol consumption). In the case of that young, gifted forward I mentioned earlier, I can say with some certainty that he later moved into even stronger drugs and that it did affect his play.

I don't think management had any idea what was going on. To be generous I would say that with but a few exceptions the general managers around the league were twenty years behind the times. Beer and booze were their staples when it came to escape from the real world. I don't think they knew the first thing about the drug scene and how more and more young hockey players felt they would rather roll a joint than chug-a-lug a beer. Certainly there was no evidence that our leaders were concerned about drug abuse; they never said a word about it. Their concern was making the playoffs, making deals, making money, and making believe there is nothing else in the world but hockey. If anyone might have known it would have been Pulford, who was a cut above the average stick-and-puck character, (he had a Master's degree) but he never said anything about drugs either.

Los Angeles was a pleasant enough team to play for and Pulford, despite his introversion, was a coach I could live with. I respected his opinions, especially his theory about winning hockey. In a nutshell, it is that goals are simply the result of good defensive play. You play well on the blue line and you'll get the puck, send it to the forward, and eventually score.

Pulford had some interesting characters to deal with, maybe more oddballs than we had on the Flyers. Butch Goring was one. A little center out of Manitoba with all kinds of speed, we called him Seed, as in Hayseed. He looked like he left the farm yesterday. His hair was long and straggly and he dressed like a farmer who had just gotten his first suit of clothes. His pants had a way of hanging back down on his behind like nobody else's I've ever seen.

They tell a story about Butch's being on the road with the Kings once when a thief broke into the room he was sharing with another guy. The robber stole every one of Goring's roommate's clothes but looked at Butch's clothes and said the hell with them.

When Goring came to the Kings he had a choice of brand-new helmets, but he insisted on wearing the same helmet he wore as a kid growing up outside Winnipeg. It was called a "Tumba" helmet because the guy who invented it was an old Swedish player named Tumba Johansson. Butchie's helmet was his trademark. It looked more like a skullcap than a helmet and had practically no padding inside.

For laughs there was Pete Stemkowski, a tall, almost pudgy center who called himself the Polish Prince. Unlike me, Stemkowski liked to kid with the referees although he didn't always agree with them. One night referee Ron Wicks blew the whistle on Stemkowski for tripping. Stemkowski stared at Wicks for a second and then said, "That's three penalties for doin' nothing. You're picking on me, Wicks, because of my looks."

"If I were," snapped Wicks, "you'd get six!"

Another oddball was Kozak, a right wing out of Saskatchewan. It was hard being pals with him because he refused to associate with any of the guys. Kozak wouldn't even sit with us in the dressing room. After every period—and even after the warmup—he would come into the dressing room, walk right past our stalls, and sit on the can.

Then there was Hutchison, the closest thing we had to the Incredible Hulk. He went 6'2", 205 pounds and was very much in love with himself. Hutch was good looking but he had the notion that his face was so pretty that it would be unfair to his audience to have it messed up, even in a fight. Instead of fighting, Hutch would use his stick in battles.

Once when we were playing in Vancouver, Hutchison got us in a hell of a jam with a couple of hookers. A few of us had just finished dinner and were walking up the street when we got to a not very elegant spot called "Hookers' Corner." We were heading back to the Hotel Vancouver, where the club stayed, when we noticed two prostitutes at the end of the street—one white, the other black.

Hutchison had been walking ahead of us and when he got to the corner the black girl approached him and said, "Ya want any action?"

He said "No thanks" and waited for the traffic light to change so he could cross the street.

Just like that she turned on him and said, "That's okay, I want to knife somebody tonight anyway."

"Lemme see that knife and I'll show you where to shove it!" Hutchison said. She didn't like that much and came right up to Hutchison and slapped him across the face. He shoved her right back. She reached into her purse and pulled out a switchblade knife and came at him. He was ready. He had taken his coat off and wrapped it around his arm for protection. All he wanted to do was knock the knife out of her hands. He kept kicking at her hand like a karate fighter and she kept menacing him with the knife. He finally got in close enough to reach her and drove her one with his shoe; just as he connected she pulled up the knife and ripped his hand badly.

There was blood all over the place. One girl turned to the other and said, "Let's get the hell outta here." She put the knife away and they started to run across the street, where they flagged a cab. We took off after them and as soon as they closed the doors of the taxi we surrounded the cab and told the driver not to move. We wouldn't let the hookers out of the car until the police and an ambulance came for Hutchison.

By the time the cops arrived the hooker, without our noticing, had managed to get rid of the knife. (The cops found it a day later on the street.) The cops checked and found out that both hookers had records and the two of them were hauled off to jail. Hutchison got eleven stitches in his hand at the hospital. The next day there were headlines all over the Vancouver papers and soon the wire services picked up the story and carried it across the continent. It was one of the few times anyone on the team took a headline away from our one legitimate superstar, Marcel Dionne.

We called Dionne "Little Beaver," a nickname Marcel was given when he originally broke into the NHL with the Detroit Red Wings. Marcel was hardly a laugh-a-minute, but he was an extremely talented player and a complicated man. He was very dedicated but very frustrated, too. He was a super shooter with great offensive anticipation and passing skills. He resented the fact that, year after year, he was destined to play on mediocre teams that had no chance of finishing first or winning the Stanley Cup. "I'd give up all the points I've ever gotten," he once told me, "to have my name appear just once on the Stanley Cup."

As good as Marcel was as an offensive threat, he was not the leader that Bobby Clarke was. Marcel was mindful above all else of getting his hundred points or so every year. In addition, the book on him was that he could be easily intimidated. If you got him good early you could finish him. I personally remember a few occasions when that was absolutely true.

Dionne was a wonderful player, but I've seen better. The player with the most talent, pound for pound, that I ever came up against was Guy Lafleur of the Montreal Canadiens. He could skate as fast as anyone; shoot as hard, make plays, and inspire his teammates in a way that few others can. Bryan Trottier of the Islanders is also outstanding. A quiet leader who will not take any guff from anyone, he likes to take the body and play a hard-hitting game in the other team's end of the rink.

Larry Robinson of the Canadiens, though not the greatest player, was a highly significant defenseman. He was one of the first to prove that a really good fighter did not have to be a goon. I realize I am condemning myself when I make such an observation, but there is no denying that Robinson brought a new dimension to the term "enforcer." He could whip anyone but he preferred not to fight and was quite content being one of the best two-way defensemen in the 1970s and early 1980s. He essentially comes to play the game but he has demonstrated over and over that, if necessary, he will step in to be a policeman as well. Barry Beck, the Rangers' big defenseman, and Clark Gillies of the Islanders are very similar in that respect.

My choice for best defenseman is not a startling one. Nobody came close to Bobby Orr of the Bruins during the 1970s. He was a marvelous attacker, could launch a play and complete it by himself, shoot hard and accurately, and, to the surprise of many, he also was just as excellent behind his own blue line. When I had the opportunity I would always keep an eye on Orr and I always learned something by watching him. For example, he had this uncanny knack of seeming to let you check him at the blue line and then pivoting in his spot and catching you out of position while he walked in home free and took his shot on goal. It was terribly sad that knee injuries prematurely ended his career.

The best goalie I ever saw was Bernie Parent, and the best playoff performance I remember was Parent's standing the Bruins (and Orr) on their heads during the 1974 finals. And talk about cool! Toward the end of the second period in one game the Bruins mounted a severe barrage but got nothing past Bernie. Then we got a penalty and Orr and Phil Esposito shot the works. Bernie produced one improbable save after the other. At a stoppage of play, he called over Joe Watson and, as nonchalantly as if he were sitting in a restaurant, Bernie said, "Joe, we should go fishing next week. Here's what we'll do: we'll leave Tuesday morning, take coffee and sandwiches and try to get there by dusk."

Parent would just grab for pucks; there would be no extra motions or big kicks. I loved playing against him in practice, because he would challenge you. He didn't even mind—as some goalies would— if you shot high on him in practice, although anyone who did had to be a little stupid, considering the injury it could have inflicted on the goalie. Bernie was so militantly cool he even took the headhunters with exquisite calm. He welcomed any challenge that simulated game conditions.

Gil Perreault, my teammate on the Sabres at the close of my NHL career, was one of the classic examples of the promising player who could have been brilliant but who just wanted to be one of the guys, and would never generate the extra effort needed for winning. It takes a certain kind of player to take a punch in the mouth to ensure the win and it also takes a certain kind of persevering player to want to score.

With Perreault the desire was not there. The fans would go crazy every time he touched the puck, but Perreault did not like the pressure; he would sooner pass than shoot. At one point he was placed on a pedestal with a Hall of Famer such as Jean Beliveau, a player who fulfilled all of his potential, under pressure, whereas Perreault skated through the prime of his hockey life without achieving the same kind of success.

Hockey is full of tragic and near-tragic figures. It took Jacques Richard, a former teammate of mine on Buffalo, almost a decade to get his act together. As an Atlanta Flame he was distracted by the money, instant adulation, and nightlife, and it was not until he married, settled down, and returned home to the Quebec Nordiques that he emerged as a player of quality in the 1980–81 season.

Pierre Larouche was another whiz kid who did not realize what hard work was required to make it in the NHL and was a lost cause for years before he came around. Reggie Leach did not come into his own, with the exception of a 61-goal season that was as much a burden as a blessing, until Flyers' coach Pat Quinn showed confidence in him and began to put him out on the ice in clutch situations.

In Los Angeles I was still getting my share of penalties—232 minutes in my first full year in L.A.—but I wasn't the same person I had been in Philly. The burden of being even a part-time goon was wearing me down. I really wasn't up for that role any more, nor could I handle it physically. My enemies were growing bigger and nastier. One night Mike Milbury, a young Boston Bruins defenseman, nearly strangled me after grabbing me from behind on the ice, and there were dozens of others just like him coming from every side—or so it seemed. There were days when I would dream of what it would be like to have the talent of a Dionne so that all I had to do was score goals. In reality, I was an enforcer getting older and more vulnerable—no more, no less.

14

Pollution
in Pittsburgh

JACK KENT COOKE, the flamboyant owner of the Kings, had a dream when he obtained me from Philadelphia. Like George Steinbrenner of the New York Yankees, Cooke liked name players and he figured they could do wonders for his beleaguered franchise. Cooke believed that with my name and my image I could help fill more seats in his "fabulous" Forum while adding some mustard to his previously bland attacking unit. While Cooke, a transplanted Canadian sportsman, didn't expect me to be King Goon anymore than Pulford did, he figured that my presence would give his timid team more courage and get more ink in the papers. I succeeded—but not that significantly.

One enforcer is not enough to bring respect to a team and, as it happened, I was the lone policeman on the Kings' beat. Since my act had cooled down from my Flyers days, I no longer had the galvanic magnetism I enjoyed in the early 1970s. The Forum attendance did rise during my stay in L.A. but it also was apparent that people weren't breaking down the doors to see me or the Kings.

My scoring record after a year in Los Angeles was modest and I believed that, all things considered, I had a decent enough year. Pulford had treated me fairly and with intelligence and that is why I was sorry when he left the team in the summer of 1977 to become general manager and coach of the Chicago Black Hawks. Nevertheless, I

169

looked forward to working with Ron Stewart, a former big-leaguer, who had replaced him.

Stewart had been a former teammate of Pulford's on the Toronto Maple Leafs and resembled Pully in personality and style. I got a lot of ice time from Stewart at the start of the new season and was feeling pretty good about myself, even though I only had two goals to show for it in eight games. By the time we arrived in St. Louis for a game against the Blues I felt I had made a successful transition from Pulford to Stewart and looked to 1977–78 with what for me was a surprising optimism.

Shortly after I had checked into my hotel room, the phone rang. It was Stewart; he wanted me to come up to his room. Could be, I figured, he wanted to have a one-on-one with each of his players. That was not unusual for a new coach. Then, again, he could be plotting some new strategy. But there was a faint strain in his voice. No. I did not want to believe *that.* I walked into his room.

"They traded you to Pittsburgh!"

He said it as simply as that. "You and Gene Carr for Hartland Monahan and Syl Apps." (According to what Derek Sanderson once told me, he deserves a little credit for the trade. At a party, Sanderson became fast friends with Al Savill, a businessman who owned a piece of the Pittsburgh Penguins. Savill asked Sanderson what was wrong with the Penguins and Derek told him that they were never the same team after they got rid of Bob (Battleship) Kelly, one of the best fighters in hockey. "You have no real, big tough guy," Sanderson said. "You should get Dave Schultz. You've got a lot of right-handed centermen. Get rid of one of your centers.") By the time I had returned to my room I was trembling. I had to phone Cathy, which I did after regaining some composure. "This time," I told her, "it's not bad news *and* good news; it's just bad news."

The trade was painful to both of us, especially the prospects of yet another relocation. In Los Angeles, I had fewer ties to the team than I had had in Philadelphia, which meant I had been able to invest time and energy in meeting new people, expanding my horizons, and laying groundwork in business. Cathy and I were in the process of getting real estate licenses and hoped to set up a business in L.A. Now, after all this planning, another move. I was furious.

Perhaps I shouldn't have been so angry. After all, those of us in professional hockey know that being traded is "part of the game," an occupational risk you must live with. The bromide sounds good in the telling but the hardship of selling a house, moving a family, and adapting to a new city cannot be soothed by clichés. I remember reading Gary Shaw's "Meat on the Hoof" and feeling for Shaw's analysis of the players being treated as commodities, like cattle being shipped from one town to another with impunity. It was a situation with which I had trouble coping, even though it was the second time around.

Compounding my dilemma were the reverberations this would have my home life. In Los Angeles my self-image had improved because my home life had dramatically changed for the better. Cathy and I had begun to share things. She was expressing herself more freely, feeling reasonably assured that I would respond and, for the first time, take her seriously in relation to hockey. I had become excited about life outside the NHL. I screened local papers for business ideas. Would all this change in Pittsburgh? I wondered about that and about what was happening to my career on the ice.

I came to the depressing conclusion that I really was not making it as a big league hockey player. Even though the Kings allowed me sufficient time to avoid goonery, I had not provided enough impact as a checking forward or as a scorer to persuade the Kings to keep me on their roster.

The sum total of the court cases and William McMurtry's investigation into violence in hockey was that the NHL had begun looking with even more disfavor on enforcers. And even if I wanted to play the policeman, my act no longer was as intimidating as it once had been. I was a frightened ice cop whose hockey skills, modest as they were, had remained static. I wasn't blinded to the handwriting on the wall—the end of my career was in sight. It was as simple and indigestible as that. Yet there remained a flicker of hope because the Pittsburgh Penguins *did* want me. I didn't have to go out and sell myself to them. Maybe, I figured, some good would come of the transfer from the Kings to the Penguins.

Once I got to Pittsburgh I didn't mind it too much. It was a blue-collar town and I figured that the iron and steel workers would appreciate me more than the beautiful people in L.A. I thought my new bosses, manager Baz Bastien and coach Johnny Wilson, would put me to good use. Baz had been around a long time and seemed to know what was going on and Wilson was a veteran coach. I was hoping that I could do something about lifting the spirit of the Penguins.

I found the comparison between the Flyers and the Penguins fascinating. Both clubs entered the NHL in 1967 as expansion teams.

Within three years the Penguins seemed on the rise—they finished second in the West Division—while the Flyers had dropped to fifth in the same section. When Ed Snider began building a bruising club in the early 1970s, the Flyers began soaring while the Penguins turned mediocre. In Philadelphia, we had a strong and stable management while in Pittsburgh, it seemed, there was a new owner (or owners) every season. More important, the Flyers had leadership on the ice in Bobby Clarke while the Penguins, almost as a matter of tradition, had become a faceless crew with no one able or willing to take command. When I arrived in Pittsburgh, I was naive enough to believe that I could become the Bobby Clarke of the Penguins.

How wrong I was. In terms of spirit, the Penguins were just the opposite of the Flyers. I couldn't believe that so many players drawing six-figure salaries could care less about the game. As for any semblance of discipline, Pierre Larouche, who had come to Pittsburgh in 1974 as a hotshot rookie center, made a mockery of it. And management never challenged him.

That was only one reason why morale was miserable. Another was our goalkeeper, Dunc Wilson, one of the worst livers I have ever encountered in the game. He smoked, he drank, he broke curfew. You name it, Dunc had done it. Once we were on a western trip with a big game coming up in Vancouver. Dunc and a few other guys stayed out all night at a disco—this, our goaltender, a very important man on the team.

I would get terribly frustrated and upset by the attitude of some of the players. I would yell and scream at them. I even got into the odd fight during practice. Pete Mahovlich had similar feelings. He had come to the Penguins in December 1977 from the Montreal Canadiens so he knew first-hand what pride was all about. He was as mad as I was but he went about it another way. After the season the Penguins had undergone a change of ownership and the new big man was Paul Martha. Pete went in to see Martha and complained about Dunc Wilson; Mahovlich didn't know that another player, Rick Kehoe, was standing right outside the door while he was doing his number on Dunc. Mahovlich said that if Wilson came back to the Penguins the following season, Pete would not. Rick told Dunc about it. When Wilson got the word he took a punch at Pete. Wilson, the ultimate loser, was sent down to the minors. (One quick sidelight: We had a player on that team named John Flesch, a big left wing from Sudbury, Ontario, who got so angry with himself after making a bad play—like causing an offside—that after the whistle he would take his stick and bang himself in the head. Once, when he played for the North Stars, he was so upset about a bad play that he banged his head on the wooden sideboards and knocked himself out cold.)

Until Pittsburgh, I had no idea what lousy coaching was all about. Johnny Wilson gave me a clue. In terms of his knowledge of the game, he couldn't hold a skate to Shero or Pulford. When we lost he would say, "I can't put the skates on for those guys." Instead of teaching us, he would say, "You guys have been playing since you were five years old, so go out there and play." Once Peter Mahovlich joined the team, we couldn't tell who was the coach—Mahovlich acted as if he were running the team.

At first I thought Wilson liked me. He said he wanted wingers who were willing to grind it out, "up and down their wings—check and play their man." That was my kind of game and I was willing to give everything I had for him. As the season progressed, I sensed that Wilson didn't care for me very much—and the feeling was mutual.

Any hopes that Wilson and I had of establishing a rapport ended after a game against the Kings. We had a 3-1 lead going into the third period but Los Angeles rallied to tie us, 3-3. It was a typical game for the Penguins; the guys couldn't have cared less whether they won or lost. I thought we should have won the game and I was angry as hell at some of my teammates who, I was convinced, had taken the night off even though they were skating around on the ice.

After it was over Wilson walked into the dressing room and said, "Good game, boys." I couldn't believe my ears. Good game? Was he kidding? I couldn't control myself and stood up in the middle of the room and said "Bullshit! It was a *brutal* game and there's no way they should have tied us." Then I turned to Wilson and said, "You're a quitter." He just walked away.

I wasn't going to quit although I knew in my heart that my career was on the decline. From time to time I would think about retiring but I knew I had a contract that extended through 1981 and I was in the best physical (if not mental) shape of my career. And, like most professional hockey players, I did not have other sources of income, nor did I have other skills. I was totally dependent on the NHL.

I couldn't help but reflect on the highs, the adulation that had been heaped on me—the celebrated nature of an athlete's existence—and I couldn't distance myself from it. Let's face it, I thrived on being recognized by the man in the street and I always got a special kick from being invited on a between-periods interview. Although this may sound hypocritical, given my attitudes about the disenchanting aspects of the game, there was so little else to gratify me and so very little to hang on to that I needed these artificial inputs. My guess is that most professional hockey players, because of their dependence on the game, have a very difficult time disengaging from the league. It is for that reason that some ex-athletes often find themselves at local dressing rooms during the days-off practices of their former teams.

Even though I had been traded twice, I was still encouraged in an odd way by the fact that the opposition fans seemed magnetized by me in as hostile a manner as they had been when I was in my Philadelphia heyday. If nothing else, my charisma had not rusted with age, nor had my penchant for getting into trouble—even when I was innocent.

In Minnesota I was sitting in the penalty box when one of the North Stars' fans came running down toward me. I had an eye on him as he approached from the upper seats, and I tried to get the attention of a cop nearby to make sure that he kept the fan out of it. The cop, unfortunately, had his back to the fan. I put my hand out to get the cop's attention and as he turned I caught that little lip on his helmet and accidentally flicked it off. His helmet went flying out of the box. It was a funny scene and I apologized immediately for it.

A wire service photographer had snapped a picture just as I had turned to the cop. Overnight a two-part photograph was sent across the continent, showing me first pointing toward a helmeted policeman and then showing the helmetless cop with his left hand reaching out toward my chest. The caption accompanying the photo described the incident as SCHULTZ VS. COP.

Cathy, Chad, and I were living in a nice four-bedroom house in a hilly section of Pittsburgh and had gotten to enjoy it. But sometime during my first season there I began worrying every time I left for a road trip. I was concerned because my son was so young and the responsibilities of child-rearing were all Cathy's. Road trips break down the sense of continuity in one's life to the point where upon my return I was literally forced to reacquaint myself with my wife and children.

This was even more painful to me because Cathy and I were getting along so well in Pittsburgh. The relationship had begun to prosper and I finally had the feeling that we were going to mature together and sustain the marriage. I cannot overemphasize the significance of that emotion because I was finally coming to realize that my marriage was more important to me than the game. I suppose that should have been the first real cue that I was becoming psychologically prepared to make my exit from hockey, but I was not astute enough to see it in that context.

I should also point out that the kids, starting with the birth of Chad, always have been a source of immense pleasure to me. When I played with them, I couldn't help but hark back to my own childhood and the primitive days on the farms in Saskatchewan. I remembered the aspects of my upbringing that disturbed me, especially my Dad's tough demeanor and, like most children, I vowed to be a better parent. Being away made it tougher. And being away frightened me, too.

The paranoia that some celebrities suffer was foreign to me until my stay in Pittsburgh. During that second season with the Penguins, I began to read stories in the papers about a killer on the loose who would break into houses, kill the husband with a shotgun, rape the wife, and then kill her. Cathy was scared to death so I bought a burglar alarm system for our house. One night, while I was on the road, Cathy heard a noise at the front door. She looked out of the window at the top of the door and was face-to-face with a head wearing a ski mask.

She screamed for help, ran upstairs, and turned the alarm on, but by this time the guy had started his car and taken off. Cathy phoned me at the hotel and I tried my best to calm her but it was obvious she had been terribly frightened. I was distraught at being away when she needed me, and it became clear to me how many hard times she must have gone through alone over the years.

When I returned from the trip I was determined to catch the intruder if he decided to come back. I studied all possible clues around the house. I could see where the guy had trampled on the bushes and plants and I knew he was a little guy because he had to stand on a box to see in through the door window. For a whole week we went crazy, wondering if he would come back. I bought a little .25-calibre pistol and installed a big spotlight so that the whole house was lit up at night. A week later a detective came to the door. He had a ski mask in his hand and a bunch of papers. They had caught the creep. He was a fellow who installed windows and window shades. Whenever he saw a good-looking woman on one of his jobs he would return to the house and do his worst.

On the ice my luck was just average. I was playing about as well for Pittsburgh as I had for Los Angeles and still was getting a hell of a lot of penalties, but I had reached a point in my career as an enforcer where I was picking my spots and when that happens, well, you're really not an enforcer any more. Like the time we played the Rangers at Madison Square Garden. Nick Fotiu was roaming around the rink like a heat-seeking missile, as he is wont to do. He would skate halfway across the rink to nail an opponent, and when he connected you were lucky to escape with your wind knocked out.

Nick wanted a piece of me and kept goading me whenever we got closer together along the boards. In my younger days I would have dropped my gloves and invited Fotiu to go a round, but now I stuck to hockey; which is another way of saying I avoided a fight. I wanted no part of Fotiu and he knew it. He ran me in the first period and took a two-minute penalty for charging. He went after me in the second period and took two minutes for hooking. Each time he made it clear he wanted me to tangle with him. No way. He was too big, too tough. I got myself a goal and we came away with a 5–3 win on the road.

The next day I came out like a hero in the Pittsburgh papers. The fellow who covered for the Pittsburgh *Press* said I "contributed mightily" to the win, "without throwing a punch." Little did he know how Fotiu had intimidated me.

If nothing else, the Fotiu incident jarred me into wondering what I could have been accomplishing had I chosen to play a different brand of hockey. Here I was ignoring a brawl and goading the enemy into foolish penalties. Here I was getting a goal and helping my team to a win. I fantasized about how I could have done this on a long-term basis until I realized that, if nothing else, there was much virtue in "if." I could theorize forever about what might have been, but now it really was too late to make any significant changes. My effort against the Rangers was a pleasant one-shot; no more, no less. I didn't deceive myself.

Nor did I deceive myself about the Penguins. Not only were they mired in mediocrity but they had other problems, to boot. I had become aware that there was a dope problem in hockey.

It wasn't until I got to Pittsburgh that I realized what the NHL's drug scene was really like. In general, until 1977 there was never any talk about hockey players and drugs. All the stories centered on football, basketball, and baseball players. Hockey players—possibly because most of them came from Canada—had a lily-white aura about them.

In August 1977 many people discovered that hockey wasn't all that clean either when Don Murdoch, a young New York Rangers forward, was arrested at Toronto International Airport for possession of cocaine. Murdoch eventually pleaded guilty and was banned from the NHL for half a season.

Shortly thereafter, Earl McRae, a Canadian writer, began probing around the NHL to find out if hockey players took dope. In October 1978 McRae published an article in *The Canadian* magazine called "Coke on Ice." McRae obviously talked to a lot of people—players and officials—because he had disclosed a set of incidents that sounded all too familiar to me. McRae never named any names but those of us in the NHL had a pretty good idea of who the parties in question were because they were so thinly disguised. At least two of the players were members of the Penguins.

McRae mentioned how an NHL club traded one of its better players because "his drug usage was affecting his performance." He told the story of a player who was caught by his club's trainer giving a teammate a quantity of cocaine in the dressing room following a practice. One anecdote that sounded all too familiar to me involved a player who was traded because of his "bad influence including drugs" on certain younger team players.

McRae mentioned a goaltender who once played a game while high on pot. The coach realized that his goalie was stoned and pulled him off the ice in the middle of a game. His comments had the ring of somebody I had played with when he said: "I'd played a couple of times in practice stoned but that was the first time in a game. I thought the grass would be good for my nerves, sort of relax me. It did. Too much."

You might be wondering what the NHL itself was doing about policing the drug scene. As far as I could determine, the league wasn't quite certain what kind of policy to pursue—extremely strict vigilance requiring a battalion of snoops, or *laissez-faire*. The league did have a former FBI man, Frank Torpey, running its security department, with a relatively modest staff under him. I often wondered whether Torpey and his men had any idea of the extent of drug use in the league during the late 1970s. The most precise figures I ever saw appeared in that article in *The Canadian*.

One of the players questioned by McRae guessed that 80 percent of the younger players in the league have smoked dope. From what I can tell, that was a reasonable guess. He added that some players use cocaine, too. I don't know about that for a fact, but then again, it wouldn't surprise me. Just looking at the kids coming out of junior hockey today, I get the impression that a lot of them are into drugs. Times have changed since I left Sorel in 1969. In those days we *all* drank.

McRae told a story that sounded very much like it happened at the Pittsburgh training camp in 1978. Al Wiseman, one of the league's security men, visited the team to make the annual "Don't-mess-with-drugs" speech. Wiseman said that the street price of cocaine was two-thousand dollars an ounce. One of the Penguins shouted from the rear, "Geez, Al, where are you getting *your* stuff?"

What happened to Donny Murdoch wasn't quite so funny. Here was a kid with the world at his fingertips. He was drafted by the Rangers in 1976 and signed a three-year contract at $200,000 plus a $150,000 signing bonus. He scored 32 goals in his NHL rookie year. He was an overnight star. Then came the drug bust and the suspension. He came back to the Rangers in 1978–79 but he wasn't the same and, finally, New York traded him to Edmonton where he was given a chance to play on a line with Wayne Gretzky, the greatest young player in hockey. Halfway through the season Murdoch was sent down to the minors; he was washed up at the age of twenty-four when he should have been the toast of the hockey world.

As far as I can tell the NHL did nothing to help Don Murdoch; nothing to steer him clear of trouble and nothing to try to rehabilitate him so that he could resume his hockey career in a positive way. That, to me, is a tragedy. I remember Murdoch's saying "I made a dumb mistake and I'm goddamn sorry!" I wonder how many other kids in the NHL are putting themselves into a position like Donny Murdoch and I worry that the league has done little to nothing to prevent a repetition of such an incident.

Hockey is backward when it comes to helping its own. You look at major league baseball and you see that it has a full-fledged program to work with those who are suffering from alcoholism; there is nothing like it in the NHL. Heaven knows, based on the drinking I've seen (and done), the league needs it.

What, then, are the responsibilities of the NHL to its players? Although athletes are paid well for their services, it seems to me that a team should bear the burden of responsibility for the athlete's well-being. It's painful to think that the old bromide "You're only as good as your last game" is a reality in this day and age. Only on rare occasions have players been assisted by owners, usually after being goaded by an aggresive players' association, forcing the owner to provide a benevolent service.

There should be a monitoring system to ensure the health and welfare of the athlete after his career has come to an end—that is, post-career counseling and lifestyle planning. I think it's an outrage that former hockey folk heroes (one of them a member of the Hall of Fame) who have become derelicts had absolutely no one to turn to in hockey for help when they began their downward slides.

15

Shrinks, Finks, Hijinks, and Sabres

OUR SECOND CHILD, Brett, was born in Pittsburgh in October 1978. As the kids grew, I got more and more pleasure from them. Chad was three by the time I started my second year with the Penguins. No longer a baby, he was developing a personality, and every so often I would wonder what it would be like if he knew what his father was doing to earn a living. I wondered how Chad would react if he saw me at a game getting into a fight. I wondered whether he would be horrified at the sight of two guys standing in the middle of a hockey arena slugging it out on skates. I remember very clearly deciding that I wanted to be retired before Chad knew what was happening to me in a hockey rink.

From time to time I would consider what might have been my reaction, career-wise, if Cathy and I had had our children earlier. What might have been my behavior pattern if, say, Chad had been three when I was in my prime with the Flyers?

I like to think I would have been a different person. Sensitive to my child and his feelings, not to mention his future attitude toward me, I am certain that I would have rebelled against Bobby Clarke and his team-only policy, spent more time with the family, and charted another course as a Flyer. I believe that the knowledge that Chad would soon be questioning my behavior would have motivated me to clean up my act, no matter what the consequences might have been. It could very well have cost me my job but, under those circumstances, I might have opted for that course.

At the age of three, Chad was just beginning to understand that "Daddy did hockey for a job" and that sometimes the same fellow he played with on a living room rug could be seen on the television screen, only this time Daddy was wearing a funny uniform.

From time to time I would project, wondering what would be my reply when an older Chad would ask me, "Daddy, what did you do when you were out on the ice?" I'd tell him that I did a lot of fighting and that I won a lot but I lost plenty, too. I would tell him that I would have preferred being a classy player like MacLeish or Perreault or Dionne, but that I didn't have the same skills as the superstars, so I did what I did best and I never failed to work as hard as I could. Furthermore, I would have told him that I violated a lot of rules of the game and was heavily penalized for the violations. And that I didn't play the game the way it was meant to be played; that I played too rough, that I lost my temper too often and that lots of people didn't like my behavior. If I had had my way, I would add, I would have played the game differently; I made many mistakes, but it's too late to do it all over again.

I would also tell him that it was tougher on me mentally than it was physically. I would tell him that even though my coaches wanted me to fight, I didn't have to play that way; the ultimate decision was mine. I wanted that role but I got carried away with it too many times and I did as much harm to my team and the game of hockey as I did to myself. These are mistakes that I must now account for if I want to be honest about my career.

I would tell him that in Philadelphia I tried to behave like Superman. When somebody attacked one of my teammates (supposedly the Good Guys), I took it upon myself to challenge him even though the opponent probably was no worse a guy than my teammate. I did it for publicity reasons. I did it because a lot of people expected it and I did it because it gave me a thrill; at least in the early days it did.

After a while I had a reputation to uphold, a role to play. I discovered that the ice had a way of changing people's personalities. There were guys who wouldn't lift a fist on the ice yet off the ice they would beat their wives or get into street fights. Me, I never had a street fight in my life, never wanted to, and hope I never will.

Not that I had gone into fistic retirement. I knew the Penguins' front office had traded for me because they wanted muscle, so I obliged every so often although my heart no longer was in it. I fought less and was more concerned about getting hurt. Once a hockey player starts pulling up because he's scared of injury he might as well pack it in. The Fotiu incident was a benchmark in my career because it showed that the intimidator was now being intimidated. Nicky Fotiu may not have realized it at the time but he did me a service simply by providing me with a good clue as to where I was in my hockey career. The opposition was wise to me and once that happens, word gets around the NHL grapevine very fast.

I became confused and depressed because I knew I was in Pittsburgh to put people in the building, yet I kept looking over my shoulder like a paranoid puckchaser. I kept wondering whether a Fotiu or a Wensink or a Milbury was going to come after me. I began feeling like a has-been at the age of twenty-nine.

One night we were playing the Bruins and one of their tougher players took a run at Ricky Kehoe, a top scorer on our team who never got into fights. I sat on the bench holding my breath, wondering "Will Johnny Wilson send me out to get that guy the way Shero would have?" Wilson never gave me the nod and I breathed a sigh of relief, although I kept thinking, "Geez, that's my job. I *should* be out there."

That knee-jerk reaction (hit my man and I'll go over the boards and get you) was part of my Flyers' brainwashing and was a behavior pattern that I never questioned. After all, if I was the designated goon—a point that was evident to one and all—I therefore had to respond to the challenge. At least that is what Shero wanted me to do when he put his hand on my shoulder and said "Schultz!" But if I had been another person, or if I had seriously wanted to challenge my role as designated hitter, I certainly could have—and I could have resisted the brainwashing as much as I wanted. Obviously, I neither wanted to nor had the insights at the time to see through the manner in which I was being manipulated.

Pittsburgh did not present the same problems—thanks, in part, to Wilson, and to the absence of the kind of winning pressure that existed in Philadelphia. If there was any joy in playing for Pittsburgh that second season with the Penguins it was that management did some housecleaning, unloading a few of the bad actors and bringing in some old friends from Philadelphia, namely Bladon, Kindrachuk, and Lonsberry. We'd win some, lose some, bobbing along toward mid-season and a nice two-week vacation early in February when the NHL All-Stars were scheduled to play a team from Russia.

The mid-season respite was welcome. With all my problems, I still felt that I could contribute something to the Penguins and I was pleased with the enthusiasm of the fans as well as my manager, Baz Bastien. "Dave," Bastien told me during training camp, "you play like that and you'll be in Pittsburgh a long, long time."

The day the Soviets were playing the NHL I was sleeping at home when the phone rang. Bastien was on the other end. Before I could even guess where I was going he said, "We traded you to Buffalo for Gary McAdam."

Cathy was downstairs. I was trembling as I walked down the steps, contemplating her reaction. As much as she had resented the trade from Los Angeles to Pittsburgh, she had gotten to like our house, the town itself, and the fact that the Bladons, Kindrachuks, and Lonsberrys were with us again. What was more, she had fallen in love with her husband all over again, a process whose seeds had been sown by our idyllic existence in L.A., where we would go for Sunday brunch in Venice, walk along the beach, and spend my days off in Disneyland. She appreciated the fact that I no longer was dancing to the Flyers' tune and that I was gradually cleaning up my act. As hockey became less important compared to the family, she began to detect the qualities in me that brought us together in the first place. Communication, which had virtually broken down in Philadelphia, had been restored and was improving all the time.

"We're gone," I told her. "I've been traded—to Buffalo."

She just about broke into tears while I buried my head in my hands and wondered what I would do next. We spent the rest of that day in a trancelike state, wandering around a shopping mall and taking Chad to a children's theater.

Pittsburgh wasn't exactly the Garden of Eden, but Buffalo? I thought briefly about throwing in the towel, then I realized how absurd it would be with a wife and two kids to support and no visible source of income. If the Buffalo Sabres were quite willing to pay $120,000 a year for my services, why not give them a try? So I packed my bags and checked into the Auditorium in Buffalo, where Sabres coach Billy Inglis assured me that my services were coveted by his club. The assurance had a familiar ring to it; something like what I had heard from Pulford in Los Angeles and Wilson in Pittsburgh. This time I was smart enough not to get my hopes up too high.

The Buffalo hockey situation was uncertain, at best, and unstable. For years the Sabres had been managed by crusty old Punch Imlach, a fellow who had built the Buffalo team from scratch and almost made them into Stanley Cup winners. But Punch got stale in Buffalo and was finally sacked in December 1978. Inglis, who had bounced around the minors for years, was the interim coach, and John Andersen who had been Imlach's right hand man, was the acting manager.

Despite the changes, there was an aura of hope about the Sabres. They had lured Rick Dudley, an old Buffalo favorite, back from the World Hockey Association, and also had launched some innovative programs, which I would soon learn about.

A couple of weeks before Imlach was fired, he hired an advisory team of non-hockey experts to help motivate the team. They were taking information from the individual players, evaluating it and then discussing it with management in the hopes of making some positive changes. One of them was a psychologist from Toronto, Dr. Ed Freedburg, and the other was a Montreal sociologist, Allan Turowetz, and I heard that both of them had played a large part in persuading the Sabres to trade for me. It seems that they told the Knox brothers, who owned the hockey club, that the Sabres needed a big man, somebody to protect the less aggressive skaters. Turowetz explained that the Sabres, unlike the Flyers, lacked a symbolic leader like myself, and that my mere presence on the bench would be worth a goal to the club every game. I hadn't heard that kind of praise since Shero.

Apart from having the "head boys," the Sabres were like most other NHL clubs. Comprising a variety of interesting social types, they had their share of serious hockey players, dedicated workers, low-profile individuals, and a smattering of pranksters. One young player on the club was the victim of one of the cruelest practical jokes I can ever remember witnessing during my hockey career.

It started after a home game when a New York State Trooper walked into the dressing room, holding a few official-looking papers in one hand and a pair of handcuffs in the other. "Your girlfriend has charged you with rape," he told the poor guy, "and I am here to place you under arrest."

The player paled and started to talk in jumbles, trying to state his case. "But she wanted it; she wanted to have sex with me; she's my girlfriend."

Meanwhile, his teammates were expressing their sympathy as the trooper handcuffed him and led him to the door, the player bawling like a baby. As they got to the door a roar went up from the dressing room, and that was when he discovered that it was all a setup. One of the players was a cousin of the trooper and had arranged the entire routine in advance. Although the victim took it well, it was clear to everyone that the "joke" had been pushed too far.

Less upsetting, but sometimes problematic, were the superstitions of several of the players. For instance, our huge defenseman, Jerry Korab, and our young right wing, Ric Seiling, both had this need to whack our goalie's pads last, just before the faceoff, as a token of good luck.

One night Inglis made the mistake of putting Korab and Seiling out at the same time. Right before the faceoff Korab skated over to goalie Bob Suave and thumped Suave's pads with his stick. Then Seiling hit Suave's pads. So Korab went back and hit Suave's pads again. Then Seiling again. Meanwhile, the referee was going crazy to start the game. All of a sudden Inglis realized what he had done and yelled to Korab, "Get off the ice," replacing him with a defenseman who didn't need to hit the goalie's pads.

I got very little ice time although the "head boys" were in my corner and it was apparent that Inglis was giving me the same song-and-dance I had heard in Pittsburgh. Nevertheless, the club played so well down the home stretch that we entered the playoffs one of the dark-horse favorites to win the Stanley Cup. Our opponents in the best-of-three opening round were the Penguins, a team we figured to beat. We lost in a very close series.

It was an incredible shock and I'll never forget the feeling in that losing dressing room. It was a mausoleum. We were like a bunch of kids whose toys had been taken away from them and who had to sit in the corner for a few hours. As I peered from one side of the room to the next, I couldn't help but think of the World War I movie *All Quiet on the Western Front*, and the shell-shocked look of the infantrymen in the trenches after a particularly explosive battle. My teammates and I seemed to be dazed, hulked over on the benches, some crying, others in a state of catatonia, and nobody said a word.

Next door, the Penguins were involved in a victorious orgy. It was the perfect counterpoint—the thrill of victory and the agony of defeat—and I knew them both.

As I sat at my stall, peeling the tape from my stockings and untying the laces on my skates, I wondered what the defeat meant for me and my future in the NHL. I figured that I had used up my last NHL credit card with the Sabres and that nobody else would want me, but I was curious what the Buffalo high command thought about my value to the team. In 28 regular season games I had scored twice and had three assists for five measly points. My playoff average was better—two assists in three games. By the time I had removed the suspenders from my shoulders and placed my hockey pants on the floor I told myself that it was time to face up to the possibility that I might not see the inside of this room—or any NHL dressing room for that matter—again. "Expect the worst," I told myself. "Figure you're saying good-bye to the bigs." I swallowed hard on that one but I had no intentions of deluding myself. My chances of returning to the Sabres were, at best, 50–50.

The Knox brothers decided to clean house that spring and signed Scotty Bowman, who had won several Stanley Cups for the Montreal Canadiens, as general manager and coach. Bowman had a reputation as a ruthless man when it came to dealing with players. The word we got from Montreal players was that they hated—but respected—the man. Everyone's fate was in his hands and one of his first moves was to fire the "head boys"; Scotty figured he was a better psychologist and sociologist than they were put together. I made out better: Bowman told me I could buy a house in Buffalo and that I would be with the team for the 1979–80 season. When fall arrived, I came to training camp in excellent shape but more skeptical than ever about my hockey playing future. Because he had made a lot of friends on the team, Turowetz came around to see the boys during the exhibition season.

Our old trainer, Frank Christie, didn't know that Allan had been canned. What followed was a scene right out of a Marx Brothers' comedy. Turowetz was in the dressing room area when Christie noticed him. Bowman was standing directly behind Christie but Frankie didn't know that. As soon as Christie saw Turowetz he asked how come he hadn't come to training camp with the team so Turowetz said, "Frankie, we were fired. We're not with the team anymore."

Frankie couldn't believe it. He said, "Impossible. Why, Bowman would never do a thing like that. Impossible. Scotty couldn't fire you guys." Meanwhile, Bowman was still standing right behind Christie taking it all in, and Frankie kept on going. "No, not my man, Scotty, he wouldn't do a thing like that to nobody. Allan, you made a mistake. Go see him. No, I'll speak to the man and you'll be back tomorrow."

Allan didn't know what to do so he finally said, "Okay, Frankie," turned around and walked out, the embarrassment showing. Bowman evidently couldn't have cared less.

Whether the team of a sociologist and a psychologist is capable of improving the performance of a professional hockey club like the Sabres is a question that remains unanswered. Yes, we did produce a winning record in the last half of the season, during which the two of them worked with the players, but I believe we may have done just as well without them. Certainly Bowman thought so and the following year, after the "head boys" had been sacked, the Sabres' effort and results were just about the same as they had been in the previous year.

Bowman was regarded by some hockey critics as the best coach in the game. He ruled by intimidation—a phrase not unfamiliar to me. Bowman's brand of intimidation featured words backed by a high decibel count. It was a coaching style that I did not appreciate. His theory of coaching by fear was not new but it had lost its novelty. He would single out one player, such as Rick Martin—one of his favorite scapegoats—and browbeat him something awful. Bowman would launch his tirade in normal tones and then proceed to get louder and louder until the victim wanted to crawl through a hole in the floor.

To persuade a defenseman to play a tougher brand of hockey, Bowman would call him a pussycat in front of the entire team in the hopes that the message would get the player's *machismo* going and would induce him to go out and knock heads. I remember Scotty berating our fine young goalie Donnie Edwards one night in the dressing room after Edwards had played a poor game. Donnie told me it was one of the most humiliating experiences in his life. Shero could get more out of a player with a little tap on the shoulder than Scotty could with all his noise pollution. If a player had a bad game or hurt the team in some way, Shero would try to work with the guy until he straightened him out. Bowman's solution was to trade the player.

Bowman obviously turned Buffalo upside down and I didn't help my cause once the exhibition season started. I began playing intimidated hockey, more so then I had ever done in my professional career. My mental set was more like it had been when I played junior hockey in Swift Current than it had been when I became the Hammer in Philadelphia.

I remember an exhibition game we played against the Boston Bruins. Instead of preparing myself in the old way, scanning the Boston lineup to see whom I might have to handle and doing it in a positive way, I became preoccupied with the thought that the Bruins were a bunch of really tough players—Stan Jonathan, Al Secord, John Wensink—and I didn't want any part of them.

No more fighting for me. I desperately wanted to walk away from the punches—and keep on walking. Every time I took the ice that night I looked over my shoulder, fearful that a challenge would come from Wensink or Jonathan, one that could permanently ruin me. With that kind of stupid thinking (by hockey standards), I was unable to concentrate on my playing and, as a result, my performance suffered. There were no more doubts: I was washed up.

I didn't go running to Bowman with that announcement but just did my best to help the team without getting myself into trouble. Bowman played me here and there a bit more. Once in St. Louis he gave me a couple of shifts and I tipped a shot from the point into the net. It was my 200th NHL point. And my last. In fact I never played a major league game after that. A few days later Scotty called me into his office and it wasn't to tell me how well I was playing.

He said, "I want to send you down to Rochester."

The Sabres' farm team was within driving distance of Buffalo and Bowman already had a few guys commuting between the two cities as a punishment for not playing well. "We've already sent [André] Savard and [Jacques] Richard down there so you can commute with them."

My heart dropped down to my toes. Rochester. The minors. "Look," I pleaded, "instead of having me commute why don't you let me practice with the Sabres and just play with the Rochester team. This way I'd be available if you need me."

Bowman didn't buy that. "Well, yeah, that would be all right," he said, "except that it wouldn't be fair to Savard and Richard who are commuting, too. Once we get rid of those two then you'll be able to come back."

I knew he didn't mean it.

16

Good-bye to All That

Long before I even considered retirement Cathy used to kid me about it. She would say, "Dave, why don't you quit and get a paper route." It was good for a laugh but we did have two kids, I was only thirty, and while Rochester wasn't exactly the end of the world, it wasn't Philadelphia either.

The summer of 1980 was upon us and I still had a year to go on my fat contract. I knew that Scotty Bowman wanted no part of me but there had been rumblings that a couple of teams still might want to take a chance with me. Every so often I would hear that the Flyers wanted me back; I never believed it, and I turned out to be right. Shero was coaching in New York with the Rangers and he would be asked about me from time to time. He would hint that the Rangers might want me, but nothing came of it. Only one club appeared genuinely interested and that was the Winnipeg Jets, who were managed by John Ferguson, one of the great fighters of another NHL era. The Jets had finished last and showed no signs of getting out of the cellar for 1980–81. I couldn't get enthused about busting my butt for them although I would have been pulling in a nice bit of change.

Cathy was very supportive, especially when you consider all the trauma she had put up with since we had gotten married and I had signed with the Flyers. "Dave, it's your decision," she said. "As far as I'm concerned one more year is okay. I just don't want you being tossed around the minors or winding up down in the International League or somewhere in the sticks like that."

When I had originally arrived in Buffalo I recalled what Phil Esposito had said when he was traded to the New York Rangers after years of great service to the Boston Bruins. He told his friends that he saw the trade not as Boston wanting him less but as the Rangers wanting him more.

I tried that rationale when I was moved to Los Angeles and then to Pittsburgh, but the excuses had run out by the time I suited up with the Sabres. A player's value in this game can only be measured by the amount of time he spends playing it. While not giving me the amount of ice time that I wanted (very little, to say the least), every one of the teams, from the Kings to the Penguins to the Sabres, tried to convince me that my value as an enforcer, sitting on the bench, looking tough, more than compensated for my inactivity on the ice. I had a very difficult time coming to terms with that. I remained convinced that there was a hockey player within me; that my potential was not limited to abject goonery; that given a reasonable chance to concentrate on hockey and forget about enforcing I was capable of performing in the manner of a good checking forward. I saw how Bob Gainey did it for the Canadiens. Like myself, Gainey was big and strong but, unlike me, he did very little fighting. He was a hard checker who earned his pay by keeping the opposition's top guns from scoring. Gainey never scored very much but nobody seemed to mind as long as he was doing his checking. That is precisely what I felt I could do, which is why the bench-sitting role caused me a great amount of frustration.

The game lost its meaning for me and the highs were replaced by severe feelings of mediocrity and a sense of aimlessness. Nobody knew this better than Cathy and I can only say that I was grateful that she didn't try to hustle me out of hockey sooner and that she allowed me to make the ultimate decision to quit.

I contacted my agent, Bill Mauer, in Montreal and told him to get in touch with Bowman. If the Sabres were willing to talk turkey I would let them buy out my contract and I would pack it in. Otherwise, I'd take a crack at Rochester for the 1980–81 season and go through the motions, collecting the big money for another year.

My heart told me not to put the skates on again but September 1980 was looming and soon training camp would open. I was obliged to be there but I prayed that Bowman would be reasonable. Early in September the call finally came. Scotty said he would release me from my NHL contract if I would settle for eighty-thousand dollars over two years. I couldn't say yes fast enough. As ironic as it sounds, getting out of professional hockey was one of the happiest days of my life.

I suffered absolutely no withdrawal pangs after hanging up my skates for the last time. On the contrary, when the NHL season started again in October 1980 I felt quite good about not being a part of it. I looked forward to establishing my own business out of my home near Buffalo and spending more time with my family. The fire that once burned within me when teams were ready to take the ice had been stilled. I had lost my desire to put on the blades "just once more." I knew I had had it.

Where once I treated my skates and my stick with the care a sculptor uses when he handles his tools, I now buried them in the cellar so far from view that I suspected I would never touch them again. Hockey, which once dominated every living moment of my existence, had now taken on the trappings of a disease. I wanted it out of my system to purify my mind for the life and work ahead.

For several weeks during the fall of 1980 I took no interest in pro hockey. I could not become a sports fan, nor did I care to try. I hardly ever watched it on television and, when I did happen to flick the dial on my TV set and accidentally came across a hockey game, I watched it for only a minute and then turned it off. It all had become very distant to me, like events taking place in a foreign land. I am sure that one reason for my reaction was my fear that the more I watched the game, the greater the likelihood I might change my mind and try for a comeback or that I would become increasingly jealous watching the guys I had played with and against. I wanted it to be distant or, to put it another way, I wanted to keep my distance from hockey.

In some ways the distance was invigorating. For the first time, I felt that I was on my own and not under the control and constant scrutiny of the NHL. Although it produced a sense of anxiety in me, it also gave me the opportunity to investigate the business world and to make an effort to involve myself in new kinds of arrangements. Most players have a good deal of difficulty in adjusting to civilian life after their playing days are over. I shared some of those difficulties, but at the same time I realized full well that my rewards would increase on a regular basis, based upon my production in the work world—a situation not very often practiced by my former mentors. The challenge to work things out inspired me and gave me the necessary courage and, significantly, for the first time in my life as a married man this challenge would be shared by my wife, Cathy.

Moreover, the respite from the ice wars gave me an opportunity to sit back and evaluate the life I lived in professional hockey. It isn't easy to sort it all out. And hardly painless. All the components that compose that history suggest an intricate web of confusions and contradictions.

Some doubts I had about my place in the hockey sun were put to rest on April 5, 1981, when I was invited to a Nostalgia Night at the Spectrum prior to a Rangers–Flyers game. The fans had been asked to pick their first and second Flyers All-Star teams and, to my amazement, I was voted to the second team. It was a touching event, being back in the spotlight with Brother Bullies such as the Watson brothers, Barber, Clarke, Van Impe, Parent, and Doug Favell. When I stepped out onto the ice after the others had been introduced the fans gave me a standing ovation, the biggest of them all.

Now that I have two young boys running around the house, it is inevitable that I think back to the effect my play had on kids and their hockey. Unquestionably, I have a sense of guilt. I know full well that young children are gullible and easily manipulated by role models. By the same token I believe that the real culprits are the coaches and parents who are in a position to supervise and curtail the youngsters' activities. For example, why do coaches at the midget, bantam, juvenile, and junior levels of organized hockey demand that their players be physically tough and "ready to mix it up"? Why are young players told that one of the ways to ensure their mobility to the NHL is through rough play? It takes two to tango.

I am not passing the buck, nor am I dismissing my involvement, which was enormous. All I am asking is that each of us reflect personally and take a look at those agencies that have a good deal to do with what we see in organized hockey. The time has come to disinfect the game of violence.

Like so many others before me, I had come to believe that fighting and assorted other forms of violence on ice were as vital to the game as pucks and sticks. This was as much a part of my education as spelling is to a schoolboy. No different from thousands of other young Canadians, I was reared on tales of hockey brutality. Has any Canadian interested in hockey not heard of the legendary Eddie Shore? A Saskatchewan native like myself, Shore is a member of Hockey's Hall of Fame. But he also is the guy who once rammed Ace Bailey of the Toronto Maple Leafs from behind during a game and hit Bailey so hard that the Toronto forward was almost killed. Bailey teetered between life and death for weeks in a Boston hospital. He survived, but he was never able to play hockey again.

Shore was but one of many hockey heroes who were glorified for their viciousness as much as their skills. Gordie Howe, perhaps the greatest player of all time, could do more with the puck than anyone. Yet when hockey historians discuss Howe they invariably mention the time he broke Lou Fontinato's nose in a hockey fight at Madison Square Garden, or the way he pulverized others with illegal elbow smashes.

This is the way it was done. At least that was the message that we were taught in junior hockey, in the minor leagues, and most of all in the NHL. Conn Smythe, the man who built the great Toronto Maple Leafs clubs, once said, "If you can't beat 'em in the alley, you can't beat 'em on the ice."

Smythe's words became gospel for legions of professional hockey players, me included. Nobody—no doubt for fear of having his masculinity challenged—ever bothered to question Smythe's philosophy. If anyone had, it would have become evident that the NHL's powers-that-be were subjugating artistry to the code of the street-corner mugger. That is wrong. Not only is it wrong but therein lies the root of hockey's problems.

If there is one reason why hockey has a black eye in the minds of the American public it is precisely because it sanctions the black eye as part of the game. More and more, critics of hockey are coming to the conclusion that the sport can stand on its own two feet without fisticuffs and without the low-grade stickwork that has contaminated it for too many years.

I am well aware that this sounds hypocritical coming from one who made his living by driving his fist into the other men's faces. But I was wrong and I paid the price others shouldn't have to pay.

Fighting does not have to be a part of big league hockey any more than fisticuffs have to be a part of baseball, tennis, or football. For too many years hockey has accepted brawls without questioning their validity or the damage that they have done to its image. The time has come for such questioning.

Anyone who watched the American Olympic hockey team sweep to a Gold Medal victory at Lake Placid must realize that a stimulating game that appeals to fans and players alike can be played without fighting. Mike Eruzione, Ken Morrow, Steve Christoff, and Jim Craig showed that, yes, there is a better brand of hockey than that displayed at the NHL level. It is good, clean, robust hockey without fighting. Anyone who has watched Mike Bossy or Bryan Trottier realizes that you don't have to be a monster to succeed.

The standard argument proferred by hockey barons in defense of fighting has been that anger that builds up after a succession of body-checks and assorted illegalities such as high sticks and elbows in the face must be channeled, so why not allow fighting?

That is nonsense. To eliminate fighting the league must first address itself to the incidents that supposedly demand a safety valve. The problem that the NHL has failed to acknowledge is the illegal use of the stick. That includes hooking, spearing, butt-ending, slashing, and interference. If the owners instructed the referees—and the coaches and players—that these infractions will be called without exception and that the rules will be enforced until such violence is once and for all eliminated, *then* positive changes would become evident.

It is necessary for the NHL to break dramatically from its past. President John Ziegler should convene all twenty-one general managers, as well as the owners, coaches, and player representatives of each team, and hammer out a precise position paper on the elimination of violence.

For starters it should provide that any penalty involving the illegal use of the stick should be increased to a five-minute major penalty rather than a two-minute minor as is the case today. Any player who deliberately injures an opponent with his stick should be suspended for no less than a month. Any player who carries his stick above his shoulder *at any time* (whether he is in contact with the opposition or not) should be subject to a two-minute minor penalty.

Strict enforcement of these rules would quickly wipe out the insidious woodchopping that leads to fights. With that accomplished, we then can presume that fighting no longer is being used as a "safety valve." Operating on that premise, it would be perfectly legitimate to abolish fighting once and for all. An NHL white paper should be written in which it is clearly stated that fighting has no more part in hockey than handling the ball has in soccer.

If players, coaches, managers, and referees all agree that all such aspects of violence will be treated as a cancer of the game that must be eliminated, I am convinced that hockey can be purified of its ills and be lifted to a new plateau of excellence.

The abolition of fighting and the elimination of excess violence would not, as some fear, have a negative effect on attendance. Granted, there are some bloodthirsty fans who attend hockey games simply to see fights, and I'm certain that if fighting were eliminated these very fans would stay away from the game. This would be good for hockey—the cretins would be replaced by a higher-minded group of spectators who are staying away from hockey at the moment because they loathe the gratuitous rough stuff. I say hockey would be better off appealing to a more intelligent, nonviolent spectator who appreciates the skills of the game rather than to a low-brow whose enjoyment of hockey rises in direct relation to the amount of blood being spilled on the ice.

To those who insist that fighting helps fatten the gate, I suggest that they check the attendance figures of teams which have been notorious for their rugged play. The Big, Bad Bruins of Boston could be Exhibit A.

During the 1980–81 season the Bruins and the Minnesota North Stars developed a supposedly keen rivalry based upon fighting—and the absence of it. The Bruins, led by such fearsome battlers as Jonathan, O'Reilly, and Cashman, appeared to have cowed the North Stars, a team that for years had accented finesse over fighting. Bruins general manager Harry Sinden had needled the North Stars, calling them a chicken team, until the Minnesotans had had it up to here with abuse.

Late in the season the North Stars paid a visit to Boston Garden; only this time they refused to turn the other cheek. At the urging of their coach, Glen Sonmor, the Minnesota players became the aggressors. The lambs became lions. Completely out of character, the North Stars attacked the Bruins at every opportunity and provoked brawls that reached riotous proportions. They did it, they felt, because they had to gain respect. According to the perverse thinking of hockey players, getting respect meant starting fights.

The event obtained excessive attention from the media and one might have thought that a meeting between the Bruins and North Stars in the Stanley Cup playoffs would lure standing-room-only crowds to Boston Garden. At least that was the theory of those who believe that fights are a big drawing card in the NHL.

But that was *not* the case. Minnesota did meet Boston in the opening Stanley Cup round. It was a confrontation that seemed to be a press agent's dream, yet it bombed. Fewer than ten-thousand fans paid to see each of the two playoff games at Boston Garden. On each night the building was almost half empty.

Individual events such as the Minnesota–Boston series of April 1981 give me no satisfaction whatsoever. Rather, they cause me to reflect intensively on the nature of the game. Is the NHL so blind that it has not been able to take a stand and to organize a position against the type of violence I personified?

There was a bit of magnificent irony following the North Stars–Bruins brawl. Lou Nanne, general manager of the Minnesota club and one of the most insightful members of the NHL hierarchy, declared that the time had come for the league to abolish fighting. Needless to say, Nanne's was a cry in the wilderness and was supported by virtually no one, least of all the Flyers' front office, which claimed during the 1980–81 campaign that the NHL was getting too soft. Instead, the Philadelphia philosophy seemed to be geared toward making the Flyers tougher than they had ever been. They had a defenseman of modest talents named Glen Cochrane who amassed 219 penalty minutes in just 31 games, an average of seven minutes per game. At that rate he easily would have broken my all-time record if he had played a full season.

The central question that needs to be answered is this: Can someone like me come along again? The answer, from my view of the league, is an absolute affirmative. As I peruse NHL rosters, I get the gut feeling there are a number of players who would like to fill the void created by my departure from hockey. Of course, Cochrane would be at the top of the list, and Holmgren of the Flyers can also satisfy the requirements. There are other enforcers still protected by the NHL's indecisiveness who escape without punishment for their actions and who will continue to terrorize those who choose to play hockey the proper way.

Eliminating that type of play should be a top priority of the Board of Governors. The league as an entity must take a firm stand against those players who would rob the game of its artistry and magic. The wishy-washy middle-range, noncommital responses of President John Ziegler demonstrate a failure to see how great hockey could be made if the goons were eliminated.

Unfortunately, the question of violence is masked by a large range of both political and financial concerns, not to mention the historical fact that fighting has been part of hockey's fabric ever since the game flowered on Canada's frontier. Considering these factors it is not surprising that a resolution to the problem is not simple. But, then again, nobody said it was. That makes the challenge all the more intriguing.

How would I have handled someone like me during those turbulent seasons of the mid–1970s if I had been NHL president? I would have been infinitely more severe in my execution of justice. I would have perceived the long-range evils of goonery and the damage that it was doing and would continue to inflict on hockey's image. I would take that into consideration when addressing myself to the consistent brawlers. Instead of fining them, I would hit them with long suspensions, which would grow as the repetition occurred. The very fact that Campbell responded in the relatively lenient manner that he did showed me and others of us who played aggressively that a slap on the wrist would be the extent of our penalties.

It would do me no good to blame society or those persons who participated as fans for all that went on in the NHL. By now you know why I did what I did and you know of my reflections and concerns, as well as my evaluation of those activities now that I have the luxury of hindsight. I would only ask that you try to understand that, for a variety of reasons, some of which are personal and others public, people become committed to a course of action and act in certain ways, not always believing in or even being able to evaluate what it is they are doing.

That was my case. I skated through the NHL confused about who I was, tormented by an inadequate home life, and unable to take stock of the hockey machinery as it hurled me through the system. You may call me a hypocrite and a cop-out artist. That, of course, is your prerogative. I have given you the benefit of my years of experience and I have tried to provide you with a perspective. If truth be told I am thankful to have had the opportunity to sit here, healthy and in one piece, to tell you my story.

Epilogue

How to Make Hockey Better

In OCTOBER 1974, just four months after the Flyers had won their first Stanley Cup, *Esquire* magazine carried an article by Jeff Greenfield. Its title was self-explanatory: "The Iceman Arriveth: Hockey Is the Sport of the Seventies." Greenfield was, at the time, expressing a majority opinion. "It has too many qualities that are in demand today," he said. Many others agreed.

"Fans predicted it," says Chicago *Tribune* columnist Bob Verdi, "players predicted it, the media predicted it, executives predicted it. Hockey was supposed to be the sport of the Seventies."

It wasn't.

The World Hockey Association, which hoped to ride the crest of the new ice boom, came—and then went bust. NHL teams began behaving like carpetbaggers. The league almost bled itself white trying to pump money into a terminally ill Oakland franchise. Two clubs merged because of fiscal failure and Cleveland, once a hockey hotbed, went right down the NHL tubes.

"In 1971," says Verdi, "hockey was too good a game to develop into this mess. Yet it became the sporting tragedy of the 1970s."

Once-mighty franchises like the Boston Bruins began crumbling. The Buffalo Sabres, a club that had known nothing but sellouts, suddenly fell victim to the no-show syndrome. Attendance in Denver, Pittsburgh, Los Angeles, and Washington has been weak enough to inspire questions about the ability of the franchises to survive. None of the three major American television networks have any interest in putting NHL games on their screens. Hockey, they will tell you, does not get good ratings. "The networks discovered," says Verdi, "that arm-wrestling tournaments and *I Love Lucy* reruns posted better numbers than the NHL."

There are several good reasons why hockey does not get the ratings or, to put it another way, does not have mass appeal to Americans. For one thing, it has become too expensive for kids to play—unless the kid's father is a millionaire.

"Hockey is becoming a rich man's sport," says Shero. "It's getting so that the wealthy families are the ones who can afford to buy equipment for their kids to play hockey. And then, when it comes time, the rich kid won't make the sacrifices to continue in hockey. He'll pack up his gear and become a lawyer or a doctor."

Obviously, hockey needs a major infusion of ideas and a transfusion of new blood. It must heed the call of such wise executives as Nanne, who in 1981 stunned the NHL governors with his proposal to abolish hockey fighting once and for all. He has made a number of other recommendations to help make it a better spectacle. "Our league sits still," says Nanne. "We never take a chance, never gamble. 'We've done it this way for fifty years,' they say, 'so let's do it this way for fifty-one years.' You never get ahead that way."

If the NHL is smart it will realize that the bottom line is artistry, not fisticuffs. Hockey, which once was the most artistic of professional sports, has become a mess; and one reason why it has become a mess is that it has turned into a game that is too fast for its own good.

Consider this: On any given shot on the net, neither the goalie, the players, nor the spectators have any notion precisely how the puck found its way into the goal. Were it not for the technology of instant replay, more than 85 percent of the goals scored in the NHL would be a total mystery to the hockey audience.

While this situation is tolerable to a hockey fanatic it has turned off hundreds of thousands of potential fans, not to mention influential members of the media who have grown disgusted with the scrambly, unartistic sport that hockey has become. One such individual is author Ed Linn, himself once a hockey devotee, who has since given up on the game for the following reason:

"Nobody ever actually sees a goal being scored," says Linn. "The goalie doesn't see it, so why should the paying customer? Ninety-nine percent of the goals come out of a driving contest in front of the net or off a rebound after the goalie has made a save. A player fires the

puck through a forest of legs and arms—and occasionally bodies—
and if he's lucky, it gets through to the net. If the player is real lucky,
the goalie doesn't see it through the arms, legs, etc., and he's got
himself a goal."

Hockey wasn't always this way. As a matter of fact it once was a
pastime that managed to meld the best elements of speed, sock, and
sophisticated playmaking in a milieu that was clearly discernible to
the viewer. In the 1920s, 1930s, and 1940s there was no secret to the
manner in which the puck found its way to the net. A spectator never
required the benefits of instant replay or slow motion to dope out the
route of the rubber. It was all there for everyone to see. Nowadays,
nobody knows what's going on—neither goalies, referees, nor spectators.

The transformation of hockey from an art form to a mishmash of
skates, sticks, and puck began in the mid-1940s. Up until then the
game was clearly defined. An offensive thrust occurred in one of two
ways: Either a player himself attempted to stickhandle the puck into
enemy territory for a shot on goal (or a pass to another teammate), or
an attacking unit crossed the enemy blue line by passing the puck
back and forth in an attempt to elude the defense. (Players almost
never fired the puck into the enemy zone at random and then hustled
after it.)

In either case the defending team was able to station itself on or
near its blue line and stop the foe either with crisp bodychecks, using
either the shoulder or hip, or by poking the puck away with the stick.
But by the late 1940s, the strategy changed. Players reaching center
ice began skimming the puck into the enemy zone and then tearing
after it while defensemen wheeled in pursuit. The offensive's style of
shooting-and-running was one of the most destructive aspects of
modern hockey; it meant that defensemen no longer enjoyed the luxury of lining up at the blue line and arranging for delivery of the
bodychecks. In effect, it removed the clean, lusty bodyblock from the
game.

Once the attacking forward dumped the puck and hustled after it,
the defenseman had no time to use his body to stop his opponent, so
he began resorting to a more practical device—the stick. Hence the
advent of hooking, hooking, and more hooking. In time the illegal
stickwork increased to such an extent that referees were hard-pressed
to call all the fouls, so they whistled only a fraction of the potential
fouls and the artistry of the game suffered even more. "What has
happened," says Colorado Rockies goalie Glenn Resch, "is that interference is now taken for granted in the game, and it has done

nothing but hurt the quality of our product. If hockey is to improve, the illegal use of the stick must be abolished. That should be the NHL's first order of business."

It is a fact of life that in the contemporary game every team employs the shoot-and-run technique, although it has such obvious flaws I find it hard to believe coaches have not done away with it as a strategic technique. Hall of Famer Doug Harvey, one of the finest puckcarriers in NHL history, analyzed the shoot-and-run philosophy with rare digust. "I consider it one of the most stupid moves imaginable," says Harvey. "When a player voluntarily gives up the puck at center ice and shoots it in the corner he is, literally, giving the puck away to the other team. To me that's like a football team punting on first down."

No less destructive to the game was the mid-1950s innovation known as the slap shot. Until the arrival of Bernie Geoffrion, Andy Bathgate, and Bobby Hull in the NHL in the early 1950s, there were two basic shots employed by attackers—the forehand wrist shot and the backhand. In using the wrist shot, the offensive player cradled the puck at the end of his stick, then snapped his wrist and delivered the puck goalward.

The backhand differed in that the puck was held on the stick with the stick on the side of the player's body opposite the side from which he would normally shoot. The rubber was fired goalward with a similar crack of the wrist. In neither case did the puck ever attain speeds of more than sixty miles per hour. In other words, the puck was always visible. The goalie saw it and, therefore, was never required to wear a grotesque face mask to protect himself from a puck he never saw.

But the slapshot changed that. By allowing a player to wind up, golf-style, to swat the puck, the league was ruling against both goaltenders and spectators. "All of a sudden," says former NHL goalie Les Binkley, "the puck became invisible. When Bobby Hull shot one at me it started off looking like a small pea and then it disappeared altogether."

If the goalie couldn't see the puck, then certainly the fans couldn't see it. And if the fans can't see the puck, then what, pray tell, is the fun of going to a hockey game?

As if the slapshot weren't bad enough, the NHL allowed even more harassment of the embattled goaltender. By the late 1960s coaches organized their strategy so that the vision of the goalie was blocked altogether. It now became fashionable for attackers to congregate in front of the net with the express purpose of blocking the netminder's view. Some goaltenders accepted the condition without protest but others, especially Billy Smith of the New York Islanders, responded by chopping at the legs of any enemy who camped near his crease. "I'm not asking for much," says Smith, "just a chance to see the puck. And if they won't let me, I'll make damn sure they pay the price with welts on their legs."

The slapshot also was destructive to style in that it enabled players to fire the puck goalward from as far as center ice. It gave mediocre players a crutch. Rather than even attempt to carry the puck over the blue line, they merely wound up and blasted in the general direction of the net. In most cases the puck bounced harmlessly off the glass and yet another attack was squandered while the spectators were robbed of a pretty offensive formation. To call the game of the late 1970s and early 1980s a mindless potpourri of helter-skelter attacks would be an understatement. By now all of the most artistic elements of the game had been replaced by the most boorishly crude techniques imaginable.

Because of the slapshot, goalies resorted to the face mask. Because of the interference and high sticks, most players resorted to helmets. Big league hockey had become a coldly impersonal game in which it was virtually impossible for a fan to relate to a helmeted superstar.

The disaster was complete. The NHL had cleansed its game of skill. No wonder attendance was down. No wonder the networks wanted no part of the NHL.

The message is clear—something drastic has to be done to make hockey better for spectators, players, everyone. Here is my plan:

• Because hockey players are larger than ever, and since rinks will never be widened or lengthened, there is less room on the ice than ever and the ebb and flow of the game is thereby curtailed. I propose that only hip checks, shoulder checks, and poke (stick) checks be permitted to stop an enemy attacker. Any form of clutching, grabbing or illegal use of the stick should be severely punished.

• Because scrambles around the net during which big forwards attempt to block a goaltender's vision produce huge traffic jams and lessen the beauty of the game, moves should be made to unclog the area around the goal crease. I propose that a "no-man's-land" be created by a twelve-by-twelve-foot box in front of the net. No attacking player will be permitted to remain stationary in the box unless he actually has control of the puck for a shot on goal or if he is accompanying a shooter. In other words, no player should be allowed to block a goaltender's vision.

• Because long shots from outside the blue line tend to eliminate good stickhandling and passing, they should be abolished. The center red line should be eliminated and players be required either to stickhandle over the enemy blue line or to pass over the blue line. Shooting the puck into the corner or the end of the rink would be prohibited.

• Because one referee is physically incapable of viewing all of the infractions that take place on a rink, a two-referee system should be used with each referee responsible for only half the rink.

• Because the two linesmen get in the way of the players and unnecessarily crowd the ice, the league should remove them from the playing surface. They should be placed in upraised chairs at each line where they would be in an ideal position to whistle offsides.

• Because youngsters who are seventeen, eighteen, and nineteen years of age are too young physically and mentally to play in the NHL, it should be stipulated that no player may skate in the majors until he reaches the age of twenty.

• Because hockey is a game that can constantly be improved, the NHL should create a permanent Quality Control Unit comprising two college-educated former players who would take jobs as coordinators of the unit on a full-time basis. These two consultants would work with a standing committee of advisors including two club owners, two managers, two coaches, two active players, the president of the league and the president of the player's union, as well as two fans. The representatives would regularly review all aspects of the game and offer constructive suggestions to improve its quality.

Obviously I believe hockey needs help. I remember when, in the early 1970s, a couple of Canadians named John MacFarlane and Bruce Kidd wrote a book called *The Death of Hockey* and those connected with the game laughed. The rinks were full then and nobody paid heed when they condemned violence and pointed out how the game had been degraded. They were right and the empty seats prove it.

But hope is not lost. Hockey can be the most exciting sport on earth and the most artistic as well—but only when properly played and administered. Tragically, it has degenerated into a sloppy, brawl-filled mess. I certainly do not deny my own contribution to the problem, which I have tried to spell out as clearly as possible in this book. I hope that I succeeded and that the NHL will, in the future, sell hockey, not blood.

Career Record

DAVID WILLIAM (DAVE) SCHULTZ
Left wing. 6'1". 190 lbs. Born, Waldheim, Saskatchewan, October 14, 1949. Shoots left. Set AHL record for penalty minutes (382) in season in 1970–71 and broke own record (392 minutes) in 1971–72.

Set NHL record for penalty minutes (348) in season in 1973–74 and Stanley Cup playoff record with 139 minutes in 1974. Broke his own NHL season penalty record in 1974–75 with 472 minutes.

Year	Team	League	Games	G.	A.	Pts.	Pen.
1967–68	Swift Current Broncos	WCJHL	59	35	34	69	138
1968–69	Swift Current Broncos	WCJHL	33	16	16	32	65
	Sorel Hawks	QJHL	–	–	–	–	–
1969–70	Salem Rebels	EHL	67	32	37	69	*356
	Quebec Aces	AHL	8	0	0	0	13
1970–71	Quebec Aces	AHL	71	14	23	37	*382
1971–72	Richmond Robins	AHL	76	18	28	46	*392
	Philadelphia Flyers	NHL	1	0	0	0	8
1972–73	Philadelphia Flyers	NHL	76	9	12	21	*259
1973–74	Philadelphia Flyers	NHL	73	20	16	36	*348
1974–75	Philadelphia Flyers	NHL	76	9	17	26	*472
1975–76	Philadelphia Flyers	NHL	71	13	19	32	307
1976–77	Los Angeles Kings	NHL	76	10	20	30	232
1977–78	Los Angeles Kings	NHL	8	2	0	2	27
	Pittsburgh Penguins	NHL	66	9	25	36	*378
1978–79	Pittsburgh Penguins	NHL	47	4	9	13	157
	Buffalo Sabres	NHL	28	2	3	5	86
1979–80	Buffalo Sabres	NHL	13	1	0	1	28
	Rochester Americans	AHL	56	10	14	24	248
	NHL Totals		**535**	**79**	**121**	**200**	**2294**

PLAYOFFS

Year	Team	League	Games	G.	A.	Pts.	Pen.
1970–71	Quebec	AHL	1	0	0	0	15
1972–73	Philadelphia	NHL	11	1	0	1	*51
1973–74	Philadelphia	NHL	17	2	4	6	*139
1974–75	Philadelphia	NHL	17	2	3	5	*83
1975–76	Philadelphia	NHL	16	2	2	4	*90
1976–77	Los Angeles	NHL	9	1	1	2	45
1978–79	Buffalo	NHL	3	0	2	2	4
1979–80	Rochester	AHL	4	1	0	1	12
	NHL Totals		**73**	**8**	**12**	**20**	**412**

*led league